FRANCHISING:

HOW TO SELECT A BUSINESS OF YOUR OWN

By the Same Author

How to Shake the Money Tree

The Tax-Conscious Investor

FRANCHISING:

HOW TO SELECT A BUSINESS OF YOUR OWN

by Robert Metz

HAWTHORN BOOKS, Inc. PUBLISHERS / New York
A STUART L. DANIELS BOOK

A section of Chapter 35 is reprinted with permission of *The New York Times*. It is one of a continuing series of small-business articles being written by Robert Metz.

To my young son Paul,
who has followed my work with interest

Contents

PART III

PART I

1

What Is Franchising?

Mention franchising at a dinner party and you'll quickly find that most of the people there are only vaguely aware of this important method of doing business. They may have watched those colorful McDonald's ads in which Ronald the McDonald clown gambols among the children and may have read somewhere that this is no ordinary chain-store operation—that the individual who owns the "franchise" is entitled to the profits from this thriving enterprise.

Quite possibly the people gathered around that dinner table may have listened to the frequent radio commercials calling for the purchase of a Carvel shop to sell the scores of ice-cream specialties offered by that franchise company.

Common knowledge of franchising usually ends just about there, for franchising is a fairly sophisticated technique of doing business—not particularly complicated, mind you, once you've grasped a few basic ideas, but sufficiently elusive so that it remains a rather vague concept for most of us.

Consequently we are surprised when we learn that more than 800 companies populate this dynamic field with perhaps 400,000 outlets and that another 40,000 outlets are opened each year.

3

Looked at another way, franchise industries make up more than 10 percent of all the goods and services produced by the nation —that total is some $700 billion—and account for more than a quarter of all retail sales.

The Importance of Franchising

Yes, franchising is and has been an important part of the business and physical landscape for many years. Consumers are surprised when they learn how often and for how long they have been in contact with businesses that are franchised operations. Franchises as we know them today go back to the beginning of this century. Louis K. Liggett is generally credited with being the man who got franchising going in its present form. In 1902 he began offering druggists the right to use the Rexall name in a joint marketing effort, a union that proved profitable for both the druggist and Mr. Liggett.

Think for a moment about what franchising means in your life:

Nearly every time you visit an automobile showroom, you talk with a franchised dealer. Most of the nation's automobiles and trucks have been sold through franchised dealers from the very beginning—even before cars were produced on assembly lines.

The same goes for gasoline and oil. Practically all service stations that sell name brands of gasoline—Esso, Shell, Gulf, you name it—are franchised. And next time you buy gas, take a good look at the tires and accessories stacked on the racks. Franchised dealers also sell vast quantities of these and other automotive products for the oil companies.

It may seem as if the big supermarket chains dominate the grocery market, but it's far from true. Forty cents out of every food dollar goes to the independents who have hookups through a wholesaler on the basis of a franchise agreement.

The nation's millions of farmers buy the bulk of their tractors and machinery through franchised dealers.

It is the franchise companies that dot the highways with the soft-ice-cream shops the kids are forever pointing to in hopeful anticipation. The soft-ice-cream business is not only dominated by franchise companies, it was originated by them.

Both number one and number two in the auto-rental field, Hertz and Avis—to say nothing of Budget Rent-a-Car, Zippy, and several others—are franchised agencies. So are several truck-rental agencies, U-Haul trailers, and most tool and equipment renters.

Carpeting, rug and furniture cleaning, and other well-known home services were pioneered by franchisers. Even today the franchise companies have a substantial chunk of the market.

Do you remember the Bendix laundries that sprang up after World War II? If you do, you may realize that "Coin-Op" laundries—and now dry cleaning—are due to franchising efforts.

Next time you drink a Coke, ponder the fortunes most of the franchised dealers in Coca-Cola have made. Ever since that first squat bottle of Coke was capped, the franchisees were there.

To round up a few others in this by no means inclusive list, think about the hearing aid and water-conditioning businesses and restaurants and motels. All are franchised in a big way. Some of these fields are dominated by the franchise companies and others have been heavily penetrated by them.

What Is a Franchise?

Just what is a franchise and how does it work? The Harcourt Brace Intermediate Dictionary defines "franchise" as—in addition to the right to vote and a right or special privilege granted by a government—"permission given to a dealer to market a certain company's products or services." That's a fine definition, but it barely scratches the surface of this complex method of merchandising.

A franchise company is one that lacks capital to compete on a nationwide basis with the chain companies and thus looks for enterprising people who have saved enough to launch a business. They offer their dealers products or services that have gained a solid reputation in the marketplace and continuing advertising support so that the name will become even better known. The franchise company has diligently polished techniques of doing business, often developed in a highly successful pilot store, and has packaged the methods so that the franchised dealer can avoid costly trial and error in establishing a business. The franchise company trains its franchisees at a company school in an intensive course so that the new dealer, usually with the on-site help of company instructors, can open his store confident of his approach and hopeful of success.

The franchise company uses sophisticated methods to choose a location that will be popular with the consumer. A hamburger shop should be on a well-traveled highway near an intersection. A cleaning store is best situated in a shopping center. In every case in which a store is involved, the franchise company studies traffic patterns, income levels, and even the ethnic makeup of the local population—to say nothing of its hard-headed look into the strength of the competition.

This then is franchising and how it works. And it is Big Business indeed.

Jerome Shuman, associate professor of law at Howard University, summed up the pervasiveness of the franchise trend when he said: "So widespread is the use of franchising that persons desiring to enter certain businesses have little choice but to do so as franchisees. Examples are gasoline and automobile retail businesses. In other fields franchising has become so pervasive that it is extremely difficult for an independent, without the economies of scale and market leverage of a franchise, to compete. Franchised outlets are increasing at the rate of 30,000 [now 40,000] per year, while the independent 'Mom and Pop' stores are decreasing because of the long hours they require and their meager prospects for survival."

Some Franchise History

Let's look into the history of franchising a bit and see how this method of doing business came to be so popular. Gasoline companies have used franchised dealers since the advent of the automobile took gasoline off the druggist's shelf and put it in a pump at the side of the road. The automobile companies probably preceded the oil companies a bit, awarding franchises to new car dealers before the oil companies stretched their own financial resources by getting local people to use their own money to set up gas stations.

However, franchising was in evidence even before the gas buggy began frightening horses and fouling the atmosphere. Prior to the turn of the century, cities granted exclusive franchises to businessmen to run public transit systems. The city fathers realized they had to limit competition so that the operators could get enough passengers to make a profit. The idea of limiting a franchise to a level consistent with profitable operation is still important.

Although Louis K. Liggett generally gets the credit for being the innovator of retail franchising, he wasn't actually the first. Coca-Cola, to name one, preceded Liggett by at least two years. Coke was concocted by John S. Pemberton in his Atlanta, Georgia, drugstore in 1886. By 1900 Pemberton's formula was being supplied in syrup form to franchised local bottlers.

Oddly enough, the big modern-day push did not begin making headway until the mid-1950's, a time when there were still relatively few national franchise companies. Some say servicemen returning from World War II were largely responsible for the boom that began then. Many ex-GI's set up their own small businesses, later recognized the potential of this great common market we call the United States, and used the franchise approach to expand on a national scale.

How Companies Are Formed

The experience of Dansby A. Council, president of the Council Manufacturing Company, Fort Smith, Arkansas, gives some insight into how these dynamic companies have been formed. He tells the story of the Handy Dan ice-vending business, a franchise that is offered both as a sideline and as a full-time business.

"When I returned to inactive duty from service as a naval lieutenant in World War II, it was my desire to enter business for myself. A long-time friend made it possible for me to establish Commercial Equipment Co., a refrigeration distributor, in

Fort Smith, Ark., in April 1946. This firm was started with $10,000 invested capital.

"In 1956, Council Manufacturing Co. was formed as a separate company. One year later, as a prelude to ice vending, the company's first automatic ice maker was perfected . . . a small-volume machine producing chipped ice [which was] successfully marketed on a regional basis.

"Because of inexperience in the national market, and a lack of working capital, we were not successful in developing a national market for the ice maker.

"Necessity being the mother of invention, we designed and tested a machine which would produce its own ice—and also be a coin-operated vendor. It was our thought that the owner of this operation would be both a manufacturer of ice and a retailer of ice, reaping two profits from its operation. The system, which was to become known as Handy Dan's, had its first test at Fort Smith, Ark., in June 1959. The market test of the vended-ice theory was successful. In fact so successful were the vending units, the small-volume ice makers could not meet the demand, even in the winter months.

"The need for larger-capacity ice makers was apparent. This led to the production of our first high-volume machine in August 1959. These are the machines now being used in our ice-vending stations. They reach capacities of 5,000 pounds of ice daily.

"The Fort Smith facilities of Council Manufacturing Co. have expanded from the initial 3,600 square feet to the present plant size of over 75,000 square feet. The Handy Dan's ice-vending system has grown from the testing phase into a system that has outlets from coast to coast.

"Once again, in this growth pattern, the need for working capital developed. A fully integrated system of distribution could not be developed without tremendous sums of money. It was very soon apparent to us that we, as a manufacturer, could not own our own distribution outlets.

"[After a false start] we set up a central sales office in Fort Smith, hired regional sales managers and, under them, district sales representatives. It might be well, at this point, to give you our understanding of a true franchise.

"At Council Manufacturing we define franchising as 'a continuing relationship in which Council provides a licensed privilege to do business, plus assistance in organizing, training, merchandising, and management, in return for a consideration from a franchisee.'

"Council sells its Handy-Dan ice-vending operations as a franchise to qualified investors. We collect no royalties and make our money from the sale of ice-making equipment . . .

"Based on our more than five years' experience in the national market, with more than 500 franchised operations . . . we are able to project a minimum return on the investment . . .

"Our method of franchising enables an individual with a strong desire to be in business for himself to avoid all of the pitfalls, headaches, and mistakes that usually accompany engagement in a new business. Through franchising, Council has been able to develop a system of distribution which could only have been accomplished otherwise by a fully integrated vertical system, which would have required far more capital than the company would be able to obtain."

Mr. Council's experiences, and motivations, are not atypical. Scores of others have perfected techniques—often through experience with a single outlet—and have applied them to the national market, sharing the financial burden with a local businessman through franchising.

What Does a Franchise Cost?

Just what kind of investment is needed?

In Council's Handy Dan operations, the franchisee's investment runs from $2,000 for an outlet suitable for a service station or grocery store to nearly $100,000 for a massive installation, such as the one in Richmond, Virginia.

Rogers Sherwood, publisher of the respected *National Franchise Reports*, says that the majority of franchises cost from $5,000 to $20,000 but that some food drive-ins may call for a $30,000 down payment and financing of that much again.

But there are many who obtain franchises for much less. Consider the small capital investment it takes to start a Duraclean

International rug-cleaning business. The down payment is less than that usually required to buy a new car—a mere $800.

Franchising runs the gamut in terms of geography as well as investments. Virtually every imaginative marketing organization without national representation must consider the benefits of franchising for rapid growth. The country is as vast as it is wealthy and the potential profits in the national market are easy to see. But the competition out in the hinterlands has frightened off those who would start chain stores. To set up new stores would require millions of dollars in capital that may not be available through normal sources. Offering franchises, with a capital contribution by the individual franchisee, is one answer to the problem. It is the motivation to be in business for oneself that enables the franchise company to tap this source of capital and recruit first-rate prospects to run the businesses.

The franchiser knows the frustration of trying to get someone to work the long hours that retailing requires. So he brings his man in as a full-fledged partner. The franchisee's own substantial investment and desire for profits spur him to work hard, thus contributing to the success of the franchise company.

Why a Franchise?

What draws the potential small businessman to the franchiser? Basically, it is the franchiser's superior knowledge. Surprising though it may seem, most people who start their own businesses know only what they have learned through years of experience as customers of other retailers. Often this misleads them into believing it is a simple matter to make a profit in a small business. The man who enters business with this misconception is very likely to become a Dun and Bradstreet bankruptcy statistic.

More and more inexperienced men sense that they can bridge the information gap more easily with the help of a franchiser. It is hard to say precisely how much better one's chances of success are as a franchisee than as an individual proprietor, but clearly they grow enormously with the backing and assistance of a strong franchiser.

Statistics show that nearly 55 percent of all businesses formed in a recent year failed by the fourth year of operation. A Uni-

versity of Missouri study prepared by marketing experts concluded that a franchise does reduce the risk of failure. A former
president of the International Franchise Association (IFA),
Donald R. Hamacher, put the matter more specifically: "Two
International Franchise Association national surveys of member
firms with about 25,000 [franchised dealers] showed the percentage ratio of franchise turnover [to be] well under 5 percent,
with actual outlet failures less than half that figure."

These are figures for the IFA, an organization that holds members to an ethical code. There are also many fly-by-night franchise companies, and the failure rate in such operations is likely
to be much higher.

Mr. Hamacher, who is also president of the 600-stand Dog
'N Suds franchise company, believes that the odds favoring an
ethical franchise firm over an independent enterprise are enormous—on the order of 20 to 1.

A good franchise company offers a boost—no question about
it—and one of their strong points is a national image, which the
company will go to great lengths to build and maintain. An IFA
description runs thus: "Frequently, the physical layout and ap-
pearances are similar in all establishments within a particular
franchise group, such as distinctive buildings, signs, colors,
packages, uniforms, bottles, trucks, and business methods."

Here's an excerpt from the Burger Chef Systems agreement
illustrating the above point: "There shall be used in the dispensing and sale of products . . . only such containers, cartons,
sacks, napkins, spoons, flavorings, and garnishments as shall
comply with specifications and standards . . . and purchased
from suppliers designated [by the franchise company] . . . and
there shall be used in the dispensing and sale . . . such signs,
cards, notices, displays, or decorations as shall be supplied or
approved . . ."

The Value of Standardization

Standardization also applies to, as the IFA puts it, "merchandise or services sold. Operating procedures and methods
are also standardized to a high degree." Chicken Delight sets
stringent rules for the preparation and serving of their meals:

Chicken dinner—one-half of what is known in the poultry trade as an average 2¼–2½ pound dressed and drawn chicken (weighing 1 pound 15 ounces to 2 pounds 1 ounce without giblets and neck), cut into four pieces according to specifications . . . a generous portion of crinkle-cut French-fried potatoes, a blueberry muffin or an approved substitute, and a fully enclosed container of cranberry sauce or an approved substitute.

Chicken, shrimp, fish, ribs and potatoes shall be cooked in plain view of patrons, and, wherever possible, in plain view of passersby on the exterior of said place of business. [The franchisee] agrees to use only fresh, refrigerated chicken and not to use preserved chicken, such as canned, frozen, or cold-storage chicken . . . that chicken, shrimp, or fish [shall not be precooked] in anticipation of orders . . . but will cook from a raw state as each order is placed.

Standardization is often very important to the franchise business because customers want to know they can rely on a familiar name for quality and uniformity of product and service. The man who chooses to disregard the set procedures is regarded as a threat to the system, and the franchiser will deal sternly with him whenever possible. It is fair to say that a good franchiser has chosen his approach for reasons that will ordinarily be translated into profits for the individual franchisee.

Here's a further example of the painstaking approach that leads to a successful franchise.

Two classmates at the Harvard Business School, class of 1950, kept in touch with each other while they followed divergent business careers. By chance, one of them, Donald W. Phillips, in the machinery-manufacturing business in Pittsburgh, read a want ad placed by a crippled shoe-repair man who was seeking any available job opportunity. Phillips got in touch with him and eventually was able to design a compact shoe-repair machine built into a counter that also included a key-making machine and a device for sealing documents in plastic. All three operations were within the capacity of the handicapped artisan. By 1956 Mr. Phillips owned three such quick-service counters. Meanwhile his friend, D. Hillsdon Ryan, had been working for a major corporation in several capitals in Europe. Ryan noticed that the cobblestone streets there quickly ruined women's heels and that it took an average of three days to get repairs. So the two men opened a heel bar in 1957 in a Brussels department store for quick "American style" heel replacement using Phillips' special equipment.

By 1965 the two men were operating in Western Europe, South Africa, and Australia with 700 "Mister Minute" quick-repair counters, which also offered knife-sharpening services and engraving work. Finally, "Mister Minute" was offered on a franchise basis in the United States. The small capital needs—$3,500 cash on a total package price of $10,000 plus 10 percent royalty against gross sales—was within the range of small businessmen.

Thus a particularly appealing franchise—one arising out of the needs of a crippled cobbler—returned to America, the land of opportunity.

Opportunities abound in franchising. If you're anxious to be your own boss and you have saved some money or can borrow, there is undoubtedly a good future for you in this burgeoning field. There are profits for the hard-working and satisfactions far beyond mere monetary rewards. A successful franchised businessman is generally a respected member of his community—whether he is a college graduate or a high school dropout. Franchising opens the doors of success to the ambitious.

To give the reader an idea of the extent of franchising within the United States, on the following page is a rundown by industry with the number of outlets and the annual dollar volume for a recent year:*

* This list is based on estimates by the International Franchise Association and on U.S. government statistics.

Industry	Franchised Outlets	Annual Dollar Volume
Auto and truck dealers	33,000	$35,000,000,000
Carpet-cleaning services	4,000	100,000,000
Gas and oil service stations	206,302	14,178,000,000
Coin-operated and regular laundries and dry cleaners	35,700	509,000,000
Grocery stores	16,000	4,450,000,000
Hearing aids	3,500	70,000,000
Moving companies	5,000	1,000,000,000
Roadside food, beverage, and soft-ice-cream shops	24,590	1,409,611,000
Soft-drink bottlers	4,000	2,001,000,000
Swimming pools	1,000	40,000,000
Temporary help services	500	100,000,000
Variety stores	2,400	150,000,000
Water-conditioning systems and services	2,300	207,000,000
TOTALS	338,292	$59,214,611,000

2

Keynotes for Success—Two Very Different Case Histories

Americans never tire of Horatio Alger stories—tales of men who have started businesses on shoestrings and have risen to financial and social prominence. No doubt the American desire for success reflects our modest beginnings. Most of us are only one or two generations removed from European social systems that pegged a man even before his birth for a certain level of accomplishment—all too often a menial existence for life. Even the school systems perpetuated rigid social and economic classes, and thousands upon thousands of talented men were left only the crumbs off the tables of the elite.

But in this country we have that wonderful quality in our society which the social scientists call upward mobility. There are few barriers to the man who wishes to make something of himself. Our society may not be perfect, but the man who has talent, drive, and strength of purpose can succeed. Social barriers can be easily overcome through business success. Business has been so worthwhile for the man of limited educational back-

15

ground in this country that millions have taken the business route to personal success.

But many thoughtful people who would like to go into business have been plagued with doubts, fearful of the risks and afraid they might put their family's well-being in jeopardy. It is a well-known fact that most small businesses fail. Thousands of men of ability who should have succeeded have not made the grade.

Small wonder then that thousands have climbed aboard the franchise bandwagon to acquire partners with proven business methods, thorough training, and a uniform product well recognized and heavily advertised as powerful insurance against failure.

The Advantages of a Franchise

"The franchise method of operation has the advantage, from the standpoint of our American system of competitive economy, of enabling numerous groups of individuals with small capital to become entrepreneurs. . . . If our economy had not developed that system of operation these individuals would have turned out to have been merely employees. The franchise system creates a class of independent businessmen; it provides the public with an opportunity to get a uniform product at numerous points of sale from small independent contractors, rather than from employees of a vast chain. The franchise system of operation is, therefore, good for the economy. . . ."

So said Judge Dawson in a famous legal opinion in the case entitled *Susser v. Carvel Corporation.*

Does a franchise offer guarantees against failure? Obviously not! The very nature of business is one of taking risks in the hope of profits. But the best franchise opportunities in America today offer the qualified person an excellent chance of success. With their preselection approach, during which men who are unlikely to make it are turned away, the best franchise companies are able to trim the risk rate to a nearly negligible point.

There are scores of franchises that offer intelligent, hard-working individuals an excellent chance of becoming successful businessmen. Your job is to make sure that you have chosen the best franchise for you. A superior franchise for one man may offer only a limited chance of success for another. What's more, you must weed out the inferior franchise opportunities, of which there are many. Let's look at two different franchises just to get an idea of the kind of warning signs to watch for. In Chapter 41 you will find a checklist that will help steer you to the best in franchise opportunities.

Two Case Histories

Let's consider the widely divergent experiences of one happily married couple in the Eastern United States. Both are alert and intelligent, but the husband's experience illustrates what everyone should look for in franchising, and the wife's experience shows how easy it is to get off on the wrong foot.

Let's call the husband Bud King. Bud, a tough-minded man with a winning manner, started in what is commonly known as the 15-cent hamburger business (but now 18 and 19 cents). Bud was wise to the ways of business. He was once a stockbroker and he knew he needed a good attorney. He also knew that he had to take certain risks if he was to have a success.

By any measure, he had uncommonly good luck with his first franchised store. He tells the story this way:

"In my first year, I probably made $10,000 over and above the $12,000 I paid myself in salary. But when I opened my second store, in a highly industrialized community of around 50,000 people, things didn't go so well. I didn't make any money there at all in the first year. The company's projections were not misleading—they warned me I probably wouldn't make any money in the beginning.

"They could have hurt me if they wanted to. But instead they allowed me to hold back money due them from the second store just to keep me going. Now I'm making money in the second store and in a third store as well. I expect to do well over $1 million in sales this year. I hope to put up another seven or eight stores before I am done."

Bud went on to explain something about his dealings with the franchiser and what may or may not have given him an advantage over other men who opened stores licensed by the same company.

"Remember that I was with them four years ago when they were smaller. I have a very close relationship with the owners. They spent so much time telling me to be careful that I took their advice on everything they told me to do.

"Whenever I open a store they have two supervisors on the premises. Both of them are in there at least a week and one stays a second week, or as long as it takes to get things going. What's more, after that if I have a problem I get on the telephone, and if they can't handle it over the phone they send a man [from several hundred miles away].

"If things don't work out in any one of their stores, they are happy to buy it back and close it up. There's no charity involved. It's only because they take pride in their operations and because they want to protect their franchise.

"They've never tried to deprive me of anything I was entitled to. And the morale among the store operators is fantastic. They have done everything for us they said they would. I think that's why their failure rate is so low. I get the feeling they are personally interested in me and in my future."

A Different Experience

So much for Bud. Now let's see what happened to Colleen. Mrs. King has a travel agent's franchise that hasn't worked out, although report she was still plugging away at it. The parent company is an old and respected regional concern that, surprisingly, still has Bud and Colleen's goodwill. Its reputation was built on its operation of company-owned outlets. Franchising was an afterthought.

The problem, oddly enough, is that Colleen got in on the ground floor, at a time when the company was still shaking out the bugs. The company has admitted to Colleen that it knew very little about the franchising business when it signed her up.

Colleen, who used to be in the advertising business, was considering a travel franchise with one of the nation's leading agencies, but she saw an ad in the *Wall Street Journal* for the regional company and decided in their favor.

"I went with [the regional agency] because they are local, and that's very important in the travel-agency business. That's still the best thing I've got going for me.

"I hate to think about the people out in the Midwest going with this agency. They're paying $30,000 for a name that means nothing out there. I've tried to have a word with the new people when they bring them up here for indoctrination, but they won't let us get together."

Colleen is a cheerful, intelligent woman who views her predicament with wry humor. She blames the hotshot salesmen for misrepresentations the company was "powerless" to prevent.

"My husband's franchise is so good that the company gets enough people by word of mouth. They don't even have a salesman."

Colleen's problems were compounded when the airlines delayed approval of fees that normally are paid from discounts on tickets purchased by agencies recognized by the airlines.

She explains:

"The international carriers finally approved me retroactively. Meanwhile I was going broke because I couldn't get domestic airline approval.

"The internationals told me that I didn't get approval earlier because they didn't have the information they needed. I sent it to the company and they said they had sent it along. Well, did they or didn't they?

"I'll tell you one thing the company did for me. They did a character check on my first manager. He walked off with $2,500.

"I'm married to this business sixty hours a week, and so far the best I can do is break even. That's fine, but how could a breadwinner make out on a thing like that? I'm not taking a salary—I haven't taken a cent out of the business.

"I still don't blame the company. The company is very good on the things they do for me directly—particularly on sales aids. Their sales aids are great. But what good is that if you don't make money on what you sell?"

Thus, in the experience of a single family—a man and wife

who had widely varying experiences—we have seen how well
and how poorly one can do with a franchise company.

Why It Happened

Let's consider why the two had such different experiences.

In both cases, they were dealing with relatively new franchise
companies. One might have expected them both to get into
trouble, for experience is a great teacher for a franchise company just as it is for the small businessman.

Bud King had the advantage of signing with a company that
was keying every effort to its franchise opportunity. The men
running the company had sufficient capital and operational know-
how to make the franchise a success. They were prepared to
grant an extraordinary amount of credit to their man when
things did not work out as planned.

They advertised heavily so that the people in the area would
be aware of the franchise. The franchise itself was based on
careful and detailed analysis of methods and markets, so Bud
did not have to experiment and learn by his own painful experiences. He received extensive training as well.

The company worked hard at developing a reputation for
excellence, and succeeded to the extent that it was never necessary for them to hire commission salesmen to find men to run
their stores. Prospects beat a path to the franchise company's
door.

As for Colleen, she joined an organization with a respected
regional name in the business of running travel agencies. However, the company entered the franchise business almost as an
afterthought. Having no experience, the company was forced to
rely on outside "experts."

One suspects that the company was sold a bill of goods by the
franchise promoter. Certainly, the travel agency's reputation suffered as a result of its unsuccessful franchise program.

Colleen learned of the franchise by reading an ad in a prestige
publication and was sold by a salesman who was working on
commission. Since the salesman had an incentive to sell as

many dealerships as possible, he overstated the profit potential —whether the company wanted him to do this or not.

The company could not deliver on its promises because it was unfamiliar with franchising and the peculiar problems entailed in this exacting business. Even the basic essential to success— the ability to deliver the necessary rights to travel-agency fees —was lacking.

In short, Colleen was stuck with a sound company that had no particular expertise in franchising. Bud found a company that was prepared to back him to the hilt with expertise and assistance.

There you have the franchise story in brief. A franchise can be a bonanza or a bust. It can offer a first-class ticket to success or a one-way ticket to the point of no return. Very probably, it will offer something in between—a route to substantial profits in exchange for your capital and your hard work.

The main thing is to protect yourself against unnecessary hardship by finding the right franchise at a price that is reasonable and within your means.

Most of the nearly 800 franchises that appear in the directories of the industry are sound, hard-headed business propositions that can help you earn a good living and then some. But there are pitfalls for the unwary, for example, high-pressure salesmen and come-on advertisements that overstate the profit potential and understate the amount of work involved.

Paradoxically, the best franchise in the world may not be your cup of tea. It can be a mistake, for example, if it doesn't suit your personality or if it requires a younger, or an older, man.

This book is designed to help you discover the best franchise opportunity for you—to help you get your money's worth and find the success you seek.

3

Is It for Me?

"The typical International franchisee is married and has two children, generally under fifteen years of age; he has had three years of college training and semiprofessional or management experience in business; he is action oriented and people oriented; he demonstrates an intellectual performance rating of bright to superior."

That profile by Al Lapin, Jr., of International Industries, which franchises a number of ventures including the International House of Pancakes, is fine—for International Industries. But it is far too limiting for the franchise industry generally, for this is a field that has brought substantial success to thousands of men of modest scholastic achievement and little business background.

Indeed, the high school dropout who has driving ambition and stick-to-it-iveness is a better prospect for some franchises than his better-educated contemporary. Many men with college degrees are looking for an easier job than the long hours and vigorous activity imposed on most franchisees. Some even feel it is demeaning to appear behind a counter in an apron, even if this may be the means to a substantial income.

Types of Franchise Owners

Owners of franchised businesses range widely in backgrounds, representing virtually every social and economic walk of life. Many franchise owners are former engineers, lawyers, teachers, civil-service workers, mechanics, salesmen, clerical workers, industrial workers, and retail store owners or employees. However, a study undertaken by the University of Minnesota found that men who succeed in franchised businesses usually have a number of characteristics in common.

Successful dealers had a more than casual knowledge of the the trick of operating and managing a business when they came to franchising. They may have possessed some competence in a technical or professional area; for example, have been a bookkeeper or had a substantial amount of experience in a field related to the franchised business. The study showed that franchisees lacking such skills generally went into highly specialized dealerships, such as soft-ice-cream or soft-drink drive-ins.

The most frequent successes were noted in franchise businesses with track records of some standing. Well-established companies with accepted brand names that were either widely known or had great potential to become widely known brought the best opportunities for success.

The university study confirms that long hours are generally necessary. The successful dealers devoted a large percentage of their time and energy to building their businesses. Many posted sixty hours a week and others as high as eighty hours. The successful were also enthusiastic, energetic, and prudently attentive to business details.

Evaluating a Franchisee's Chances of Success

While it is easy enough to find the kind of person who has succeeded, franchise companies have never developed a foolproof method of finding such people in advance. They sometimes use psychological tests. Extensive questionnaires probe the applicant's health, personal background, character, and family status. The companies also use intuition in attempting to find the best prospects. However, their best efforts are not totally successful.

Paul Gurwick, vice president of Poraflor, a franchise company that offers resin coating systems with a basic franchise fee beginning at $2,500, says:

"We have always sought to discover methods to evaluate the caliber of the potential franchisee and to be able to select those that would be successful and those that would not. However, we have sadly come to the conclusion that this is not completely possible.

"Good predictions cannot be drawn upon the basis of past or current success in other businesses, financial ratings, or whether the applicant is tall, thin, short, or fat.

"I have one dealer in mind who has a multimillion dollar business and has been at a virtual standstill with Poraflor since purchasing a five-figure franchise. On the other hand, we have dealers whose total assets consist of themselves and possibly one other man and who are continuously doing work and making excellent profits and incomes."

Let's look at the advantages of going into business for oneself. It is unfortunate but true that there are relatively few truly satisfying jobs. Of course every company has a few top spots that offer high pay and a considerable amount of authority. Then there are glamour jobs in such fields as airline travel, newspapers, and television that offer psychic rewards that may make up for a lack of advancement and high pay.

But look around you at work. How many in your organization have been able to realize their full potential? Chances are, relatively few are truly happy.

The man with the right qualities is very likely to find fulfillment in his own business. He has an excellent chance of reaching his highest aspirations and earning enough to live very well indeed. One observer who has followed the franchise industry closely says that anyone who travels across the nation and passes through different towns will find that the local businessmen are heavily represented in the best residential sections. The men who occupy those luxurious homes also serve on town boards and provide community leadership. Their opinions are respected. Their help is sought in solving local problems, and they are given responsibilities for important projects.

Most ambitious men would rather work for themselves instead of a boss because they want more control over their own destiny. But in some there is great fear and hesitation, which is natural, for if a family man leaves his job to go into business for himself, he is placing his family's welfare on the line. No man wants to do that without some assurance of success.

A Strong Appeal

And this, of course, is one reason why franchising is so appealing. The franchise industry invites you to:

"Come with us and we'll see to it that you have everything going for you that human ingenuity can possibly arrange. We offer you successful methods that have worked throughout the country. Methods that should work for you just as they have worked for hundreds of men like you who have ambition and ability.

"We'll give you extended training, which may last for weeks, in our proven methods. We'll show you how to keep your books, how to prepare our products in a manner that will identify them with those we sell all over the nation. We'll find the very best location possible so that you will have considerable traffic of good potential customers—more than enough traffic to assure your success. We'll offer you a certain number of blocks or miles of radius within which no other man will be selling our products. Our national advertising program will back up your selling efforts and we'll offer you assistance in putting together advertisements in local newspapers that will 'tie in' with this national advertising. We'll have an experienced man in your territory at all times who will drop in from time to time to answer your questions and who will help solve your problems if you call on him in for assistance."

These and many other advantages are yours if you go into a business with a first-rate franchise company. You will be operating within a framework of rules that has brought success to many men who had feared the unknown in business just as you may. You'll be your own boss even though you will have to conform in some degree to the pattern of the franchise, but this will lead to sales and profits that would probably be unattainable otherwise.

What Do You Need to Succeed?

What qualities will you need for success?

As a businessman you will be dealing with all kinds of people. Many of them you will admire and respect. Some will give you a hard time. The customer, as you know, is always right—within reason. You should be prepared to talk pleasantly even when the customer is surly and unpleasant to you.

You will be a manager in your business. You will have to manage men, money, merchandise, methods, and, most important perhaps, minutes.

You must be a self-starter. Remember, if you decide not to open your store on a particular day, it simply will not open. So if golf beckons on a sunny morn, better choose a franchise that does not require your fulltime efforts every day.

You should have some zest for paperwork. Some paperwork is interesting and some not so pleasant. But you will have to keep payroll and tax records—meticulously. Until you are able to hire a bookkeeper, you may have to be both bookkeeper and entrepreneur.

If you are lacking in business education or experience, do you have the willingness to learn that will see you through today's fairly complex management problems? Do you think you have good judgment when it comes to selecting people to work for you? Remember, once you've picked an employee you have to train and supervise him too. Do people listen to you and respect your opinions? Are you flexible enough to react intelligently when you meet unusual problems? Do you work well in the face of competition—especially unexpected competition such as a rival firm across the street?

Do you think that you spend your money wisely? One indication that this is so is the fact that you have accumulated enough money to invest in a franchise. If you are borrowing the money, look back on your past purchases for a clue to your money management potential. Are you an impulse purchaser? Do you often regret your decisions?

Remember that as a businessman, you are on your own, even when you have a strong franchise behind you. You won't have a company pension plan or hospitalization insurance; you will have to arrange and pay for them yourself. You won't have paid vacations unless you finance them yourself and have trained a good manager to fill in for you. You'll have to buy insurance to protect your business. If you fall ill, you will have to pay someone to run it for you in the interim.

In all probability you will be "married" to your business, often working sixty hours a week or more. There are franchise opportunities for men who wish to hire others to manage for them, but those are in the minority. By and large, you will find that the franchise company wants you—not someone you have hired to do the job for you. Thus you should consider carefully whether the demands of franchising really appeal to you. If they do, then you will find rewards that are likely to match your ambitions and challenges that will fulfill your aspirations.

4

How Much Cash ... and What Am I Paying For?

There is marvelous variety in franchising, which makes it possible for thousands upon thousands of ambitious men to open businesses of their own. The cash requirements vary so widely that even someone with a couple of thousand dollars can join the parade.

No franchise company wants to take a man without an investment. They've found that people with a stake in a business tend to do better than those who have none. But it is surprising how very little is required to convert a man from an employee to an entrepreneur.

You may have heard the Carvel ads. A store here or a store there is available for just $5,000 cash. Or a General Motors dealer who is putting in a rent-a-car agency might be looking for a partner—an owner-manager to run if for him. You will need only $2,500.

A brand-new Shell station could be yours for as little as $12,000 —your investment in merchandise and gas—or even less.

Shell has on occasion helped a man into the station business for about one third of what it takes to stock it because they had faith that he had the ability to make the station pay.

For those with substantial capital, the sky is the limit. The General Motors dealer might be extending his credit as much as $250,000 to get enough cars to stock the rental agency. The big hamburger stands and other restaurants can also cost a pretty penny, but the small roadside stands like Carvel do not take much cash. McDonald's requires $53,000 in initial capital. Mr. Steak requires $35,000, but this can come from investors. The owner-manager must put up at least $5,200.

How Much Money Do You Need?

Thus, if you can borrow, you may be able to get into a substantial business that might otherwise be closed to you. You should ask the franchise company whether they permit outside investors to put up part of the cash for you. If you do take this route to buy a franchise, be sure to get a good lawyer to set up the arrangements so that ultimately you will own the business in large part.

Ordinarily, the franchise company will give you a realistic estimate of the amount of money you will need to get going. Members of the International Franchise Association are pledged to avoid overstating potential profits in the early stages and usually are careful to point out how much you will need to live on in the meantime—before the profits begin to carry you along.

Question the franchise company carefully on the question of money. It should willingly offer convincing documentation—enough to convince your banker and your lawyer—that their licensed dealers do as well as they say they do. Make sure that you understand how you can afford to live during the first year, when the business may break even or even show a loss. Remember that in the eyes of the state you are not unemployed once you open the doors to do business. To qualify for unemployment checks you must be actively seeking a job.

Consider the experiences of Alex, a businessman who decided to shift his enterprise to a franchised rental agency.

"A man who doesn't put aside $9,000 or so for living expenses

when he opens one of these operations is heading for trouble."
Alex said that a man with a rental shop in a heavily populated
area should make it, although he knew a man who did half again
as much business as he did himself and yet did not make the
franchise company's projection of profits.

Question Those in the Same Business

Keep this vital point in mind. Once you have decided on the
kind of franchise you want, visit a number of other franchised
dealers in the same business, particularly those who are in areas
similar to the one in which you will be located. The reliable
franchise company with nothing to hide will urge you to follow
through on this plan and will tell you where to find their dealers.

You may want to use the checklist in Chapter 41 when you
question their dealers. It will help you cover key points regarding potential profits and problems you can expect to encounter
in your new business.

Be sure to find out how much the dealers have made—including salary and whether they were able to make profits in the
early years. Find out what kind of assistance the franchise company gave them if they had financial difficulties in the beginning. Find out if they have unpaid relatives in the business or
if they have found other ways to trim their costs not available
to you.

Do you have sources of additional money if you should need
it? Do you have parents or in-laws who can extend help if you
and your family need it in the early years of your new business?
Have you securities you can pledge for loans? Can you get a
second mortgage on your house?

One of the most common causes of failure in a new business
is too little capital. Don't let this contingency spoil an otherwise promising future.

The leading franchise companies have now set up codes to
help their dealers avoid disappointment and have established
exacting standards to determine whether they can handle the
financial burden in the beginning. The companies have pro-

cedures to help their dealers over the rough spots by advancing them merchandise and making various adjustments to keep the business going.

The legitimate franchise company is as concerned about your success as you are. It wants you to succeed because your profits are the best guarantee that the franchise company itself will continue to be a profitable enterprise.

Now that we've considered the question of your initial cash commitment, let's look into the continuing financial obligations to the franchise company.

Other Financial Commitments

After you have paid the initial fees for the franchise itself and the costs of equipment and inventory, if any, you will have to pay a percentage of your gross revenue on a continuing basis for the right to use the franchise. At least that's the way most franchise companies operate.

It many cases you will also pay for supplies—priced so that the franchise company can make a profit on the merchandise. (Lately, franchise companies have come to rely on percentages of gross revenue from their dealers as an alternative to markups on supplies because the courts have limited the franchise companies' rights to act as exclusive suppliers to their dealers.)

Profits on the sale of supplies are still, however, a major source of income for many franchise companies. Where special formulas are involved, such as in the ice-cream and soft-drink fields, carpet cleaning, glass tinting, supplies must as a rule be purchased from the franchiser. But the companies that use this source of income are careful not to overcharge for their supplies. Many turn from this source of income completely. As Harry J. Sonneborn, president of McDonald's Corporation, puts it:

"We know that, theoretically, we could make more quick profits if we were in the supply business . . . On $15 million worth of paper products alone, we could be making about $1.5 million. But by doing so, we would be tying our success to how much our franchisee buys from us and not on how much he sells . . .

and succeeds . . . We prefer to stay on the same side of the fence as our local partners, to make a profit on his success and not on his inventory."

We have already seen that the franchise company often profits from the sale of equipment and from initial charges, usually called "fees." And we know that the franchise companies very often lease equipment to the dealer at a profit rather than sell it outright.

At any rate, whatever technique is used, you—as potential franchisee—are concerned with the question of how much you can make after all charges are deducted. Once again, you should visit other franchised dealers so that you can determine whether the franchise company's charges are fair.

Some companies charge for tax and accounting services. You may be asked to pay a percentage of your gross for a national advertising campaign that is conducted on behalf of all franchised dealers.

Some Specific Charges

Here are a few actual examples of specific franchise-company charges:

Robert Half Personnel Agencies, Inc., charges $7,500 for the franchise, of which $2,500 must be paid at the time the agreement is signed. The remainder is payable at a rate of $250 a month starting with the thirteenth month of operation. If the office is closed for any reason, the franchised dealer's obligation is terminated. In addition, the franchisee must pay a percentage of gross receipts varying between 5 and 7 percent, depending on how early the franchisee joined the system. The offices that opened when the franchise was new pay less than the later offices, which presumably benefit from the earlier promotional efforts to familiarize the public with the Robert Half name.

The franchise package offered by 60 Minute Cleaners costs $35,000, with the company willing to finance $20,000 of that sum over five years. While the interest charge was originally 6 percent, there is now a line in their literature stating, "Balance is to be financed at prevailing interest rates." (Interest rates, as you know, have risen dramatically, and most financing charges will reflect this change.) The company also gets a "management services fee" equal to 6 percent of sales.

The soft-ice-cream franchise companies often require regular payments from their dealers based on the number of gallons of mix purchased. American Dairy Queen, which has recently shifted many stores to straight percentage-of-gross payments, charges some dealers—particularly those who serve soft ice cream primarily—so much a can for the ten-gallon mix containers.

Apart from the percentage-of-gross charge, perhaps the most common franchise-company charge is a levy for advertising expense. After all, it is important to be associated with a company with a well-known name, and perpetuating that name before the public is a costly business.

Midas Muffler charges its franchised dealers 2 percent of purchases as a contribution toward the company's sales-promotion program. Dairy Queen has a voluntary promotion program; the dealer must belong to the program to get local support.

Each member of the Hertz Rent-A-Car system makes contributions to a fund that is used for sales promotion, advertising, and related programs. Payments are made monthly, and determined in accordance with the following yearly rates, given for a recent year: $205 a year for each passenger car used for transient rental, $17 for each passenger car used for long-term lease, and $27 for each truck used in the business.

United Rent-Alls charges the franchisee $1 per month for each $1,000 of equipment in his inventory as a contribution to the advertising program. The company also contributes to the program, to the extent of 20 percent of franchisee payments.

Franchise companies often offer discounts to encourage their dealers to purchase supplies from them rather than from other suppliers. Franchisees in one organization are expected to buy all their initial inventory and 60 percent of their additional inventory from the franchise company. At the end of each calendar year the dealer receives a credit equal to 2 percent of his sales if he meets the 60 percent requirement and 3 percent if he buys at least 75 percent of his needs from the franchise company.

In some contracts the prices of the items to be purchased from the franchiser are specifically detailed. For example, MUGS UP's agreement specifies the price of the company's special-strength root-beer concentrate and sandwich mixes.

Under the Chicken Delight franchise agreement the dealer agrees to buy specified service items solely from Chicken Delight. In turn, the company agrees that the prices for the items shall be reasonable—and no greater than the amounts indicated in the contract. Any future price increases are limited to 10 percent in any six months' period. In the event that prices have to be increased, the franchise company agrees to furnish evidence that their costs have also increased. Purchases of batter used to coat the chicken before frying must also be made exclusively from the franchise company—again at reasonable prices.

There you have it, then, a rundown of the kinds of charges you can expect to pay. But remember to get in touch with individual franchised dealers to learn their actual experience in the field. For the key question is not the charges, but whether you can make a good living with a particular franchise company.

On the next two pages are two examples of basic franchise costs and continuing fees for two completely different organizations— Sheraton Inns and the Weather-matic Company, an organization in the business of installing lawn sprinklers.

These examples are reprinted from the literature of both companies.

SHERATON INNS, INC.

For an inn which is in operation, the initial fee, which is due upon execution of the License Agreement, is as follows:

Up to 125 rooms $7,500

For each guest room in excess of 125,
$100, up to a maximum initial fee of $12,500

Continuing Fees

There will be a continuing fee of twenty five cents (25c) per room per night or four percent (4%) of room sales, whichever is greater. The continuing fee is based on the number of available rooms and not occupied rooms. Continuing fees are payable monthly. There is no separate advertising assessment; the continuing fee covers your inclusion in Sheraton advertising.

Sheraton's Reservation System
Reservatron II

All Sheraton Hotels and Motor Inns must participate in Sheraton's electronic computerized system known as Reservatron II. The cost of this system is apportioned among all Sheraton properties, and the fee for all Sheraton Inns is Two Dollars and Fifty Cents ($2.50) per available room per month. Reservatron II gives the system's available rooms, eliminating the need for an individual property to have Teletype or Telex machines. There are no other charges connected with Reservatron II; installation, message costs, and training are all included in the monthly charge.

WEATHER-MATIC DEALER INVESTMENT SCHEDULE
Effective March 1, 1968

INITIAL FRANCHISE INVESTMENT

Training/orientation fee	$ 1,100.00
Advertising/sales promotion package	560.00
Media "lift-off" advertising program	1,000.00
Initial material inventory	840.00
Total	$ 3,500.00

EQUIPMENT REQUIREMENTS	*Cash Plan*	*Finance Plan*
Truck	$ 2,250.00	$ 400.00
Trenching machine/trailer	1,000.00	100.00
Laborers' tools	200.00	200.00
Mechanics' tools	150.00	150.00
Office equipment	865.00	865.00
Drafting equipment	160.00	160.00
Total	$ 4,625.00	$ 1,875.00

WORKING CAPITAL REQUIREMENTS

First-month operating expense	$ 1,000.00
Your living expenses while in training	300.00
*Round-trip air fare for Dallas training school	200.00
Operating reserve	4,000.00
Total	$ 5,500.00

*Will vary according to distance from Dallas

TOTAL INVESTMENT REQUIRED	*Cash Plan*	*Finance Plan*
Initial franchise investment	$ 3,500.00	$ 3,500.00
Equipment	4,625.00	1,875.00
Working capital	5,500.00	5,500.00
GRAND TOTAL	$13,625.00	$10,875.00

5

How Much Can I Make?

"Of the franchised dealers interviewed, three out of four felt they had realized their profit expectations, and in several instances . . . expectations had been greatly exceeded."—From "The Franchise System of Distribution," a report prepared by the University of Minnesota for the Small Business Administration.

Running a franchise business is somewhat like taking a ferryboat. You wouldn't go just for the ride, but it's a pleasant way to get where you're going. Similarly, most people who go into business for themselves do it for the pleasure of being their own boss. But they probably wouldn't do it unless they believed they could make a better living than they could by working for someone else.

So if you are buying a franchise to be your own boss, all well and good. But you might just as well be boss of a $20,000-a-year business as one that returns $10,000. After all, you want the most profitable franchise you can get for your money.

As soon as you start checking into some of the ads you've been reading, you'll find you've got a strong factor in your favor: there is lots of competition among the franchisers for good people.

Excellent franchises are there for the asking if you meet the requirements.

The Odds in Your Favor

Perhaps this story will give you an idea as to just how heavily the cards are stacked in your favor. A couple of years ago a major food-service chain spent $14,000 advertising for qualified candidates to run their stores. They found just two. A spokesman for Partners for Profits commented, "More striking is the fact that this is a well-known, long-established firm with high profits whose recruitment problems should be minimal."

Yes, franchising is still growing by leaps and bounds, and as a result, you're in a "buyers' market." That's the general picture. Now let's get down to specific cases.

It is probably fair to say that the more money and time you invest, the greater the return you are likely to have—over the long run. Yet there are all kinds of opportunities that require little capital and still return a good living. For instance, if you are willing to enter the door-to-door selling field, Watkins Products, Inc., may be for you. Watkins, which distributes cosmetics, vitamins, spices, and similar items, is looking for distributor-managers to recruit and train twenty to sixty salesmen through sales conferences, contests, and sales assistance, and to supply them with merchandise.

Watkins has a salaried training program, and your $3,000 inventory of supplies can be taken on a consignment basis. Your potential income is probably $11,000 to $12,000 a year.

But unlike businesses in which it is possible to lose money indefinitely, you're a cinch to make *some* money with Watkins so long as you put forth an effort. In fact, some would regard Watkins as a job. And like a job, the rewards are limited—as is the investment.

Probably you're looking for bigger stakes and may be able to make a more substantial investment. Perhaps you have your eye on a hamburger stand, doughnut house, rental center, or even a Puppy Palace.

Puppy Palace Enterprises, Inc., had six outlets in and around Philadelphia when it began franchising in 1967. The concern now plans a 750-store franchising operation.

The company states, "All puppies sold by the chain carry an unusual ten-year guarantee against accident, sickness, and death. Store owners are initially asked to invest a minimum of 50 percent of the total price of $15,000. This provides everything needed to commence business in leased premises. Financing assistance is also available for the conversion of existing pet facilities.

"Individual stores' annual volume is estimated at from $100,000 to $200,000 with a net of 19 percent to 28 percent. This is over and above the 5 percent royalty on gross sales charged by the home office for continuing guidance."

If you're really interested in a big potential, try Burger Chef Systems—just one of several highly successful concerns in the 15-cent (but now 18 and 19 cents) hamburger business. They pay you very well indeed to attend their school at the Indianapolis headquarters, presumably out of the $25,000 minimum you've put up in cash to buy the $48,500 franchise.

By one account, they'll have you "going out of your mind" from their vigorous training. You'll be expected to remember the "twenty-five points of effective counter selling" while serving burgers at a mock-up Burger Chef counter. You have to get all that down pat in three weeks, but the effort should be worth it.

If everything works out as planned, an average store with a $4,000-a-week gross could put you in the $30,000-a-year class, assuming the competition for the hamburger dollar doesn't get too tough in your neighborhood.

However, that's not the limit to your potential riches. As you've already seen, a good franchiser is not letting you in so that you can hire a manager, but once you are in and prove successful, the company may let you buy more franchises and hire managers to run them. If you eventually owned ten Burger Chef stores, for example, you could easily net $100,000 a year, having financed the additional stores through profits piled up on the earlier ones. According to one analysis, such success in the hamburger business is not a pipe dream. All the McDonald's stores in Washington, D.C., are owned by a single, hugely successful franchisee who started with one stand.

Just to give you an idea of the kind of return you can expect, here are some random figures from a representative franchise operation, Ben Franklin Variety Stores. Ben Franklin, which has nearly 2,500 stores in operation in all parts of the country, sells notions, household supplies, clothing items, and miscellaneous everyday articles in a fairly low price range.

Location	Annual Sales	Total Income & percent of sales		Investment required	Percent back on investment
Southeast	$144,815	$18,590	12.8%	$53,000	34.7%
Mid-South	88,077	13,259	15.1	40,000	33.2
Southwest	91,803	9,794	10.7	41,500	23.6
Mid-Central	165,210	25,600	15.5	57,800	44.3
East	333,206	41,036	12.3	86,000	47.7
Midwest	151,498	17,720	11.7	59,800	29.6
Mid-South	88,773	12,843	14.5	40,000	32.1
Mid-Central	91,520	13,055	14.3	41,500	31.5
West	150,799	20,711	13.7	59,800	34.6
Midwest	241,461	35,900	14.9	66,800	53.7
East	140,248	22,621	16.1	53,400	42.4
East	127,658	13,701	11.3	47,000	29.2
Mid-Central	126,999	20,598	16.2	51,200	40.2
West	196,555	25,890	13.2	56,500	45.8
Northwest	155,030	18,889	12.2	59,800	31.6
Southwest	93,167	12,192	13.1	41,500	29.4
Mid-South	121,629	13,063	10.7	47,000	27.8
West	129,256	13,028	10.1	51,200	25.4
East	284,142	33,061	11.6	75,200	44.0

Here's a profit picture drawn up by Schwinn Bicycle Company, the nation's largest bicycle manufacturer. Schwinn in effect has worked backward in the franchising field, using franchise agreements as a method of eliminating unqualified (nonproductive and inefficient) accounts while it seeks out promising new dealers.

Schwinn says the examples below are based on actual operating statements submitted by Schwinn dealers. They assume a market potential of at least 35,000 people in the middle-to-upper income levels and a store-rental cost of $300 a month for a 500-bike-a-year volume and $400 a month for a 1,000-bike-a-year volume. Also assumed are a man-and-wife team for the smaller stores (500 bikes) with an additional one or two part-timers for larger stores; Schwinn says that a 500-bike store can go to 600, 700, or even more bikes without a proportionate increase in investment or operating expense.

SCHWINN 500-BIKE SET-UP

Investment:	Inventory: 100 bicycles	$4,000	
	Parts and accessories	4,000	
	Store and shop equipment	10,000	
			$18,000

Sales per year

Merchandise dollars		Gross profit	
500 bikes	$26,500	$6,500	(at suggested retail prices)
Parts and accessories	20,000	6,700	
Labor	5,000	5,000	
	$51,500	18,200	
Estimated operating expenses		9,000	
Owner's income before taxes		$9,200	

SCHWINN 1,000-BIKE SET-UP

Investment:	Inventory: 150 bicycles	$6,000	
	Parts and accessories	7,000	
	Store and shop equipment	15,000	
			$28,000

Sales per year

Merchandise dollars		Gross profit	
1,000 bikes	$53,000	$13,000	(at suggested retail prices)
Parts and accessories	40,000	13,300	
Labor	10,000	10,000	
	$103,000	$36,300	
Estimated operating expenses		21,100	
Owner's income before taxes		$15,200	

Schwinn reports that they now have about 3,000 dealers, of which 534 have become high-volume accounts selling over 500 bikes a year, and that they are operating "clean, modern, and up-to-date dealerships." At the present rate of growth, Schwinn expects to have 1,000 of these high-volume accounts by 1970.

A Postscript on Profits

Chalk up another plus for the successful dealer when he sells his franchise business. He's been piling up a stake year by year that may not really show until he sells out. And this is something you have to look forward to as well as a substantial income.

Item: A Dairy Queen dealer earned $10,000 a year for ten years and never took less than a three months' vacation in Florida. He finally sold his busy little store in 1964, making a $20,000 profit, in effect adding $2,000 a year to his past earnings (and at a lower tax rate).

Item: A restaurant owner who was an expert at picking prime locations usually sold his stores within a few years. He once sold a store that was still celebrating its grand opening, making a five-figure profit. Over a lifetime he built an estate of $250,000 largely through his build-and-sell tactics—to say nothing of the comfortable living he earned in the meantime.

It's impossible to set forth a sure-fire guide to profits on the resale of a small business, but one thing is clear: franchises, by and large, are more popular on the resale market than independent businesses. Indeed such is the popularity of franchising businesses that they have put the independents in the shadows. One business broker reports that a man who owns one of the few remaining soft-drink distributorships in the East, a business that earns $50,000 a year, is unable to find a buyer. He cannot convince those who have looked at the business that it earns so much money with relatively little work. "He keeps the books, hires the delivery men, and they do the rest," is the way the broker put it.

The popular Mr. Donut shops reportedly sell for three times their annual earnings after the first year. Assuming you rang up profits of $20,000 a year—which is considered a reasonable figure—your store would be worth $60,000 after a year of successful operation. You'd have about $25,000 cash in the business and another $20,000 in machinery. At those prices, you would be ahead at least $15,000, and even more if the buyer picked up some of the equipment financing.

Robert Half, an expert in sums and digits, is even more optimistic. He's the certified public accountant who gave his name to a personnel-agency franchise that specializes in finding jobs for accountants and other finance experts. Half told a congressional committee studying franchising that his successful franchises are worth seven times annual earnings. Thus, one paying the franchisee $35,000 a year would be worth $250,000.

By contrast, liquor stores, one of the most popular of independent businesses, normally sell for only 30 to 45 percent of annual sales. The average store in New York City grosses upward of $150,000 a year, so such a business would be worth $45,000 to $67,500.

It's a little like the difference between renting an apartment and buying a house. After many years of renting you have nothing to show for your payments but rent receipts. The house will have a cash value. Of course the house involves a little more time and effort on your part, as will a franchise business. But isn't it worth it?

The point, of course, is that a good franchise is worth more than you paid for it. All the risks of building and opening have been taken. The location has proved to be a winner, and the community has shown it will support the store.

You're not going into the franchise business with the idea of selling out, of course, but someday you may want to. The equity you are building is a nest egg for your future.

6

The Importance of Training

If the prospect of having your own business frightens you a little, you'll be in good company. Fact is, hardly anybody knows very much about the business he is entering when he puts his name at the bottom of a franchise contract. You might, for example, have worked in a gas station as a youth or clerked in a dime store, but unless you are an exception, when you open your soft–ice-cream store or your rental agency or whatever you do, it will be a new experience.

Franchisers recognize this problem and have set up training programs to offset this inexperience with a concentrated dose of their know-how. This may be delivered at the home office, or it may be on-the-job training in a working store—either company owned, or operated by one of their successful dealers.

Some of these training periods last a relatively short time—a few days of concentrated activity—and others are quite long. Some take up several weeks of your time, and you may have to travel to the company's home office at your own expense. Some franchisers believe the man should pay his own living costs, and they use his willingness as a test of his seriousness of purpose. Others see it differently and will help defray your expenses while you are learning the trade.

Mr. Donut actually pays trainees a fair salary during the weeks of training. It is almost unheard of for a franchiser to charge a fee for their instruction. If the franchise you're considering lists a charge for tuition, put a question mark over it.

In any event, get a clear-cut understanding of the training you are entitled to and make sure that the contract spells it out in detail. Your lawyer can see to that.

Before we look at a couple of training programs, one long and one short, let's look into the question of training after the fact.

How Franchisers Help

The best franchisers follow a policy of keeping their dealers informed of new developments and ideas. They keep traveling supervisors on the job to help dealers meet unexpected problems. The first order of business for the traveling men is to help you open your store. Very likely, you'll find that the company will put one or two men with you in the beginning—for a few days or for as long as a couple of weeks—just to get you off and running. After that, the supervisors will probably be at your beck and call when you run into problems. Once again, be certain that the company's post-training commitment is put in writing.

Remember that the franchiser is just as interested in the success of your store as you are. He's going to do everything within reason to keep you going and to realize the profits you both expect. If you don't make any money, neither does he over the long pull—whether he takes his share through fees, royalties, or payments for supplies you buy from him.

Here is what the marketing director of Burger King Corporation says about the success of that Florida-based self-service hamburger chain: "We have over 300 successful restaurants. We are interested in a record of 100 percent success, and we work to make all franchisees make money."

Evidently, the company makes good on its word, and the news has gotten around. Burger King claims that they have never had to advertise for prospective franchisees.

The even larger, Indianapolis-based Burger Chef Systems (over 850 limited-menu restaurants in forty-two states and Canada) is worth looking at for its training methods.

Burger Chef trainees have sunk a minimum of $25,000 into their franchises by the time they unpack their suitcases in the Hoosier capital, so their hearts are in it. (They get their money back if they cannot pass the course.)

The training is what the teachers call "structured," and everybody is expected to do it the way they teach it. Burger Chef says there are twenty-five points of effective counter selling, and it drills this message into the trainees through a variety of teaching aids. There are teaching machines and a closed-circuit television system that records the gaffes trainees make while standing behind a Burger Chef counter pushing burgers out to "customers."

The instant playback shows with merciless precision all the mistakes the trainee has made, all the rules he has broken. As a Burger Chef trainee, you would be trying hard to get that burger to the customer within forty-five seconds.

After your demonstration the instructors may point out that you forgot, for example, to ask the customer courteously, "May I help you, sir?" or that you jammed a five-dollar bill into the cash box instead of laying it beside the register so there will be no question over whether it was a five, a ten, or a one.

You have to learn the system well enough to be able to tell the people you will employ how to keep the store running. Burger Chef insists that the level of your success will depend upon how well you master *their* method of doing things.

The training goes well beyond the burger window. You will be expected to learn how to assemble and take apart a condiment dispenser and to do chores that you might balk at doing for your wife. Once you are through schooling, you'll be given a thick orange manual to comfort you on the firing line.

There you have an example of a relatively long training program designed to teach you everything you need to know.

You can be sure that Burger Chef and most other franchisers that offer extended training include some basic instructions on record-keeping procedures. They will not expect you to become an instant accountant or expert bookkeeper, but you will be expected to keep whatever records they have prepared for your use.

Several owners of franchises who were interviewed in connection with this book complained that they were not taught anything about keeping daily accounts. Clearly, these franchise companies presumed that the dealers were sufficiently schooled to handle any problems and that training was unnecessary.

If you have doubts about your ability to run a fairly complicated business, be sure that the franchise you choose doesn't require skills that are beyond you. Discuss it with some business friends or with your accountant and lawyer before you sit down to sign a franchise contract.

The Schwinn Training Program

Let's look at a shorter training program, such as the one that Schwinn Bicycle offers. The dealers spend just three days with company instructors, but the program is considered thorough and effective in conjunction with the other assistance the company constantly offers its dealers.

Schwinn's vice president Ray Burch is highly regarded in the franchise industry for his training know-how and marketing skill. He believes training is the key to success in franchising and that the public has learned that the franchised dealer is well trained and "knows his business better."

Mr. Burch argues that franchised dealers "maintain higher standards and more courteous service" than most of their non-franchised competitors. It's that financial stake again, he says, and goes on to explain that Schwinn finally decided to give up selling bikes in all chain and department stores, "even the very finest," because their employees were "not interested" in Schwinn's training and therefore "just couldn't be taught."

By contrast, the investor-dealers bring intense concentration to their studies, Mr. Burch has found, making it possible to cram in a lot of information in a relatively short period of time. A franchised dealer is so eager that it is possible to set up long days plus evening sessions, and "He'll be there . . . He didn't come to be entertained . . . he came to learn. After-hours get-togethers last well into the night."

To give you some idea what to expect from a thoughtful training program, here are the Schwinn principles. A well-run program offers three broad objectives: first, to qualify the franchisee as a "true expert" in the product or service offered; second, to "indoctrinate" the dealer with a sincere desire to render outstanding service to customers so to enhance Schwinn's trademark in the store and in general; third, to "assure the success, the well-being, and the future security of each franchisee and his employees."

Sales Techniques

With regard to sales techniques, Mr. Burch states; "In sales training, for example, we teach and emphasize *demonstration*— not merely a test ride of a Schwinn bicycle but a physical demonstration of the special quality-construction features that make Schwinn Bicycles different from other bicycles—such things as the Schwinn double-thickness tubular rims, which are not only lighter in weight but also five times stronger than ordinary single-thickness rims. Here the dealer learns how to use the bicycle parts on the Schwinn demonstration board, and how to ask the prospect to twist a half-circle section of an ordinary rim, which is easily twisted, then try to twist a similar section of a Schwinn tubular rim, which is quite strong and rigid.

"He also learns to point out the differences between Schwinn's solid forged-steel front forks and the hollow, tubular forks used on other bicycles; welded-on versus bolted-on kickstands; and how to demonstrate Schwinn's stronger construction by standing on the chain guard and sitting on the rear fender. He not only learns how to do these and other demonstrations, but he also learns the proper words to use to explain them in terms of consumer benefits. He learns from sound slide films, from manuals, and from actual practice in our sales school classes.

"Our Schwinn sales-training classes also teach methods of guiding the dealer through the six steps of a Schwinn sale, from the approach to service after the sale, courtesy in customer contacts, and courteous handling of complaints and adjustments under the Schwinn guarantee."

(It's worth mentioning in passing that Schwinn's approach includes something unheard of a few years ago—carpeted bicycle showrooms, which the company says make an "astounding difference in customer behavior and in sales. The same customer who used throw his cigaret butt on the floor and haggle over the price now carefully uses the ash tray, speaks softly, and cheerfully pays the price.")

Sales and Service

In Schwinn's world, there are two areas in which its dealers must be expert—sales *and* service.

"Our Schwinn service schools teach service procedure by having the dealers or mechanics actually do each repair and service job, using the recommended equipment.

"The method used in our service school classes is learning-by-doing. First, the instructor explains and demonstrates to the class the operation of a component such as a coaster brake or three-speed hub. Then he shows how to disassemble it and diagnose the possible causes of faulty operation. He then shows how the repair is made and the unit reassembled, adjusted, and tested. Each trainee then repeats the process at his own bench, and the instructor grades each one on each component he repairs. If he gets a passing grade on the three-day course, he receives a Schwinn-Trained Service Certificate. If he doesn't pass, he can attend another class and try again."

In addition to this formal training, Schwinn supplies sales and service manuals, a monthly dealer paper, and other educational materials.

So you see that training includes some time with the company and, usually, some time in your own store. However, there are instances when franchised dealers get into a business and find that they do not know enough about it or, worse yet, do not particularly like it.

You might set out to learn the business you are considering by taking a job with a successful man in the chain you like. Mr. Burch maintains that this is one of the "great strengths" of franchising—the almost universal willingness of franchisees to help one another. "Some of our better Schwinn dealers are glad to let other dealers work in their stores to learn the business. Very often the successful franchisee is far more effective in guiding and influencing a new franchisee than anyone from the home office."

So take it from there. Perhaps you ought to consider a bit of moonlighting while you are considering giving up your job to go into franchising. Get yourself a second-shift job in a franchise business and work there for a few months. If you are still sold on the franchise after you put in the time, you will be well along the road when you take the formal training offered by the franchise company. You will also have gotten a good idea of the problems and advantages of becoming a member of that particular franchise family, so when you get behind that counter you'll easily slide into the routine and begin to enjoy being your own boss.

7

The Uses of Advertising

You can't listen to a radio or watch television these days without becoming aware of franchising. You see McDonald's colorful clown, Ronald, pursued by an army of kids; in the East you can hear Carvel extol its "ice-cream supermarket"; Avis constantly reminds you that the company is "only number two" and therefore must "try harder."

These advertising campaigns are designed to keep the company's name before the public at all times, and the three mentioned have certainly been successful. If you have children, you know what it is like to pass a McDonald's without stopping when the kids are in the car. Think of the many times you've driven up to a soft-ice-cream store just to quiet the back-seat din.

You may have rented from number one, but you'll never forget the Avis slogan, and, given the chance, you've probably checked the ash trays of an Avis car to see if they stand by their cleanliness creed.

All this advertising fits more or less into the "image making" category. It is one of the best things you'll have going for you when you open your own franchise business. Indeed, without the "brand name" identification you get with a franchise, you would have very little to show for your investment. The company may help you learn the business and set it up for you so that you can operate it in a fool-proof manner, but it's the Avis sign over the door, the Mary Carter name, or the Esso medallion that will draw in the trade.

The Mark of Merit

Franchise companies of merit all have effective advertising or promotional programs. In well-managed franchises, the advertising programs extend beyond radio and television into national magazines, local newspapers, and into the related area of sales promotion.

One reason you'll be interested in the franchise company's advertising program is because you will probably be asked to contribute toward the local part of it at least. You may also have to pay into the national advertising program in some instances.

Keep this point in mind: local advertising may be much more important to you than national, or vice versa. For instance, national advertising that does not reach the people who shop with you is of no value whatever. Suppose you are operating in a small city where there is only one television channel. A strong national advertising program carried by another network is a total loss to you.

If you have a flair for sales promotion, you may prefer a franchising company that gives you considerable leeway in spending your advertising dollar. Some companies collect the money and advertise as they see fit. Others, Burger King, for one, go the other way. Burger King insists that its dealers allocate 2 percent of their gross sales on local advertising, but does not itself spend the money. It's up to you. Thus you have a considerable degree of control over the local program and what it does for you. You must, however, get approval of the advertising "copy" from Burger King.

Local Tie-ins

Franchisers generally encourage dealers to "tie in" local advertising with what they're telling the folks on TV. For example, if Howard Johnson's is plugging fresh peach ice cream, you're likely to get more mileage out of your advertising dollar if you do too, and say "Buy it here." The national advertising tells the customer what to buy; your local ad tells him where to buy it.

Burger King isn't the only company that calls for a 2 percent budget for local advertising. Several franchisers suggest 2 percent of sales. Thus, if your dealership grosses $150,000 a year you should spend $3,000.

There may be occasions when you will want to budget more for local advertising. Suppose, for example, it turns out that your store is not quite so well located as you had anticipated. Maybe the state is tearing up the highway near your store and disrupting the traffic pattern. You may want to spend over your budget to hold your customers, to tell them the best alternate route to get to your store. Or stiffer-than-anticipated competition may be the reason you ought to jack up the ad schedule.

Your Franchise Sign

Once again, be sure to place your franchiser's sign where it can be seen—the national advertising campaign will be stressing the name. Franchisers generally encourage dealers to place ads in the Yellow Pages, a surprisingly effective means of advertising locally. Remember, the telephone company is your "partner" in this project as they tell people to "Let your fingers do the walking . . . through the Yellow Pages." The day you throw open the doors to your new establishment you will want the neighborhood Boy Scouts out in force distributing handbills and premium offers.

Ordinarily, the franchiser will provide the necessary advertising copy and scripts for television commercials and will give you instructions for their use.

Here's how Martinizing, the 2,500-store dry-cleaning company describes its advertising and promotion program:

"Consistently, Martin supports its franchised store operators with the industry's largest year-round program of advertising in the United States and Canada. This support is one of the most important keys to your successful business operation.

"To introduce your store to the neighborhood, Martin gets you started off right by furnishing a Grand Opening Kit with a full array of tested material.

"For many years Martin has been strengthening the 'One Hour Martinizing' brand name with strong advertising campaigns in top national magazines and Sunday newspaper supplements. 'Martinizing' dry cleaning also has been promoted coast-to-coast on network radio . . . and on network television as well. In fact, during the past several years, Martin has sponsored network television's largest continuous program of dry-cleaning advertising.

"To make the national advertising program more meaningful in your store, Martin furnishes tie-in posters, circulars, counter cards, and window banners. Also available to you are ad mats for local newspaper advertising, and local television and radio commercials.

"As a franchised 'Martinizing' dry-cleaning store operator, you can count on this support all year long, year after year."

As you see, then, advertising is not limited to the more familiar settings—radio and television, newspapers and magazines. In a well-coordinated effort, it extends to posters, hand-outs, and even the things a salesman says ("Can I suggest the weekly special? You've seen it advertised on TV"), all tying in with the advertising campaign.

The Sheraton Motor Inns and a $6 Million Campaign

Let's look at one more effort from top (*Time, Newsweek,* and *New Yorker* ads) to bottom (maps, posters, and mailings); in this case, Sheraton Corporation's $6 million effort to market its services. Let's say you've just dropped $12,500 on Sheraton's counter and pocketed a license to run a Sheraton Motor Inn. Some of the folks who will be walking up to your registry will undoubtedly be there as a result of that $6 million advertising effort.

Sheraton spends $1 million to get reservations. Ads are placed in magazines and newspapers, pasted on billboards, and run on radio and television. The ads urge people to call Sheraton for out-of-town reservations. Sheraton hotels and motels can take reservations for other Sheraton Inns through their instant room-finder service, thanks to a computer that lists all available rooms in the system. The computer list is revised each time a transaction takes place—in an instant the room that has just been rented is dropped from the computer memory.

In the lobby you would have tent cards, directories, posters, and the like to remind guests to call ahead for the next night's lodging. Meanwhile, similar aids are working for you in other Sheraton Inns down the road.

As a Sheraton innkeeper, you would be chums with your Shell dealer—Sheraton lets Shell's 6 million credit-card holders charge at Sheraton Inns and runs joint promotions with the giant oil company through maps, posters, mailings, and so forth. Shell-station men are instructed to refer business to Sheraton Inns.

As a Sheraton man, you would be offering the company's "Guaranteed Company Rate Program," which guarantees a specific rate (selected by each Sheraton property) to employees of more than 2,500 prominent corporations that are members of this program.

Meanwhile, the Sheraton salesmen are out beating the bushes to drum up convention business. You might not get much of this, but any overflow from a nearby city would be told there was a Sheraton Inn in your vicinity. Sheraton's national convention department maintains an up-to-date IBM card file of basic information on national associations and convention groups. Convention leads from these files are constantly distributed among Sheraton Hotels and Motor Inns.

Sheraton is out for tour business too. Salesmen from the organization talk with tour operators, travel agents, and others in the business to work out incentive plans set up by large industrial organizations. Meanwhile, Sheraton sets up tours with airlines, bus companies, railroads, and steamship lines.

Your Sheraton sign will certainly remind passersby that you are a link with the big hotel chain they have been hearing so much about. And that is the central point in this discussion of advertising and its effectiveness to you, the man behind the counter. Whether you're a Sheraton innkeeper, a Kentucky Fried Chicken man, or a Midas Muffler operator, you've bought your franchise largely because of the importance of the name and the way it is being kept in public view.

When shopping for the right franchise, keep in mind the costs of advertising and compare them with that done by competitiors. Be especially concerned with the effectiveness of the advertising.

Ask your mother-in-law, your golf partners, your kids, and your club members what they think of the company whose banner you're thinking of flying, for they are your potential customers. If they haven't heard of the franchise, the advertising behind it is probably not as effective as you need.

8

How to Be Sure Your Location Is a Good One

You've seen stores like this a thousand times—dimly lit and uninviting, buried on some side street far from the bustle of life. How, you wonder, did the owner ever decide on that location? Well, he may simply have decided to open a store in a building owned by a relative or friend. Or perhaps the community has changed since he started—from a neighborhood of thriving shops and heavy population to an economic backwater as families moved into other areas.

Or maybe the man is a success after all. It could be that he does most of his business at the homes of customers and his shop is merely a mailing address or a staging area for his workmen.

But that's rarely the case. Even plumbers and electricians like to show the public an attractive storefront when they can. They know that a location across from a railroad station or near the center of town is a drawing card because passersby are reminded that they need service.

You can bet that franchise companies consider an excellent

location an essential building block for success. They want a location that will help you pile up revenues to make money for them *and* for yourself. They're not trying to stick you off in some undesirable site that nobody knows about.

In fact, franchise companies are so concerned that you may end up in a spot where trade is light that they demand veto power over your choice of a site. Some won't even let you choose. One company tells its prospective franchisees, "We *must* approve your location. You *might* know a successful location. We *do* know how to pick them."

The Art of Site Selection

Site selection is an ever changing art. Ben Franklin, the variety-store people, approach site selection by preparing a town survey for each community where the company plans to put stores. Company officers pore over population and economic data and look into the business set-up of the town in general. They make a detailed analysis of retail trade in the community. Competition is carefully studied, and estimates of probable receipts are prepared. Ben Franklin is particularly interested in what the existing variety stores are doing and whether the town can use another. The data is compared with similar studies put together for other towns of like size and character.

On the other hand, if you are interested in an International Industries franchise you might have to wait until site-selection work is completed before you pick out your franchise. International has over a dozen different franchise businesses.

Al Lapin, Jr., the top man at International, says that the company evaluates the economic and social structure of the community at hand, the closeness of the site under consideration to other businesses and shopping areas, and the number of cars that will pass the store. The company studies local building codes to see whether there are restrictions that would prevent International from building, say, a House of Pancakes or some other International franchise store. Not only is International interested in getting you into a site that is "right" for franchising, it is also interested in picking the right type of store.

"In certain locations, for example, research could indicate that a Copper Penny Restaurant would be more suitable than an International House of Pancakes. We are also in the field of franchising equipment rental stores (United Rent-All), business schools (Sawyers School of Business), women's apparel shops (House of Nine), and an orange drink (fast food) operation called Orange Julius, to name a few."

Remember, though, that no matter how effective the work done by the franchise company, you're the one who is going to be running the store. Once a site is under consideration, go to it and make your own study.

One franchisee, whom we'll call Harold, persuaded A to Z Rentals to let him open a store fronting on the Atlantic Ocean. A genial man with twenty-five years' experience in greeting the public in his own stores, Harold realized soon after he opened his shop that he was in the wrong spot. A to Z had argued that the effective trading area—the distance people were willing to drive to rent his tools—was about three miles. Some 70 percent of the business came from within that area. Obviously, the Atlantic Ocean blocked half his market.

"I'm going to move closer to their homes," Harold said. "If I move two miles from here, I should get a minimum 35 percent increase in business with my present inventory."

Harold's mistake was a costly one. Instead of making A to Z's projected $7,000 profit in the first year, he broke even. In a better location, he expects to meet the company's long-term projection. "My $30,000 tool inventory should bring me roughly $15,000 to $16,000 in annual net profits."

Don't feel that mistakes in site selection are inevitable. There are lots of things you can do to backstop the franchise company's choice of site.

The Value of Your Own Market Research

Take some tips from Sam Shapiro, who has never owned a franchise business but has learned a lot about personal market research. Sam started out with plenty of handicaps. He entered the United States from the steerage compartment of a Trans-

Pacific liner in 1920 and didn't understand a word of English when he landed on the West Coast. It was years before the canny Russian immigrant was able to scrape together enough money to buy a kosher delicatessen. He had migrated East and bought his store in the Bushwick section of Brooklyn.

Over the years, through a succession of stores Sam put together a system of market research with general relevance for small store operators. Here's the way he describes it:

"When I find a promising spot, generally in a shopping center, I drive around for one or two miles and look at the names on the mailboxes in the various apartment houses. I always check to make sure there are Jewish people in the neighborhood.

"Then I go around to stores that are already open and see how they do. Then I go around and ask certain people [shoppers] whether they think the location would make a good spot for a delicatessen.

"Then I go and speak to the landlord and try to work out a good deal. I have to take a long lease. I have always protected myself with long leases, because if I should decide to sell the business, the buyer will want time to recover on his investment. In the past I have usually asked for fifteen years. I got twenty years the last time."

Sam has owned and sold at high profits several very successful delicatessens.

It will be worthwhile for you to find out whether or not there is a market in the immediate neighborhood for the product you will be selling. Chances are, most of your customers will come from within a few miles. If you have a product that is special—for example, delicatessen is most popular with Jewish people—be sure that the kind of people who use your product live nearby. A soft-ice-cream store would be more popular in a neighborhood of many children than in a section populated by developments for senior citizens.

Other Considerations

Then, with the competition in mind, see what stores have already opened in the neighborhood. Consider what happened to a franchise dealer who bought a Chicken Delight franchise in a neighborhood of small stores:

Let's call the franchise owner Bill. While Bill has invested more than $20,000, the several competing stores in the neighborhood have invested much less. His competitors cater to a few blocks of walk-in trade in a predominantly Negro–Puerto Rican section of a major city, while Bill must blanket the area with delivery service. Under the franchise agreement he is not permitted to feed people in the store.

The competing stores can prepare chicken (to be eaten on the premises if the customer pleases) in five minutes. Similar orders take Bill fifteen minutes. While Bill offers a limited menu, primarily of chicken, the competitors offer a surprisingly large variety of foods.

One competitor, Burt, has a store a few blocks away that specializes in poultry and fried foods. Burt is open eighty hours a week, knows all his customers by their first names, and is understandably proud of the quality of his food.

While Bill can't break even on $1.49 chicken dinners and $2.10 spare-ribs dinners, Burt makes a profit on a $1.39 chicken dinner and a $1.59 ribs plate. Several other competitors also charge less for their meals.

Bill maintains two delivery cars to serve his clientele, while his competition does not deliver. Bill must service scores of blocks, while his competitors concentrate on a few.

Bill has considered raising his prices so that he can operate in the black, but the strength of the competition and his already higher prices make this course seem questionable.

Careful market analysis—checking the competition—should have told Bill that he was getting into a difficult area. He has been trying to sell his store for many months now.

After you have checked the competition in the area you are considering, make sure that you are getting a lease that will make it possible for you to conduct profitable operations over a number of years.

Here are some sources of information that will help you evaluate the site when you plan to open for business. Ask your newspaper, your Chamber of Commerce, bank, or town planning board for maps, recent population figures and trends, and for retail sales data.

Find out how big the city fathers expect the town to get in the near future. There will be more highly useful information of this sort that you would think. How do you suppose banks, shopping centers, civic planners, and other big spenders of business and community funds decide to spend their millions? If you make a few phone calls, you'll soon find who has the information you need within your community.

9

Rents and Mortgages

Let's say you're thinking of going it alone. You've found what appears to be an ideal location, and you've got a fine product. Then you approach the landlord. He wants $500-a-month rent and a long-term lease. He insists that you pay even more in the years ahead under "escalation clauses."

What do you do about it? It is very difficult for anyone to say just what rent you should pay—unless that somebody is your partner in profits, the franchise company.

Most likely your franchise company has faced this problem over and over again in locations very like the one you're considering. It's just one more problem they can help you solve.

Suppose you're looking at a spot in a sunny community in Florida. The franchise company probably has stores in several similar communities with the same kind of population and similar traffic patterns. The company will know how much rent is appropriate in terms of the number of dollars you will be dropping into the cashbox.

It's the franchise company's job to reject sites where the landlord wants too much money. It's not like the old days, when franchising was still in its infancy and a few unscrupulous companies accepted exorbitant rentals on behalf of their dealers in order to compete in a particular market. Dealers often found that no matter how much they made, they couldn't do well enough to offset the burdensome rent. But things have changed.

Rents That Are Right

Today franchise companies look for locations at rents that will enable you to succeed. No franchise company wants to lose an outlet—or a dealer either, for that matter. If the dealer fails, the franchise company will probably lose money on the equipment. Like as not, the dealer has borrowed money from the franchise company to buy his equipment.

If the franchise company tries to fill the store again by signing up a new dealer, the second man will want to know why the first one failed. Thus the franchise company will try to avoid the first failure, getting you a lease at a rent that will give reasonable assurance that the profits it projected for you will materialize.

Look for comment on rental costs in your franchise material. Somewhere there should be a breakdown of anticipated revenues and costs. If the company has not offered such a breakdown, ask for one. Also request breakdowns of the revenues and costs of stores the franchise company has in the vicinity.

If the franchise company then offers you a location where the rent is higher than those shown in the statements, ask how you are to make up the difference. Higher volume? A smaller royalty payment?

If you have the option of picking your own location, be sure to listen to the franchise company's advice. The company will be able to tell you whether you can afford the location you like. Shopping centers have great appeal, and you may have your eye on a bustling center a few miles from your home.

True, you're going to get a lot of traffic—that's what the shopping center is there for. But the shopping-center management has spent a lot of money setting the center up and is likely to demand a high rent, *plus* a percentage of your gross sales.

One franchise company that has tight profit margins and requires unusually large display space says that it ordinarily tells its dealers to steer clear of such locations.

On the other hand, don't talk your franchise company into going along with a location on a side street just because you've checked with the landlords and found the rents to be low. You may go out of your mind before customers find you. Or you may have to advertise every week at heavy cost to bring the public into your out-of-the-way location.

Do You Have to Build?

At this point, you're probably wondering whether you will have to put up your own building. The answer is, normally no. It depends, of course, on the franchise you are interested in. Dairy Queen, for example, once had a policy of selling its franchises for a fee and leaving it up to the dealer to build a store. The company would supply the plans, the dealer found a contractor, warned him the company would not tolerate significant changes in the red barn-type structure, and then he looked for a bank to get a construction loan. Dairy Queen recently perfected a pre-fabricated building that the company now, in most cases, puts on the site.

Keep this in mind. Many businessmen think of their mortgage payment as "rent," and therefore a deductible expense. However, the tax collector sees it differently. Only that part of the monthly mortgage payment that is interest and real-estate taxes can be deducted from your taxable income.

When you lease, the entire amount is deductible as a cost of doing business. But some businessmen will still prefer to own their buildings. They could be right—land values have risen spectacularly over the past decade or so.

Let's say you are interested in a Mr. Donut store. These New England specialty shops are ordinarily put up by the company on land purchased by the company. The company then rents the shop to the dealer.

But let's look to the deep South for a variation that is not uncommon in the franchise business. Jack's Hamburgers, Inc., tells dealers that they may buy their sites if the company approves the location. "The majority of our franchisees have found it advantageous to arrange the lease of land and building from private investors. This is no problem where there is sufficient security behind the lease and the rental is sufficient to provide a satisfactory return to the investors."

Where land and building are leased, you can begin operation of a Jack's store with as little as $13,500 cash. The forty-store hamburger chain says that the $13,500 includes a down payment on equipment if the equipment purchase is financed and that the company will assist in arranging for equipment financing if desired.

Who Signs the Lease

One question frequently asked by individuals who want a franchise business is whether they might not pay less rent if they let the parent company sign the lease directly.

The answer is, not necessarily. Real-estate income is an important part of the earnings of some franchise companies. In a recent report on Tastee Freez Industries, Inc., a soft-ice-cream franchise, the company's public relations counsel made this statement:

"Importantly [for the buyer of Tastee Freez stock], Tastee Freez can expand without seeking new capital. It leases its sites and its structures. It still stays in the real-estate business through subleasing at a 25 percent markup in rental to the operator. It goes without saying that the capital investment becomes considerably higher for those companies which buy sites and own buildings."

Now that we've seen some variations on the real-estate question—the way different franchise companies handle the key matter of finding you a place to set up shop—let's look at the typical situation. What does the franchise company normally do for you on real estate?

Phil David Fine, former deputy administrator of the Small Business Administration, sums it up this way:

The franchise company locates a site that experience suggests will be a successful location for a store;

The company leases the spot for a minimum of twenty years and pledges its credit as a guarantee of the lease;

The company hires a contractor and arranges to have him build the dealer's store;

The company arranges to finance the construction of the building and to guarantee its payment;

The company supervises construction of the building;

The company purchases, installs, and pays for the fixtures to be used by the dealer in the store.

We've already stressed the fact that rent is a key factor in your quest for profits. Now let's look at rent in terms of your business expenses in general—what you'll be spending your money for after you snip the ribbon on Grand Opening Day.

Hickory Farms

Reprinted on page 68 is a profit-and-loss statement for a Hickory Farms of Ohio store, the "just plain folks" franchise that features pungent cheese cut from a wheel and something called a "beef stick." The stores—over 100 of them—feature attractive barnlike exteriors and, on the inside, weathered boards and wagon-wheel light fixtures. They're just what you'd expect to see at a county fair—which is by design. The stores originated out of an idea developed at cheese stands set up at fairs and expositions.

Hickory Farms take a lot of cash—at least $33,000—but with that and some luck, the company predicts that you will be writing up the kind of profit figures shown here—one of three statements shown in literature distributed by Hickory Farms to prospects.

PROFIT AND LOSS STATEMENT
For the Year 1966

		Percentage to Gross Sales
Sales	$161,361.25	100%
Cost of Sales		
Inventory beginning	$10,271.01	
Purchases	83,614.19	
Total available to sell	93,885.20	
Inventory ending	12,440.74	
Cost of Sales	81,444.46	50.47
GROSS PROFIT	79,916.79	49.53
OPERATING EXPENSES		
Payroll	13,051.62	8.09
Rent	9,924.59	6.15
Franchise Fees	9,690.29	6.01
Advertising	2,558.43	1.59
Freight	4,190.65	2.60
Store Supplies	3,901.92	2.42
Office Supplies	74.62	.04
Utilities	1,497.82	.93
Telephone	665.03	.41
Postage	2,021.26	1.25
Repair–Maintenance	41.01	.03
Insurance	558.57	.35
Legal-Auditing	625.00	.39
Depreciation	1,521.77	.94
Dues and Subscriptions	883.72	.55
Taxes–State and Local *		
Taxes–Payroll	957.68	.59
Travel-Entertainment	99.76	.06
Auto Expense	739.00	.46
Miscellaneous Rents	400.00	.25
Miscellaneous Expense	269.01	.17
TOTAL OPERATING EXPENSES	53,671.75	33.28
PROFIT FROM OPERATIONS		
(Before owner's draw)	26,245.04	16.25
Other Income		
Discount earned	339.34	.21
Miscellaneous income	492.09	.30
TOTAL OTHER INCOME	831.43	.51
TOTAL NET PROFIT	$27,076.47	16.76

* Not reported.

10

Financing Your Franchise

If you've ever asked a bank for money when you really needed it, you'll probably get a smile out of that wry bit of American wit: "A bank is an institution that will lend you money if you can prove to their complete satisfaction that you don't really need it."

Even in this day of high excitement over the growth of franchising, the banks haven't begun to appreciate the opportunities to be found in the field. Those big oaken doors are often closed tight to the business hopeful.

But that's what is so wonderful about the well-run franchise from your point of view. You don't really need a bank to finance the bulk of your investment. Yes, most good franchise companies can do the miraculous: through a combination of lending facilities they can provide you with most of the capital you need to become a dealer.

Where else could a man of limited means—one who probably never had $10,000 in cash to his name—find a way to finance a business worth upward of $50,000?

This ability to help the dealer get the necessary money to embark on an important business career is the real romance of franchising—and the reason why franchising has been called the last frontier of the small independent businessman. For in these days of ever rising costs and more sophisticated business methods, it has become more and more difficult for men to start business on a shoestring. Profitable business opportunities usually call for a substantial investment, one that, in all probability, will be beyond the means of most.

Mr. Donut's Plan

With franchising, the all-important question of how to raise the money is largely solved. Every day men of small means sign as dealers with major franchising companies with cash investments of less than $10,000. Mr. Donut, for example, asks for a cash down payment of $10,000 on a $45,800 lease-and-equipment package, but adds, "Smaller down payments can sometimes be arranged . . . for qualified applicants."

Meanwhile, in this period of heavy competition for qualified dealers, the giant oil companies have found it increasingly difficult to attract operators. The oil business has been in a decided backwater—a relatively unglamorous field at a time of stardom for the hamburger, doughnut, and soft ice cream. The result is that highly attractive service station locations are available for, as one franchise industry expert put it, "not one thin dime in down payment."

The financing terms at Mr. Donut, like those of most franchising companies that offer to carry their dealers, is decidedly short-term, in this case, forty-two months at 7 percent interest. The idea is that the business should net enough income in that period of time to pay off the loan.

Another franchise agreement might call for a much larger down payment, say $25,000, and an agreement on your part to pay off the balance—another $25,000 in two years. You would pay $12,500 in each of the first two years out of your earnings.

An expert on the subject, Phil Fine, partner in Fine & Ambrogne of Boston and former deputy administrator of the Small Business Administration under President John Kennedy, said that, generally speaking, the rate you would be charged would be "pretty closely related to the prime rate." The prime rate is the rate that banks charge their customers with the best credit ratings.

As a man of unestablished credit in the eyes of the bank you would be refused a loan, but a franchise company with a good credit rating gets very close to the best rate the bank offers and in turn passes the savings along to you.

Three Basic Financing Plans

Mr. Fine explains that there are three basic ways in which dealers pay for their franchises. First there is the man who walks in and is told it will cost him $45,000 for the whole shooting match; he sits down and writes a check. It's as simple as that. The only problem from the standpoint of the franchise companies is that relatively few men are able to do this. However, some prefer a man who has to borrow to buy the franchise because it tends to make him more diligent and harder working.

The second approach is more or less as we have outlined. He goes to one of the major franchise companies, pays whatever they ask as a down payment, and the company takes care of the rest. The larger franchise companies will accept the new dealer's note on the balance. The company may put the note in the vault and take payments from the dealer as due, or it may "discount" the note, that is, sell it to someone else at less than the full price. If the company follows this practice, the dealer will have to pay a somewhat higher interest rate to cover the "discount."

There is still another way to skin this particular breed of cat. The franchise company—possibly pressed for cash itself if it's expanding rapidly—will take you to the Small Business Administration for a loan. First stop, though, would be at your neighborhood bank—just to get a refusal of a loan. Under the law the Small Business Administration cannot help you unless you have been refused by a bank.

After that, the franchise company will probably send one of their men to the regional Small Business Administration office to give you moral support and help you with the somewhat complicated forms you must fill out.

The Small Business Administration

Now you're talking about a possible long-term loan, because the Small Business Administration is permitted to lend to small businessmen for periods of up to ten years.

If you are about to sign a franchise agreement, the SBA, as it is known in business circles, will make you a dandy loan—on half the money. This can be a drawback. Let's say you need $50,000. They would put up only $25,000 on a seven-to-ten-year loan. They will try to get a bank to participate on the loan, but this is not essential. The SBA will ask the franchise company to co-sign the loan.

Now the question arises: Where do you get the rest of the money? It may be that the franchise company will be able to get financing on some of the equipment you must buy—possibly from the supplier of the equipment. Suppliers want to sell equipment, they have financial strength, ergo, they lend the purchaser the money to buy the equipment.

But even the franchise company will want you to have some cash of your own in the business, preferably a sizable amount. So the problem is still money. Where can you get it?

You May Have Hidden Assets

You may have hidden assets that have never occurred to you. First stop may be that indulgent Aunt Fanny who always knew you'd make good. She may be eager to help you. Be sure to offer her interest to cover what she loses when she takes the money out of the bank.

But don't stop at Aunt Fanny. Every member of the family who can be approached should be approached. Set the terms up in a legal way. Have the papers drawn up by your lawyer and see to it that you make regular payments. You're not trying to beat Aunt Fanny out of the money, and you want her to know that.

Perhaps you'll want to back up the agreement by taking a second mortgage on your home. This has been done successfully in many families. We're assuming, of course, that you've re-financed your mortgage already, if possible, so you can't get any more money from the bank on the first mortgage.

This is a time of high interest rates, but if you are confident that you can succeed in your own business, you shouldn't hesitate to refinance your mortgage at 7 percent or a bit higher, *if you can raise a substantial amount of money this way.*

Other Ways to Finance

Dig those life insurance policies out of the safety-deposit box. Perhaps you are not aware that "ordinary life" or "whole life" policies, and "endowment" policies especially, have what is known as "cash" or "loan" value. Often a policy that has been in effect for some years will be good for thousands of dollars of capital for your business. Talk it over with your insurance agent. Better yet, to avoid an argument with him (after all, he works on commission), write to your insurance company direct and tell them you want to borrow as much as you can.

So long as you keep paying the premiums, your loan will not affect your life insurance coverage unduly. If you should die while the loan is outstanding, your beneficiary would collect the face value less the money you still owe the company.

Don't overlook this fine source of cash. You'll pay interest on the loan, it's true—even though it's your own money—but the interest rate will be less than half what you would pay for a straight signature loan at the bank.

Naturally, if you have securities—stocks or bonds—you'll be able to borrow against them. Let the bank know you are borrowing to go into business, and it will lend up to 65 percent of the market value of the securities. The loan rate on this sort of transaction will come to you as a pleasant surprise. The bank has *security* in hand and can afford to let you have a low rate.

Keep this in mind, though. If the market value of the stock falls drastically, the bank will ask for more security. Blue-chip stocks might be safer, if you have a choice, than the so-called glamour issues, which tend to fluctuate dramatically.

Perhaps you have cash in a savings bank that you have vowed not to touch; you're saving it for a "rainy day." You can keep the money on deposit and take a passbook loan against the full amount, either with the savings bank or any other bank, savings or commercial. You can't touch your savings because the bank keeps the passbook. The bank will give you a payment book with "tickets" to mail in with your checks as you repay the loan each month.

A passbook loan is also very cheap. You can borrow your own money in this manner for about a 1 percent "net" interest cost, that is, the money in the account continues to earn interest, but it will be applied against the loan and you will be out of pocket only the additional 1 percent.

If you belong to a credit union, don't overlook this fine, cheap source of funds. You can use this lender so long as you or your wife is working for an employer where a credit union is established. Under federal law the limit on credit-union loans is $850. However, if you later decide to quit your job and go into business, the loan is still in effect and you just continue with the payments.

While banks are likely to be unwilling to lend you money when you are about to go into your own business, for the first time, they may feel differently in time. Once you've been operating and are doing reasonably well, you may then be eligible for a bank loan. The reason you weren't a serious candidate in the beginning is because the banker could not answer the all-important question, "Can he manage a business?" Months later—or at least a couple of years later—when you've got things humming, you have more or less proved that you can.

(Don't let the likelihood of a rebuff keep you from approaching a bank before you go into business. Banks do finance the bulk of the small businesses in this country. There is a strong possibility that you will need the banker later, so get acquainted with him. Even if he cannot help you finance the opening of your business, he should have many helpful suggestions that will guide you in evaluating business propositions. He may even be able to send you to private investors or to other sources of risk capital that you do not know about.)

How to Borrow from a Bank

Approach the bank in a professional manner. Nothing is so disconcerting to a banker than a loan candidate who comes in without records or who is vague or evasive in his manner. You're a businessman and a potentially successful one. You should have financial statements that will give him the whole picture—who you owe and who owes you, how much other debt you have and how much you are making. Give him the works.

Take him into your confidence. Answer his questions in an earnest, straightforward manner. Give him every opportunity to conclude that you're a good risk, so that he can make the loan. If he's not impressed with your ability to organize your financial affairs for his inspection he will doubt your ability to run a business.

He will want to know precisely what you intend to do with the money and how you intend to repay it. If you need money for a new delivery truck, tell him so. If it's for working capital, don't keep him in the dark. If your profits have not reached expected levels, give him a factual projection based on your volume of business and your costs to show that your earnings are growing, that the means of repaying the loan are at hand and not pie in the sky.

During the early phases of your business, the banker will still seek collateral for his loan—something valuable that he can fall back on if you let him down. Perhaps you can offer him a second mortgage on your home. He'll ask if you have any savings that he can lend you money against—a passbook loan. Have you securities that you haven't already pledged?

If he's really convinced that your business is firmly established, he may be willing to lend you money on your signature. An experienced banker comments:

"It is quite obvious that only an established business can rely on unsecured borrowings. A new business, lacking the history of a product of merit or a stable earnings record, must offer security. Outside of cash, the most liquid assets are accounts receivable and inventory. Assuming that credit has been intelligently authorized, the accounts receivable are, of course, the more liquid because the inventory has already been sold. Not being able to get unsecured credit, the new enterprise will probably find it desirable to supplement working cash by borrowing on accounts receivable."

Some Borrowing Case Histories

The American Bankers Association, a trade organization to which virtually all the nation's fourteen thousand commercial banks belong, has prepared a manual for bankers to help them evaluate would-be borrowers. Here are a few examples with some relevance for a franchise dealer:

A personable automobile mechanic purchased the service station where he had been employed; the price was reasonable in view of the poor earnings record of the previous owner. The mechanic had saved about $5,000, which he invested in the station. Increased patronage led to the employment of two men and his cash position was falling. His financial problem was solved with a $2,500 bank loan payable in twenty-four months. While the bank took a chattel mortgage on the equipment, his ability and industry were the underlying values.

A restaurant owner lost his lease and was forced to seek a new location. This meant additional equipment and modernization expenses. His past record in this type of business indicated that he had the ability to operate his business profitably and should be successful. The cost was $10,000, of which he paid $5,000 in cash. A loan for $5,000, amortized over a five-year period, permitted a start at the new location.

A drugstore operator wanted to take over the store adjoining his premises so that he could open a soft-ice-cream business. Total cost: $10,000. He would not be in a position to use more than $2,500 of his own cash without impairing his working capital. His problem was solved with a bank loan for $7,500 for five years, based on his honesty, industry, and good prospects for sufficient earnings to meet the monthly installments.

A fast-delivery chicken take-out store needed a second delivery truck. The truck would expedite deliveries and increase the dealer's earning power. A down payment of 50 percent was furnished, leaving a balance of $4,000, which he financed over three years. A bank loan was approved and a chattel mortgage taken on the equipment.

These examples stress the bank's desire for proven business ability and its demand for collateral where possible.

The American Bankers Association cautions banks to avoid lending money for overlong periods, suggesting that loans be paid off over one to five years. The loan period would depend on such factors as the anticipated flow of funds in relation to the amount of the loan and whether the business is seasonal, in which case monthly payments can be adjusted to meet business peaks and valleys. (Soft-ice-cream dealers take note.)

The association comments that the risk of making loans to small enterprises is higher than to large corporations. Rates reflect this difference in the magnitude of risk. Rates are generally pegged at or near the upper end of the lending scale and are usually stated on a basis that suggests a rate roughly half that of the actual interest charge. This is a complicated but important concept. Rates are higher than they appear because they are calculated on the basis of the total sum borrowed. In fact, you have the use of the total sum only in the first month, because you begin making monthly payments thereafter. The effect of this "amortization" is that you have, on average, a little better than half the money to use over the full term. (In the last month of a one-year loan you have just 1/12 of the money.) Since you are using just half the money on average, the effective rate of interest is almost double the stated rate.

You are well advised to avoid the high-rate lenders—finance companies and similar lenders—until you really need them. You may be short of cash to the extent that you simply must borrow to keep going. If you should reach this point, remember that the finance companies are honest—but by no means cheap.

Avoid Loan Sharks

Whatever you do, do not borrow from a loan shark. The smooth-talking guy who walks in and offers you money—cash, as much as you need—is probably a loan shark. Loan sharks like nothing better than to lend money to a small businessman.

Once they have hooked you, they do not like to let go. They will keep offering you money until you are working for them in a business you once called your own.

Long before you consider going to a finance company, the place to turn is to your franchise company. Suppose you have been in business for six months. The crowds didn't flock to you as you had dreamed they would, but the business is moving along nicely and you see signs of a break-even in the forseeable future—say six months.

Remember, your franchise company does not want you to fail. It wants you to be a big success, and if the situation is promising, it will do what it can to help.

Eugene P. Foley, head of the Small Business Administration, had this to say about the franchise companies' attitude toward dealers:

"Firms engaged in extending franchises are fond of saying that they will not permit a franchisee to fail if it is at all possible to save him. Allowing for some exaggeration here, there is evidence that, prompted by self-interest, franchisers will go to extraordinary lengths to shore up a weak outlet.

"One of the results, I am told, is that the reported failure rate among franchisees is less than 1 percent. Here again, we must be cautious; but regardless of the validity of this particular figure, it seems to be a safe assumption that the casualty rate among franchisees is lower, far lower, than that among other small businesses."

Delayed Payments

What can the franchise company do for you once you are underway? Lots of things. You'll remember that earlier in this book we talked about a man named Bud King, who owned three hamburger restaurants. Recall how in the beginning the second store did not do as well as the first, and Bud became cash-poor as a result? The franchise company allowed him to delay making payments due the company, thus in effect "lending" Bud additional cash.

This is a common approach used by franchise companies to help their dealers. Find out if the franchise company you are interested in will lend you money to start and offer you assistance later if you need it.

Let's say you are having trouble getting off the ground. A concerned franchise company may decide to deliver supplies to you on "consignment," that is, you pay for what you sell when you sell it. In a sense, this is what the hamburger company did for Bud.

Value of Future Accounts

Following another avenue, the company may permit you to turn over your accounts for collection. For example, if you sell Mrs. Jones, a nice, slightly forgetful lady, a sprinkler system, you won't have to wait until she remembers to sit down and do the bills. You "pay" the franchise company by giving the company the papers and letting the company wait for Mrs. Jones to take pen in hand.

Meanwhile, you've paid the company without drawing on precious cash. The company will charge a reasonable fee for acting as collector, of course.

The company you choose may follow both roads in coming to your assistance, but this is something you should discover before you make your decision.

Most of the well-known, well-established franchise companies have the resources to be very helpful both before and after you open your business. Make sure yours is one of these. Before you make your final choice, prepare a list of questions for the finalists based on this chapter to find out how far they are willing to bend the reed to come to your assistance. It may mean the difference between success and failure later.

PART II

SOME WELL-KNOWN FRANCHISES AND WHAT THEY DO

Generalities are fine when you are trying to get a grasp of a subject, but before you can make a choice as to the specific franchise business you wish to run, you need to know something about the different types of opportunities.

With the help of knowledgeable people in the franchise industry, the author selected twenty-five of the top companies for detailed consideration. (There are many other opportunities equally good that could not be covered.) You will find considerable variety in the list and sufficient information to help you decide in general which type of franchise is for you.

The bulk of the information presented came in response to twenty specific questions the author posed to the management of each franchise company. A number of the companies approached did not wish to answer certain pointed questions, and those companies are not included in the book. Others answered some questions cautiously or in a sketchy manner but are included because they represent an important aspect of the field and gave specific answers to the most important questions.

In certain cases companies were unwilling to make profit-and-loss statements available for an average franchise unit. Therefore not all accounts of specific franchises supply parallel information.

If a franchise in which you are particularly interested is not covered, refer to Chapter 41, "Making Your Final Decision." Guideline answers to the twenty questions are given. Submit these questions to the franchise companies you are interested in and compare their answers with the information about the companies in this section and with the guideline answers.

The fact that a company is included in this book does not constitute an endorsement of the company or its policies by the author.

11

Shell

Have you ever thought of a service-station franchise? Perhaps it's not the most glamorous route to franchise success, but it is certainly one of the most stable, and it can be highly profitable. But most important, it offers one of the least costly ways of entering a substantial business. You can do it with as little as $3,000 capital.

Service stations are certainly among the most plentiful franchises in the nation. Oil companies are constantly looking for new dealers, and there are always profitable opportunities available. What's more, oil companies are so eager to satisfy the ambitions of their men that some will transfer a successful man who is running a relatively small outlet to a station with greater profit potential.

You've heard of turnkey operations. Well, the service station is usually just that. If you are to go into a new station—and new ones are available practically all the time—you will be trained and delivered to a shiny building on a well-traveled corner and given the key.

Normally, your sole investment will be in gasoline, equipment,

and the stock on the shelves—tires, spark plugs, etc. While you will need $10,000 to $15,000 worth of merchandise and equipment, chances are you will recover that entire investment within a year. What's more, if you impress the oil company that you're their man, they'll help you finance the merchandise, reducing your investment to practically nothing. (However, even the Small Business Administration in its new program to encourage minority groups to go into business insists on a 15 percent investment, believing this to be sound practice. Most oil companies will want at least that much capital from you.)

You can bet that the oil company is going to give you all the help it can to start you on the road to profits, because it is making a major investment in your station. The land will cost $100,000 to $200,000, and the station itself may cost nearly $100,000—pumps, major equipment, and toilets installed.

And that, perhaps, is the rub—if there is one. Normally, the service-station dealer has nothing to sell if he leaves the business—except, of course, his stock of tires, equipment, and so forth.

On the other hand, if you want to buy your own land and build the station yourself, you can. Then it's yours. But beware. In this dynamic society of ours, highways are often replaced or moved. Towns that once got transient business are bypassed and the stations in town suffer heavily. If the oil company owns your station, you are probably in the clear. They'll happily relocate you. If you own the station, it's your problem.

Now let's look at the oil company that has been conducting perhaps the most aggressive program to acquire new dealers —Shell Oil Company.

First, what does the modern service-station operator do for a living? Shell says that basically he's manager of the three M's—men, money, and merchandise. He'll pump gas—so as to meet his customers and establish rapport. But the mechanical work—if he takes it on—will be done by others for the most part. He'll work sixty to seventy-two hours a week and somewhat more than that the first year because of the problems involved in getting underway. He'll put in a six-day week.

If he's a really good manager, he'll hire and train people so that he can get away two days a week. If he finds he has to be there seven days a week, chances are he's not the right man for a service station. It's a year-round business, but, Shell says, he must take a week or two off if he is to keep up his morale. "This vacation, of course, depends upon whether he has trained somebody to take over for him."

He'll find that the summer months are ordinarily the busiest, but in some areas of the nation, December will be his best month. Typically, a dealer is between twenty-five and forty, is married, and has children. The oil companies eagerly seek family men because by and large they are more stable and do a better job. Chances are, he is a high school graduate and may even have some college. Shell has many college graduates. However, the company also has many operators who did not finish high school, and a man shouldn't think he'd be excluded from consideration just because of this. He needs a level head, lots of go, and the ability to manage the three M's.

He'll need, on the average, four full-time people. Some stations use part-timers, but their time must add up to that of four full-time employees. Some dealers have fifteen to twenty people working for them. They sell a lot of tires, batteries, and accessories and do a lot of service work—tune-ups, brake jobs, wheel alignment, and so forth. Ever wonder how much gas goes through the pumps in a typical month? About 35,000 gallons in an average station, and some run to 100,000 gallons and more.

Oil companies do not charge a franchise fee, nor do they collect a royalty fee. Their profit is derived from the sale of petroleum products and, often, from TBA (tires, batteries, and accessories) that they sell to their dealers.

A rental is charged for the land and service-station facilities, generally based upon gasoline gallonage. Shell usually gets 1.75 cents per gallon, but this varies depending upon the facilities.

There was a time when gas stations dispensed gas, lubricated cars, and did little else. Today many gas stations carry on extensive mechanical services and increase their profits considerably as a result. Any investment in tools and related equipment for auto repair and allied services will come out of the dealer's own pocket. The oil companies permit the allied repairs and services, and Shell, for one, encourages it.

Shell says that $10,000 or $12,000 will normally cover the investment in a Shell station's merchandise—which is all the dealer must pay for. Here's how Shell's James Graybill puts it:

"We would lend the man $5,000 to $6,000—half the money required—and we do it all the time. The amount we're willing to lend depends on our estimate of his ability to succeed.

"On isolated occasions we have gone all the way, but feel it is good business practice that a man have some of his own money in the business. Naturally, we prefer a man with a full cash investment, as he has no discouraging payback obligation."

Financing, if required, is often through Shell. Sometimes, however, the dealer gets the money through a personal loan or from friends or relatives.

Shell believes that its product advertising is among the most extensive in the industry, spending $20 million a year. The company pays for all national advertising and will split the cost of advertising in local media 50-50 with the dealer. However, Shell finds that most dealers don't use local advertising. "They feel our national advertising is so extensive that they don't need it," Mr. Graybill says.

A few Shell dealers who carry on extensive sideline activities such as auto body work earn $50,000 a year and many are in the $20,000 to $30,000 bracket, but they are of above-average ability. The average dealer earns in the neighborhood of $12,000 a year, but few ever go broke. A recent study of the service-station industry by the American Petroleum Institute showed that less than 1 percent of a sample group resulted in a business failure.

But before a man goes into the service-station business he must be trained. The number of training schools operated by Shell gives an inkling as to just how extensive this business is: Shell has forty-five centers throughout the nation. Each dealer gets four weeks' training. He is taught station management and how to operate his business profitably. Shell encourages dealers to hire at their own expense an outside bookkeeping service to take care of tax payments and prepare monthly profit-and-loss statements.

A few of the training centers are adjacent to a service station, but most buildings have been put up specifically for training purposes. The franchisee is taught financial management and merchandising and how to handle personnel. There is no charge for this schooling, and the prospect is paid $75 a week while at school. Most applicants are within driving distance of a training center. Under some conditions Shell will pay the applicant mileage expense and a per diem to cover expenses if he lives beyond a reasonable distance from the training center.

You can be sure that before the station is picked, Shell has done a great deal of market research to rule out failure due to location. Among the factors the company checks out are traffic count, whether the business will come from a residential or industrial area, and whether the area can support the station. While territories are not exclusive in the service-station business, Mr. Graybill comments, "You can be sure we won't build unless there is a sure potential. Our improvements to the land run $80,000 to $90,000, and we commonly pay $125,000 for land and even as much as $200,000. What's more, if by rare mischance the location turns out to be a dud anyway, we'll relocate the man if he is good. If he's reached the top potential of his station and is unsatisfied, we'll move him to a better station."

Mr. Graybill said that occasionally a man has run two stations successfully, but that Shell discourages this. "We find that most men learn that running a service station isn't an easy job. He's better off if he confines his activities to one outlet."

Occasionally Shell will get a woman dealer, usually a widow whose husband was a Shell dealer. This is usually the only way that a family can continue a service-station business, since the oil company reserves the right to cancel the lease on the death of the dealer. Shell does not actively seek women dealers, although it doesn't rule them out. "It just isn't a woman's type of work," Mr. Graybill says.

The company takes retirees who are physically and mentally qualified. The company finds many excellent dealers from among the men who retire at a relatively early age from the armed forces—mostly in their early forties.

Shell also seeks members of minority groups. "Our service stations are located in all parts of the country. If we have a station in an area where there is a heavy concentration of

Mexicans, we want a Mexican in that station because he fits into the group and speaks their language. We do this sort of thing everywhere."

Shell has scores of available stations, and in most areas of the country. The company is building new units constantly, and there are retirements at all times. Others leave the business for various reasons.

Mr. Graybill sums up Shell's franchise opportunity: "A service station is probably one of the greatest opportunities in America today for the person with limited capital who wants to go into business for himself. The rewards are great. He should be able to get his entire investment back the year he starts—it's hard to equal that."

Shell presents the following stories of men with different backgrounds who, Shell says, are all making good money today as dealers.

Blayne Swift, an experienced businessman of San Bruno, California: "I graduated from the University of Iowa and spent a few years in the Air Force as a fighter pilot. During the 1950's, I had my own construction tool company. But I was spending too much time on the road, so I decided to try something else. I looked into such things as vending machines, ice-cream parlors, and— you name it. I might add, I made quite a survey of service stations. I picked Shell because I feel, in this area, at least, they're far the most aggressive. Also, I'm sold on their product. I went into this unit with $7,500. And in my first full year of operation I made a profit of $16,000. I don't know of any other business where the risk is so low and where the return can be as great. My wife is all for it. I spend a lot more time with my family than when I was on the road. I'm part of the community, and I take part in such things as the Lion's Club, Chamber of Commerce. I feel that I'm an independent businessman just like the man who runs the supermarket or the bank down the street. And I'm accepted as such."

Tony Rebustillo, a former service-station employee of Miami, Florida: "It was twelve years ago when I first came to this country from Cuba. I could hardly speak one word of English. So I

had to start with washing cars. Then finally I got my own station.
I didn't have too much capital, and a lot of people trusted me, so
I felt obligated. I was working seven days a week for awhile. I
mean that really did make it hard on me, but I was happy, because in the first month I showed a $500 profit. After that, it was
$700, $800, and over $1,000. Then everything came easier. I paid
everybody and hired more help. Now we're number one on tires
in the whole district, and we pump about 84,000 gallons a month.
I know other dealers in different companies, and when we start
talking about the kind of deals they get, actually I think Shell is
the best. I wouldn't be anything else but a Shell dealer."

William Docchio, a retired serviceman of Orient, Ohio: "I retired after twenty years in the Air Force. I went into real estate
for awhile, and then I heard about this station. The books looked
pretty good, so I made the move. I actually knew nothing about
the service-station business, other than being a customer. Of
course, the Shell training school helped me a lot. Especially the
sales instruction. Was my service experience a help? Definitely.
It helped me with keeping records and supervising employees. I
find this a fascinating business because of all the different kinds
of people you meet. I'd say our future looks bright. We're ahead
of last year's gallonage, and I'm very pleased with Shell. I never
knew they were so dealer oriented. They bend over backwards
to help."

Robert Cain, once an aircraft-industry supervisor, of Arlington,
Texas: "I started working part time in a service station to see if
I'd like it. I did, so I finally bought it out. The main reason was
to better myself, which I feel I certainly have. I had that station
—it was with another company—for a few years. And then it
looked to me like Shell was coming on pretty strong. So I made
the switch and took over here. It's been very good right from the
start—in fact, better than I expected. The Shell training school
was a big help. I didn't think it would be, because I thought I
really knew the business. But they showed me a better way to do
lots of things. I'd recommend Shell to any dealer. They're on the
ball as far as commercials to the public, product-wise, and they
build some of the finest installations I've seen anywhere."

SHELL OIL
Monthly Operating Statement: Typical Set-up

	Sales	Cost of Goods	Gross Profit
Sales			
Gasoline (40,000 gallons)	$14,760	$12,260	$2,500
Oil and A.T.F.	680	374	306
Tires and tubes	960	740	220
Batteries	220	132	88
Accessories and parts	1,440	864	576
Lubrication	145	—	145
Labor	1,000	—	1,000
Miscellaneous	160	95	65
TOTAL	$19,365	$14,465	$4,900

Expenses			
Wages	$1,800		
License and taxes	150		
Insurance	110		
Depreciation	55		
Supplies and tools	60		
Station use	45		
Special service	50		
Stamps/premiums	340		
Advertising and promotion	40		
Rent	700		
Laundry—Uniforms	55		
Maintenance and repair	22		
Utilities	110		
Discounts and refunds	15		
TOTAL	$3,552		$3,552
		NET PROFIT	$1,348

12

Robo-Wash

Robo-Wash, Inc., offers an opportunity for the man who would like to own—but not be tied down by—a franchise business.

Robo offers a fully automatic car wash that takes just two minutes. The equipment cannot be left untended—Robo looks for people who are mechanically inclined—but it can be operated by a single attendant during the normal 8 A.M. to 6 P.M. day. (The work week is six days.)

"A dealer must have capable people operating his unit if he is not present. A maintenance checklist helps the person managing the unit in the dealer's absence," the company states.

But let's study this operation from the beginning—from the moment the customer pulls into the driveway—just to get an idea as to how much work and effort is involved.

Typically, the customer drives to a coinbox mounted just outside the Robo-Wash bay. He deposits either 50 cents for a wash or 75 cents for a wash and wax. The car is then driven by the owner into the bay, and the front wheels activate a pressure switch for wheel, under-fender, and chassis sprayers. When the left front wheel reaches the correct-position switch, the Robo is activated.

The Robo follows a guide in the bay floor and circles the car four times. The driver stays in the car. During the first two cycles the Robo sprays a solution of warm water and a specially developed detergent on the car at a nozzle pressure of about 550 pounds per square inch to loosen the grime.

In the remaining two cycles, the car is rinsed with plain, soft water. If the extra 25 cents has been deposited, wax is applied automatically at the time of the first rinse cycle. Upon completion of the wash, most customers drive away and allow their cars to dry in the air. However, most Robo locations have a drying area for those desiring to wipe their cars. Paper "chamois" are generally available from a vending machine for either 10 cents or 25 cents. At most locations the use of a vacuum cleaner is also available, at 10 cents for five minutes.

Robo-Wash units are operated in the biggest cities and in some of the smallest towns. The individual operator and one of the company's area distributors work together to choose a suitable site for the operation. Various factors such as population, traffic flow, size and adaptability of property are considered. Robo recommends one bay of Robo-Wash equipment for every 10,000 people in cities over 50,000 population and one bay for every 5,000 people in smaller cities.

The dealer's order for equipment is submitted to the distributor, who sends it along to headquarters. It is shipped directly to the dealer by bill of lading and sight draft payable to the company.

Robo has a lease program for dealers who need financing and describes itself as "very flexible" in meeting dealer financial needs. Financing is arranged through the leasing company.

The dealer's total investment is generally about $20,000 to $25,000 for a single-bay installation and $40,000 to $50,000 for a double-bay installation, exclusive of land and the cost of Robo-Rinse equipment—$3,700 for a single bay and $4,500 for a double.

The Robo rinse system is designed to help obtain a relatively spotfree wash without wiping, especially in areas where the water has a high mineral content. The Robo water-reclamation system costs an additional $4,200 whether for a single or double bay. It will reduce water consumption by about 50 percent and lower water-heating and detergent expenses.

Special accessories include aluminum and glass wall panels, vacuum cleaners with a coinbox, paper "chamois" vending equipment, down-draft forced-air furnaces, winterizing kits, and under-floor heating equipment.

The company provides detailed engineering and architectural plans and at start-up time the assistance of a field engineer. All accessories, replacement parts, and buildings for Robo-Wash equipment are purchased by the company from outside sources.

The company or its distributor will conduct inspections from time to time to make sure standards and policies of the company are being followed.

The company charges 8 cents per car, for which it furnishes wax and the patented equipment to apply the wax. Robo also charges a royalty of 4 percent of gross receipts to pay for advertising and research and development conducted by the company. (The dealer is furnished with a complete bookkeeping service designed to fit his needs.)

Robo states: "We advertise on radio, national TV, newspaper handbills, and billboards." The 4-percent-of-gross-receipts royalty fund is used to advertise in the dealer's locality with the assistance of a national advertising agency. The company guarantees that it will contribute as much or more to the fund in areas from which dealer contributions are received.

To ensure quality and uniformity, Robo insists that its franchisees use the approved and recommended detergents and waxes. The dealer is furnished with Prestone Jet Spray Wax, a product of Union Carbide, and Robo's patented wax-applicating machine. The detergent—many have been tested and none have equaled in Robo's view the one used—is purchased from Keystone Chemical, a company that Robo acquired in February 1967.

The dealer pays no franchise fees until he actually begins washing cars.

Let's say that you set up a double-bay unit that costs $50,000 all told. You will recover your investment, the company maintains, in from three to five years. This would mean a yearly income on your investment of 20 percent on the stretched-out basis—$10,000 a year. In three years you'd be earning 33 percent on your money, or $16,500 a year. Thus the franchise offers a substantial additional income to a man who has other interests and a good living for individuals whose needs are relatively modest. Add-on locations can obviously be handled, and the Robo operation lends itself to a gas-station installation as a source of additional income to the proprietor.

Before the new dealer opens his car wash, he will attend a free service school in Kansas City. He must pay his own room and board. In addition, meetings are held regularly throughout the country to acquaint dealers with advertising and promotional ideas and tips on maintaining the equipment.

Robo says that most successful dealers have a working knowledge of mechanical equipment and develop a "great deal of rapport" with their customers. The company encourages its dealers to engage in civic affairs. The typical dealer is forty years old, married, and has a college education. "He's a businessman with a knowledge of how to run a business," the company says.

Under the Robo-Wash contract, the dealer's heirs can inherit the franchise should he die. The term of the franchise is ten years and is then renewable annually. The dealer is free to sell the franchise to a man approved by Robo-Wash.

There is a lot of competition in the car-wash field, but Robo believes it is number one. "Our dealers have experienced little trouble with competition coming into their areas." In fact, Robo is still actively seeking new dealers, as there are "2,500 counties which still do not have Robo."

The franchise is open to one and all, so long as the company is convinced the individual can do an "acceptable job of running a car wash."

Robo comments: "Robo is still in its embryo stage. There is still a tremendous market that the car-washing industry has yet to tap. Robo, in its short life, has made many people realize that it makes them have a greater sense of pride to ride in a clean car especially if . . . at little effort and at nominal expense."

13

Western Auto

Western Auto stores are probably as familiar to you as the corner drugstore, for there are more than 4,000 of them coast to coast and they have been around a long time. The company is celebrating its sixtieth anniversary, and it's had franchised dealers since the mid-1930's. The company is practically a living history of franchising.

Western Auto opened its doors to answer a need spotted by George Pepperdine, a $15-a-week bookkeeper. He had noticed that Henry Ford was selling the Model-T "Tin Lizzy" without such "luxuries" as windshields, tops, bumpers, and headlights.

What better way to cash in on a growing market? There were 300,000 automobiles in 1909—most of them Henry's Lizzies.

Pepperdine wasn't able to stock any parts. He had no money. But that didn't stop him. He had a printer turn out circulars, which he mailed to a list of auto owners he got from bankers and other businessmen in town and in surrounding areas. His only investment was $5 for postage. Then he waited. The orders soon began to come in. As they did, he bought the merchandise to fill the orders, neatly solving the inventory problem by avoiding it.

The business grew. Auto mechanics were rare in those days

and the Model-T spawned a nation of handymen. Ford owners quickly learned to change a tire in minutes and to take down an engine and replace the bearings in an afternoon.

The Model-T, simplicity itself, brought orders for tools and spare parts in abundance. Few of the weekend mechanics wanted to go to the city for their parts. So Pepperdine's service was good news. Customers preferred to leave the driving to the mail department.

And that's how Western Auto began. But there were crises in the early days. The first big one came in 1927 when Henry Ford dropped the Model-T. This was stunning news for a business that often billed its early catalogs "Ford Owner's Supply Book."

In a prideful moment in 1919, Western Auto actually assembled a Model-T from its own stock for the Texas State Fair. The only things drawn directly from Ford factories were the motor block and the chassis.

But the Model-T setback proved to be a blessing in disguise. The line was expanded to include parts for all automobiles. Not too many years after that, the company expanded the line again to get away from dependence on automobiles. By the early 1950's, Western Auto was offering a full line of hard goods including major appliances and related merchandise—much of it sold under Western Auto brand names. But mail-order profits remain important.

Western Auto has offered its customers credit since 1934, and the company became one of the early franchisers when its first "Associate" store was opened on May 5, 1935, in Fredonia, Kansas.

With sixty years of know-how going for it, Western Auto is one of the most conservative franchises a man can choose. It offers the dealer enormous volume buying power that will put your store on a strong competitive footing with other stores in the area. You will be able to price your merchandise attractively and still make a substantial profit.

Western Auto makes its profits through the sale of merchandise to its dealers. There are no franchise fees or royalty payments. The company does charge $25 a month for the bookkeeping service it offers its dealers.

Western Auto advertises nationally in leading magazines and supplies advertising materials for use in local newspapers. Before each of the eleven annual sales events, the company is prepared to supply, at a cost of about $40 per thousand, advertising tabloids for dealers with their store name and address imprinted on them. The dealer makes his own decision as to how he will distribute the tabloids and does this at his own expense.

It will cost you about $10,000 in cash to establish your own Western Auto associate store. The minimum investment is about twice that, varying with the size of the community, the competition, etc. Western Auto will handle the lending arrangements to finance the balance of the purchase price through its own acceptance, which deals exclusively in dealer loans.

New dealers are given two weeks' formal classroom training at no charge at one of the five company training centers. (Room and board are the dealer's responsibility.) The school teaches principles of store management, display, merchandising, time-payment selling, bookkeeping, inventory control, and all other phases of the business. After that, Western Auto advisers are there to help. There is no charge for their visits. A Western Auto sales representative who lives in your area will contact you periodically to counsel you on your operating problems.

Western Auto's guarantees on their products add considerably to the sales appeal of your merchandise and do not raise the price.

Western Auto says that its successful dealers are personable, and that some even border on the extrovert. They are mostly married, high school graduates, self-starters. The company has had many dealers for their entire careers, and the average age is over fifty. Young men are, of course, welcome.

The stores are usually open six days a week for normal retail hours. It's a twelve-month-a-year job, but vacations can be arranged once the dealer has trained his staff. The stores can be run as family enterprises in the beginning. As volume grows, however, the profitable store will add employees to become even more profitable.

Western Auto helps select store locations and bases its decision on a number of factors. The size of the community is taken into consideration, the competition, pedestrian and automobile traffic, etc. It prefers a corner location where there are already established stores. Generally speaking, franchises are located in communities of 1,000 population or more. The company stresses that to earn an adequate profit, your rent must be in line with the sales potential. It offers you and the owner of the building a suggested lease form, drawn up especially for Western Auto stores, which, the company says, "gives practical protection to both."

At present there are locations available in all states.

If a dealer decides in the future that he wants to sell his store he may. Western Auto must approve any buyer who would like to assume the franchise. The franchise itself may not be sold, since the dealer paid nothing for it. Western Auto will handle the transfer without charge to either man. The heirs have the right to sell the store should the dealer die. The franchise is good until terminated by either party for good cause.

Western Auto has no restrictions on retirees or on minority groups. All are welcome, the company says.

In a brochure Western Auto lists histories of a number of stores that trace their beginnings back to the original franchise grants in the mid-1930's. A. A. Anderson of Fredonia, Kansas, who bought the first Western Auto franchised store shortly after it opened, summed it up: "The Western Auto dealer program proved itself many years ago. It's a program that offers the energetic businessman great opportunity—opportunity that is as great today as it was thirty years ago!"

On page 104 is a profit-and-loss statement indicating the kind of results a successful dealer can hope for. The salaries are paid to employees. The owner's earnings come out of the net profit.

WESTERN AUTO

Merchandise sales	$150,000.00	100.0%
Cost of sales (including freight)	107,100.00	71.4
Merchandise gross profit	42,900.00	28.6
Handling charges—service income and other	3,600.00	2.4
Total Income	$ 46,500.00	31.0%
Expenses		
Advertising	$ 6,150.00	4.1%
Bad debts	750.00	.5
Utilities	1,200.00	.8
Telephone and telegraph	450.00	.3
Repairs	200.00	.2
Travel	150.00	.1
Misc. expense	300.00	.2
Postage and supplies	750.00	.5
Delivery expense	1,050.00	.7
Service expense	750.00	.5
Accounting and legal services	600.00	.4
Salaries	8,850.00	5.9
Rent	3,300.00	2.2
Depreciation	1,200.00	.8
Insurance	600.00	.4
Taxes	1,350.00	.9
Total Expense	$ 27,650.00	18.5%
NET INCOME	$ 18,850.00	12.5%

14

Budget Rent-a-Car

How much money does it take to put a man into a thriving auto-rental business? Would it take $60,000 or $125,000 or even $250,000? Would you believe $5,000? You won't make a million at that price, but if you've got little capital and are looking for an opportunity that improves with time, this may be your cup of tea.

Budget Rent-a-Car offers this opportunity. As you may know, Budget is the car-rental agency that proved new cars could be rented for 30 to 40 percent less than the major rental firms were charging—largely through a franchised agency setup that avoids heavy supervisory expenses.

For your $5,000 you won't be the prime licensee, but that's to your advantage. Here's how it works: Budget, which is now licensing new-car dealers exclusively, encourages the car dealer to take on an "owner-operator" as a partner. The dealer makes the major investment. (Cars cost $3,000 each and he may buy as many as 75 or 100.) You put up the $5,000 for your franchise.

Budget, which is presently interested only in General Motors dealers, can find a dealer who will let you share perhaps 20 percent of the profits on an auto-rental business. Take no less. Jules

Lederer, the dynamic founder of Budget Rent-a-Car, says that the markets into which Budget is now moving indicate a normal initial setup in which a General Motors dealer could become a licensee with twenty to twenty-five cars.

"A good operation makes $500 to $600 per car per year after expenses," Mr. Lederer states. He envisions a setup such as this: A GM dealer in, say, Bridgeport, Connecticut, with the minimum number of cars at the beginning, twenty to twenty-five, operates the auto-rental business right out of the auto agency. You, with a 20 percent profit stake in a minimum operation, would be paid from $600 to $700 a month for running the agency. Profits should run to about $15,000 a year after all expenses. Your 20 percent of the $15,000—$3,000—would be added to your owner-operator's salary of approximately $8,000, so you would make about $11,000 in the first year. As more cars were added, you would make more money, naturally. If the business earned a total of $25,000, you would get $5,000 out of the profits, for a total of $13,000.

Budget gives thorough training, and the 20 percent owner-operator is included in the program. The training takes place in a nearby Budget agency. You spend two weeks at this agency and another two weeks' training in your own Budget agency.

"A Budget expert will be in the vicinity to hold your hand and help you over the rough spots," Mr. Lederer says.

The General Motors dealer who is your partner is going to promote the rental business because it gives him exposure to potential new-car customers. Once a man has driven one of your cars for a couple of days or so, he is likely to become a customer when he is ready to buy.

If you join the Budget organization as an owner-operator with an auto-dealer partner, you will find that you are in a six-day-a-week business and you will have to hustle. "This is a young man's business—it requires a lot of energy," Mr. Lederer says.

15

Snap-on Tools

For the mechanically minded, the Snap-on franchise must surely offer one of the most challenging and satisfying of businesses. Snap-on represents that old but always refreshing story of the triumph of ingenuity over antiquated methods. In 1920 the company developed an interchangeable socket wrench that soon became the standard in the industry.

Today's mechanics and do-it-yourself buffs are so used to the interchangeable socket that many would be surprised to learn that mechanics once had to have dozens of wrenches with "tight" or fixed handles in order to conduct a business. Bolt sizes varied in an age of nonstandardization, and the very bulk of this tool inventory presented a significant problem in itself —to say nothing of the cost.

When the two founders of the company, Joe Johnson and William A. Seidemann, began their quest for business, their assets were limited. They had developed the interchangeable socket—a high-quality steel product and a twisted steel handle —and had rudimentary machining equipment. Things were so tight in the beginning that the two men would strip to the waist and work around the bending block for hours wrestling the steel rods into Snap-on handles.

In time, as their tools gained acceptance, the operation grew and today it includes seven factories that turn out 6,000 separate items.

Snap-on dealers do business out of vans. Their line includes socket wrenches and handles, screwdrivers, hammers, pliers, open-end and box wrenches, tool-storage units, pneumatic and electric power tools, wheel-alignment and balance equipment. They also sell a complete line of automotive electrical-testing equipment. Every year Snap-on adds from 300 to 400 new tools, many of them "specials" needed in servicing particular models of new cars.

The Snap-on franchise is free for qualified individuals, and the dealer pays no fees or royalties to the company. The company furnishes some bookkeeping and other record forms to the dealer without charge, and its field managers provide assistance in keeping these forms and in all other phases of the operation. Frequently, the dealer's wife helps with his records.

Snap-on Tools has long offered a business opportunity to the relatively capital-poor aspirant. The company looks primarily for good health, honesty, a strong desire to succeed.

The average Snap-on dealer is forty-three years of age, married, and has children. He usually has at least a high school education; however, Snap-on has a number of successful dealers who have less education. The company looks for affable men who are self-starters—men who can build and maintain good working relationships with their many customers. The company stresses a helpful attitude as the keynote to dealer success.

The dealer will purchase his tools from Snap-on Tools. Snap-on makes its profits from these tool sales.

The dealer benefits from Snap-on advertising in a wide variety of trade publications directed to specific automotive and industrial fields. The cost of the entire advertising program is borne by the company. New products are frequently featured both in advertising and in news stories published in these trade journals. Advertising reprints are provided to dealers so they will be aware of the tools the company is featuring.

Inside view of a Snap-on Tools truck

Since you will be working out of a van, this "store" is perhaps your most important sales tool. Your initial investment in a van is much lower than would be required to buy or rent a building. The company says that a good second-hand van can be purchased at between $900 and $1,500. A new van would cost $3,000 to $5,000, depending on its size. Van maintenance is much lower than the operating expenses of a building. You pay nothing for heat and electricity, and no real estate taxes.

With the display van, you seek out the customer. There is no waiting behind a counter until the customer comes to your store.

Your van will be big enough to allow immediate delivery on most items. The vans contain what the company terms "eye-appealing" displays that lead to many impulse sales—just like impulse purchases at stores.

Your inventory of tools will run about $4,800, and the company recommends that you spend somewhat more—buying a new van if you can afford it. You should also have enough capital in reserve to cover emergency needs, although the company says most dealers never have to fall back on this cushion. As you can see, if you buy a used van, $6,000 will cover you. What's more, if you have trouble getting financing, Snap-on will either throw their credit behind you at your bank or help you directly.

Snap-on is confident that a dealer who makes regular weekly calls on 75 to 100 customers can make a good living—and will wind up in the top 10 percent of the nation in terms of income. They say that a successful dealer should do $75,000 annually in sales and spend $46,500 for his inventory of tools. Truck-operating expenses, Snap-on says, should cost roughly $2,100, leaving the dealer with a net income of about $26,400.

An average dealer would produce sales of about $40,000. After expenses, the net income on this volume would be in excess of $10,000.

The company says that a survey by *Motor Service* magazine showed that each independent repair shop, new-car and truck dealer, and fleet operator spends an average of $18.41 per week, or $957.32 a year, on tools and equipment. Each service station offering repair service spends an average of $12.02 a week, or $625.04 a year, for tools and equipment and each mechanic spends an average of $4.91 per week, or $255.32 a year. The average territory has a total sales potential of $220,000—perhaps three times what the dealer can handle.

"It has been proven that regular weekly calls on from 75 to 100 customers produces much closer to total potential per call and is instrumental in a successful franchise operation," says Snap-on.

But success depends on many intangibles as well. One dealer, the company says, can be "highly successful" after three or four years. Another may require quite a few years to mature. The main thing is an intense desire to succeed. The degree of this intensity, the company says, is almost directly proportionate to the success of each man.

Snap-on offers free training through sales managers who work in the dealer's own home, so there is no expense for room and board. The dealer gets instruction in business fundamentals and related subjects, and the manager is constantly available to help with problems. There are training films, instruction booklets, and a monthly magazine, Snap-on News, to give the dealer valuable support. The sales manager is available to give instruction to the dealer's customers in the use of complicated equipment, thus reducing the time a dealer must spend away from his primary activity—selling.

The dealer can earn a reasonable income by putting in a forty-hour week, but most successful dealers work more than that. Some work evenings in order to contact customers who work the late shifts, and many make calls on Saturdays.

Snap-on is a year-round business, for the dealer must keep his customers away from the competition by making regular calls. Some successful dealers find that the best way to manage time off is to take short vacations throughout the year and plan a lengthy vacation only when business permits.

That bane of business, personnel, is no problem for the Snap-on dealer. He will be working his franchise alone. His family may help keep the van in good condition, polishing and cleaning it, and help with record keeping and telephone orders.

Should the dealer retire or give up his territory for any reason, the company will hire a successor. The dealer has no salable interest. However, the franchise agreement provides that all new Snap-on stock can be returned for full credit whether the dealer retires, leaves for another reason, or dies.

There are not a great number of Snap-on franchises available as of this writing. In all, there are 1,400 territories and many have a waiting list of men desiring to take over a territory.

There is competition for tool business, as you would expect, and Snap-on says it meets this competition with "top quality" and dealer services. Dealers do not discount prices to meet the competition.

Here's another important point. The company stresses that it does not compete with its franchised dealers through sales to jobbers, hardware stores, mail-order houses, or any other business.

The company likes to promote from the field, and field managers are chosen from the ranks of successful dealers. Branch managers are selected in turn from the numbers of efficient and productive field managers. Division-manager positions can follow, as can general-office executive positions.

"This method of filling managerial positions offers the dealer excellent promotional possibilities and a career with a bright future," the company states.

16

Puppy Palace

If you've ever lost a puppy to illness or a hit-and-run driver, you know what it's like to live with a family that has lost something irreplaceable.

In these days of high-cost pedigreed dogs, you know that it also means a substantial financial loss. Not long ago a family lost their dachshund pup, Fred Baby, from that virulent disease of cats and dogs, distemper. It was a fairly long illness, lasting almost as long as the family had the dog—some five weeks. When it was all over, they had spent the purchase price once over in medicines, veterinary fees, and boarding.

The children were heartbroken, and the parents tried to find another dog to replace their pet. But as they checked into it, they learned that another dog—even a full-grown animal permanently vaccinated against disease—could well become a victim of distemper, for sometimes the vaccination doesn't take. The worst way to find this out is to bring another dog into a home where a dog has recently died of distemper. For complete safety, the family was advised to wait several months before getting another dog.

What has all of this to do with Puppy Palace? Everything. Puppy Palace sells dogs that have been carefully selected from purebred stock. The shops see to it that the temporary vaccine (permanent vaccine is not safe for very young puppies) will last ten days or more—long enough for even the busiest of families to get the puppy to the veterinarian for complete protection.

This is the guarantee of Puppy Palace: "Any purchaser who follows the instructions regarding vaccinations listed on the back of the guarantee gets full protection for six months in the event the puppy dies of an illness within that period."

Should the purchaser lose the dog within two years for any cause, even if it is run over, stolen, or runs away, Puppy Palace will give him a 40 percent discount on a new dog of the same price or 40 percent of what they paid originally against the purchase of a more expensive dog. Thus if they paid $100, they would get a $40 credit against the purchase of a new puppy. The guarantee goes even further than that. If the dog dies or disappears within ten years, Puppy Palace will allow 25 percent of the price of the first dog toward replacement with a dog of similar or higher price.

This is an extraordinary promise in a business in which the merchandise is commonly sold on an "as is" basis. As Puppy Palace says in its business-opportunity brochure: "You can be certain that customers who take advantage of the refund will remain your customers."

Let's look in on a Puppy Palace franchise holder. Frank Madalone had already been in business for himself when he discovered Puppy Palace at the Franchise Show in New York City's Coliseum. He had been earning about $12,000 a year in a soft-ice-cream business and supplemented this by driving a school bus during the winter months for $6,000.

Always fond of puppies (his own five-month-old English sheep dog, which he "fell in love with right in the store," is always there with him), he was captivated by the prospect of making a living doing something he really loved. He opened a Puppy Palace in Roosevelt Field Shopping Center in Garden City, Long Island. The business has been unusually successful. Officials of the company say his may well be the most successful of all the Puppy Palaces in existence as this chapter was written.

(Puppy Palace had 85 outlets at the end of 1968, and plans 350 before 1971.)

Frank's shop has three of Puppy Palace's famous "love rooms" where families can get acquainted with their tentative choices. Even if the family later decides they have chosen unwisely, the dealer will take the pup back in a full-value exchange within seven days.

Frank says that the most rewarding thing about the business is that he's not selling a "dry product." (The pun was accidental but appropriate, as we'll see later.) "It's very touching with the kids. I had a blind kid in the love room the other day, and his parents bought him a German shepherd. It broke me up. I'd have given him the dog if they hadn't taken him. We're not really selling puppies, we're selling love."

That point cannot be stressed too strongly, because it goes to the very essence of the business. Another Puppy Palace man, Jack Frost, an ex-steelworker in Allentown, Pennsylvania, who nearly tripled his income with a Puppy Palace, put the point somewhat differently: "I have sixty salesmen in the store—all of them puppies." Most customers sense this immediately, that it's the puppies that do the work, and any prospective dealer who doesn't share the view that puppies are pretty wonderful had better not pursue the idea of a Puppy Palace dealership.

The company wants dog lovers only, and Puppy Palace founder, Norman Docktor, a man whose life has been devoted to the pet business, and his associates will see to it that dog lovers are the only ones who get franchises. Docktor has been described by an associate as a rugged man who is nevertheless "very soft-spoken and sincere. A true pet lover." He is also a stickler for cleanliness.

The cages in the Puppy Palace stores are designed so that droppings fall through the cage onto newspapers covered with grit. The newspapers are replaced several times a day, beginning with a thorough cleaning before the store opens in the morning, usually at ten o'clock. After a puppy is sold, the Puppy Palace personnel scour the cage with brush and cleaner.

While Frank Madalone employs his brother as a salesman, a girl who feeds and tends to the dogs, and a porter, all full

time, he still must perform the disagreeable tasks from time to time when an employee is absent or the shop is unusually busy. But as far as Frank is concerned, it is a small price to pay for the privilege of owning a delightful and profitable business. He works long and hard, though. He's there seven days a week, fifteen hours a day, except Sunday, when the normal closing time of 9:30 P.M. is moved up to 6 P.M. The shop is operated year-round.

Puppy Palace dealers pay a franchise fee of $35,000 to $38,000. For that money, the company says, it will furnish a "fully-stocked, fully-decorated store," a lease, and one month's intensive training in Philadelphia, along with the inventory of dogs, kennels, and merchandise to get you off the ground and an "unending" supply of replenishments.

To herald the new dealer's arrival, Puppy Palace offers full-page newspaper ads and publicity releases, which are more than likely to lead to newspaper stories, for dogs are better "copy" than the merchandise found in most new stores. There will be an opening-day promotion, possibly with a clown and a ribbon-cutting ceremony. Puppy Palace puts a consultant in the store for the first two weeks to help serve your customers and assist in ordering and displaying your merchandise.

The home-office support continues after that with public relations, training, consultation, purchasing, advertising, and other services at your disposal. If you run into problems, Puppy Palace says, "Call us up."

As Puppy Palace tells the story, you will be specializing in the most profitable side of the pet business—purebred puppies. A poodle that costs you $50, for example, sells in the store for $150. A deferred-payment plan puts the costliest breeds within the customer's reach.

You will also sell profitable items such as health, grooming, and training aids, toys, collars, and clothing for dogs. You will provide grooming services too, establishing your store as a specialty center for anything the well-bred dog might want. In short, you will develop the reputation as a dog expert (which will be fully deserved before you are in business more than a few months).

The Puppy Palace management regards turtles, goldfish, birds, and other small animals as low-profit items that waste store space and selling time and that "water down" that very important "specialist" image that means so much to a franchise holder, and especially to a Puppy Palace dealer.

If you're worried about the cost of feeding several dozen ravenous puppies, Puppy Palace says "Don't. Livestock turns over about twenty-three times a year, so the cost of feeding and caring for each puppy takes very little from your profits."

"Dry-goods volume is also high. It is not unusual for a customer to purchase about $70 worth of dry goods along with his puppy. Your markup on this merchandise—almost all of it bearing the Puppy Palace brand name—would be at least 100 percent."

Remember, a puppy needs a bed, several chew toys, two or more varieties of shampoo, at least one brush, and vitamins. He will need medicines for minor ailments and various kinds of house-training sprays. He'll need food supplements and, of course, a leash and collar.

As grooming will be part of your Puppy Palace service, at the training school you'll learn how to groom even the fanciest poodle. People who bring their dogs in for such care often leave with a shopping bag full of dog-care items for home use.

Naturally you pay for these carefully designed profit-making programs. The Puppy Palace royalty fee is 5 percent of your gross profit, and a substantial 7½ percent of your gross will be charged for advertising support.

You must buy your supplies from Puppy Palace, but why not? You get substantial discounts on their merchandise. Your customers will soon learn that they can buy certain items only at your store. Your profit, Puppy Palace spokesmen say, will be at least 20 percent higher on Puppy Palace items than on any other brand.

Your training at the Philadelphia headquarters is included in the $35,000 to $38,000 capital requirement. So is your room cost while you are there. You have to buy your own meals.

At the Puppy Palace school you receive what the organization calls "concept indoctrination." You are schooled in the

history of the company and its reasons for specializing exclusively in dogs. Your indoctrination also deals with the Puppy
Palace image and how to maintain it. The marketing training
emphasizes the value of advertising, promotion, and publicity,
and explains the reason for certain designs for stores, packaging,
and trademarks.

The dealer is taught a basic knowledge of all breeds, including their dominant physical, mental, and psychological traits.
He learns how to evaluate good breed types and their state of
health, and, very important, how to maintain records required
by the American Kennel Club. (Each dog is given a special
collar that prevents misidentification on the pedigree.)

A Puppy Palace dealer learns about the company's packaged
products so that he can recommend the right ones to each customer and build repeat sales—an important profit consideration.
He learns about differences in product quality, about pricing, and
about the nature of competitive products. There is instruction
in selling technique, inventory control, personnel management,
profitability accounting through holding controllable costs in
check, bookkeeping, and an "all-important" lesson in the operation of a cash register. Then he gets on-the-job training in an
established Puppy Palace.

As for credit, Puppy Palace has a close relationship with
Girard Trust Company in Philadelphia, which has financed
many Puppy Palace dealers. No matter where you borrow the
money, you will have to raise at least $10,000 to $15,000 in
cash. You can't get all the money from a bank.

Puppy Palace spokesmen were asked to evaluate the profit
potential for the first, second, and fifth years in business. They
said dealers should be able to make (including their own
salaries) $25,000 in the first year, $27,000 in the second, and
$30,000 in the fifth. In 1968, a good year for business in general,
the *least* profitable Puppy Palace was said to have earned $20,000
for its owner.

Where you set up your Puppy Palace would be up to you and
the company, depending, of course, on availability. In any event,
the company will place you in a busy shopping area on a site
serving a population of at least 50,000. Local taxes, zoning

regulations, availability of utilities such as gas and sewers, store dimensions, and ease of alteration are other factors that the company site-selection men take into consideration.

As the company puts it: "Your site may be in a shopping center, or it might be in a downtown metropolitan area. It will always be in an air-conditioned, clean, modern structure. And you must approve the site personally. The national stature of Puppy Palace [the company is now owned by Mars, Inc., the maker of M & M candies, Mars Bars, and Milky Ways] and the experience of our staff enables us to negotiate leases at rates that are usually far more favorable than the individual business-man could obtain by himself."

Building owners usually require a co-signer on their leases. A Puppy Palace spokesman said that the company is willing to co-sign for its dealers.

A Puppy Palace dealer who wishes to retire can sell his store to a buyer approved by the company.

The company has a death-clause policy giving the dealer's heirs the right to sell the store. The company has no policy excluding widows or retirees who might want a Puppy Palace franchise. The company has stores in operation that are owned by women and by retirees. One Puppy Palace is operated by two Negro partners.

At present there is no direct competition from a rival fran-chise, but there are pet shops in some localities that do special-ize in puppies. Puppy Palace protects their dealers' territories from competition from other Puppy Palace dealers, as territories are exclusive.

Every Puppy Palace store is planned around a basic design created by a retail-store architect. A large sign outside the store bears the Puppy Palace symbol—a white long-eared puppy under an enormous crown in red and white—which customers recognize from the company's ads. Stores are usually at least 1,500 feet square, and are characteristically "clean, spacious, and uncluttered," and in the center of each are "movable 'shelf islands' neatly stacked with packaged goods such as vitamins, sprays, and shampoos."

As for the wearers of the crowns, they are in kennels that are never glassed in. Some physical contact with each animal, the beginning of the emotional "chemistry" that leads to a sale, is possible through the bars of each kennel. And when the customer enters the love room and that lively bundle of fur begins to sell himself, you, as the dealer, would be watching through Dutch doors until the puppy cons the customer into signing on the dotted line.

The furry salesman could be a cairn terrier, a fox terrier, a cocker, or even a bloodhound. Puppy Palace selects dogs from hundreds of breeders in the United States and Europe, thus giving the company's dealers access to forty-three or more breeds. There are usually twenty-five different breeds in a dealer's stock. A dealer has ten days to return to the breeder any dog that arrives in poor health.

As Puppy Palace says, you would become a puppy expert, offering a specialist's service. You would make the heart-warming promise that is part of the key to the Puppy Palace success: "We sell you the right puppy—or no puppy at all."

PUPPY PALACE

Projected Profit Potential

Net sales	$100,000	$150,000	$200,000
Percentages based on net sales	100.0%	100.0%	100.0%
Purchases	42.0	42.0	42.0
Gross profit	58.0%	58.0%	58.0%
Operating Expenses			
Salaries	10.0	10.0	7.5
Franchise fee	5.0	5.0	5.0
Advertising	7.5	7.5	7.5
Store expenses	10.0	8.5	8.0
Administrative expenses	4.0	3.5	3.0
Total expenses	36.5%	34.5%	31.0%
Net operating-profit percentage	21.5%	23.5%	27.0%
Net profit (before taxes)	$21,500	$35,250	$54,000

(A) *Depreciation on equipment not included.*
(B) *Figures based upon existing franchise operations.*
(C) *Figures based upon model 1200-sq.-ft. store.*

17

Dunkin' Donuts

Perhaps as much as any other franchise, Dunkin' Donuts represents the American dream come true. Look through the roster of franchises in this book. How many offer a man an opportunity to get into a substantial retail business requiring no previous experience and just $20,000 cash?

The doughnut business offers a particularly fine opportunity for the school dropout to succeed in a big way—those who had to begin work at an early age rather than go to college; those who are willing to work long hours and who have no aversion to work with their hands; salesmen, cab drivers, waiters, policemen—people who know how to deal with the public.

For that's almost a profile of the successful Dunkin' Donuts franchise dealer, and if you look at the first man aboard this enterprise you'll agree that it is fitting that this kind of man should be a success.

William Rosenberg was an eighth-grade dropout who fought his way up the ladder starting as a Western Union messenger who pedaled his bike the fastest to the most lucrative telegraph client in downtown Boston. That was during the Depression, and the $18 a week he made was welcome in a family of six.

He was fourteen when he started and he's been on the move ever since.

Soon after the war he decided he wanted to be his own boss, and the way he set about this paved the way for his franchise company. He had been a chief union delegate in a defense ship-yard and was asked to stay on as a coordinator of surplus dis-posal. But he turned his back on this advancement to be his own boss. He set up a shoestring venture to deliver coffee at factory gates in Massachusetts.

Arising at 3:30 A.M., Bill brewed fifty gallons of coffee on the kitchen stove, and then prayed that his aging truck would start in the frigid New England winter and keep going until his day ended sixteen hours later. Even then, as he began to add trucks to serve the growing business, he insisted that his few employees wear distinctive uniforms so they wouldn't look like "peanut peddlers."

Within three years Bill and his brother Leon had stretched $1,100 in war bonds into a 140-truck factory-catering service that included running twenty-five in-plant cafeterias. One of Bill Rosenberg's big items in those early days was the doughnut.

One day, after a discussion of quality control, he is said to have shouted the word "doughnuts" three times and enthusi-astically laid out what was to become the business philosophy behind Dunkin' Donuts.

Realizing that 40 percent of the catering service business was in coffee and doughnuts, he concluded: "Everybody likes dough-nuts, but nobody's doing anything about them. When times are good they're a snack. Comes a depression and people buy them instead of a steak. They've got everything going for them: eggs, sugar, shortening, everything. Why, you might say they're the staff of life."

It wasn't easy to convince bankers, suppliers, and even some of his best institutional clients; they thought the idea unsound. His partner, an accountant, wanted nothing to do with the idea. (Later, however, he started a doughnut chain of his own.)

Today, according to Dunkin' Donuts, Americans consume half a billion dollars' worth of doughnuts a year—due in no small measure to the pioneering efforts of William Rosenberg.

How does a man decide to become a Dunkin' Donuts dealer? Here's the way it happened to Ed Voss of Gary, Indiana. Ed is an unusually cautious young man who finally settled on a Dunkin' Donuts franchise after three years of careful investigation of a number of franchise opportunities. He had been a lower-level member of management at the Youngstown Sheet and Tube Company when he became convinced that he wanted to be his own boss.

"For about three years [my wife and I] had been kicking around the idea of going into our own business. Since my skills were limited to management, we decided that a franchise might be the ideal thing so that we could utilize the skill of a large company, yet own our own business. After checking the franchise opportunities available at that time, we broke it down to what we could afford, what we liked, and what we had the proper background for. We discovered that Dunkin' Donuts could fit just perfectly into all three categories."

Ed Voss's shop is a Mom and Pop operation in a way. His wife, Lois, is very important to the operation. She sees to it that the coffee urns, the floors and counters, the display cases and windows are spotless. Ed personally supervises the doughnut baking. Ed and Lois weren't faced with the prospect of uprooting their family (they have four daughters) and moving to a new community. Luckily, they found an ideal location just five minutes from their home in Gary. In the first eight months of operation the store grossed over $100,000, so the long hours and hard work (flour sacks and dough must be pulled, tugged, and lifted) paid off. At that rate, the store would gross $150,000 a year. Figuring a $6,500 salary for the owner, a business of that size would produce profits, before payments on the equipment, and interest charges, of $33,360 a year.

Like everyone else who becomes a Dunkin' Donuts man, Ed Voss attended what is called, drolly enough, Dunkin' Donuts University in Newton, Massachusetts. While the school is not on a par with a liberal arts college—the graduates are qualified specialty bakers—the people who do the psychological testing of the candidates have impressive educational credentials.

The school, beneath a Dunkin' Donuts shop, is nevertheless

a serious learning institution. Those who successfully complete
the course—the dropouts get their $12,600 down payment back
—are not only doughnut bakers but have learned the rudiments
of operating a store as well.

Dunkin' Donuts trains 120 students every year. After five
weeks, the student is expected to produce 160 dozen doughnuts
in nine hours. The students are given a written examination on
the financing and management of doughnut shops, and they
take Dunkin' Donuts' famous pledge to make doughnuts fresh
every four hours and coffee every eighteen minutes. It is not
uncommon for those attending the school to bring along wives
and children.

Recipes for Dunkin' Donuts were developed in 1948. As
William Rosenberg once explained: "We started making our
own doughnuts in 1948, hiring a Swedish master baker who
had become a doughnut specialist. People kept saying they
were the best doughnuts they ever ate. The reason, besides the
formula, was that we were selling so many so fast that they had
to be made fresh constantly."

By the time you are enrolled, you'll probably have a good
idea where you want to set up business. "After extensive research with thoughts to traffic, population, shopping habits,
etc.," Dunkin' Donuts selects the site, but subject to the approval of the dealer so that you get a site that is well suited
to you.

The thought of swinging open the doors for the first time
will seem less forbidding when you know that there will be a
training crew in the store to help you get started. They will be
at your beck and call thereafter to give advice and help as you
need it. That's the way Dunkin' Donuts explains its policy of
letting you be "on your own, but not alone."

Here are some qualities that Dunkin' Donuts wants to see in
a man:

He is capable of being his own boss;
He is willing to work hard to achieve success;
He is in good health;
He has drive and stick-to-it-iveness;
He is level-headed and shows maturity in judgment;

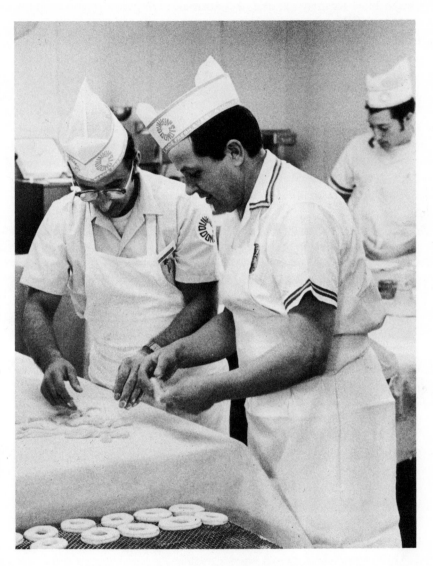

Preparing the donuts at a Dunkin' Donuts shop

He is willing to accept responsibility;

He likes to meet people and to make friends;

He is willing and able to learn new ideas;

He has a competitive spirit;

He has the enthusiastic backing of his family;

He takes pride in accomplishment;

He wants to be financially independent.

That's what Dunkin' Donuts expects of their dealers. What can you expect of Dunkin' Donuts? High ethical standards, among other things. The company has long been in the forefront of the drive to raise ethical standards in the franchise industry. In fact, William Rosenberg was one of the founders of the International Franchise Association, trade group for the industry.

Here's an example of the progressive steps Dunkin' Donuts has taken to build dealer loyalty. In the past a number of franchise companies were criticized for the charges they imposed on their dealers. Some dealers say that there are franchise companies that mark up their supplies unduly and insist under the licensing agreement that the dealer buy from them. Dunkin' Donuts no longer insists that the dealer buy mixes, paper products, and certain food items exclusively from them. The dealers are allowed to shop for the best possible deal from approved vendors.

Dunkin' Donuts' chief source of income is a 4.5 percent royalty on gross sales.

Here are the cash requirements published by Dunkin' Donuts and earnings estimates for stores with different sales volumes:

DUNKIN' DONUTS

CASH REQUIREMENTS FOR FRANCHISE
Down payment on equipment $12,600
Payable as follows:
At signing of Franchise Agreement
   and Equipment Service Agreement ....$ 1,000
At signing of lease 6,000
Within 10 days of signing of lease 5,600
                         $12,600
Working capital 6,600
Covering expenses as follows:
1. Your living expenses while in training
2. Salary and expenses of employees during training
3. First month's rent
4. Grand Opening advertising and give-aways
5. Utility deposits
6. Deposit on lease of signs
7. Freight on equipment
8. Other normal working-capital requirements
9. Sales tax where applicable
Total cash requirement (*excluding extra for lease security or
contribution to construction where required*) $19,200

COST OF EQUIPMENT
Down payment $12,600
Financed over 3 years 22,400
Total cost of equipment package $35,000
(*plus purchase of Dunkin' Donuts pylon sign and roof sign*)

Dunkin' Donuts stresses these other facets of its services:

Architectural, construction, and design services. Professional control assures you a modern, air-conditioned shop, with a colorful, inviting exterior and interior which attract customer traffic.

Finest laboratory-tested shop equipment. All equipment furnished you is selected on the basis of fast, quality production, long-life reliability, and minimum maintenance.

Complete training at Dunkin' Donuts University. For you and your employees.

Use of exclusive formulas and ingredients. Your products are made from highest-quality donut mixes, and our secret blend of the "world's finest coffee."

Continuous supervision and counsel. Our donut-maker specialists, operations and accounting departments, and general management provide you continual assistance.

Proven product appeal and variety. Your profit-making products include fifty-two varieties of donuts.

Planned promotion programs. Dynamic advertising—using television, radio, newspaper, and store displays—and special merchandising and promotion campaigns keep the public "Dunkin' Donut"-conscious.

In summing up, Dunkin' Donuts talks about the $50 million parent corporation, Universal Food Systems, Inc., which backs up the franchise operator, and concludes, "The franchise operator benefits from the best of the American way of life: encouragement of his entrepreneurial spirit abetted by modern technology and management counsel."

DUNKIN' DONUTS
ESTIMATED EARNINGS UNDER VARYING SALES LEVELS

	$2500. per week Amount	%	$3000. per week Amount	%	$3500. per week Amount	%	$4000. per week Amount	%
Annual sales: (1)	$130,000	100.0	$156,000	100.0	$182,000	100.0	$208,000	100.0
Cost of sales:								
Food	$ 35,100	27.0	$ 42,120	27.0	$ 49,140	27.0	$ 56,160	27.0
Payroll (2)	33,800	26.0	37,700	24.2	41,600	22.8	45,500	21.9
Supplies	5,200	4.0	6,240	4.0	7,280	4.0	8,320	4.0
Total cost of sales	74,100	57.0	86,060	55.2	98,020	53.8	109,980	52.9
Gross profit	55,900	43.0	69,940	44.8	83,920	46.2	98,020	47.1
Deduct—Operating Expenses:								
Rent (3)	$ 13,000	10.0	$ 13,420	8.6	$ 15,240	8.4	$ 17,060	8.2
Depreciation	5,100	3.9	5,100	3.2	5,100	2.8	5,100	2.5
Utilities	3,900	3.0	4,680	3.0	5,460	3.0	6,240	3.0
Advertising	2,600	2.0	3,120	2.0	3,640	2.0	4,160	2.0
Cleaning-laundry	2,600	2.0	3,120	2.0	3,640	2.0	4,160	2.0
All other expenses (ins., taxes, etc.) (4)	11,250	8.7	12,420	8.0	13,330	7.3	13,980	6.7
Weekly service fee (5)	5,850	4.5	7,020	4.5	8,190	4.5	9,360	4.5
Total operating expenses	44,300	34.1	48,880	31.3	54,600	30.0	60,060	28.9
Operating profit	11,600	8.9	21,060	13.5	29,380	16.2	37,960	18.2
Cigarette vending income	650	.5	700	.4	750	.4	800	.4
Net profit before income taxes	12,250	9.4	21,760	13.9	30,130	16.6	38,760	18.6
Add—Depreciation:								
Equipment and sign 8 yrs.	5,100		5,100		5,100		5,100	
Operator's salary incl. in payroll above	6,500		6,500		6,500		6,500	
Total cash earned by operator before equipment, sign and related interest payments	$ 23,850		$ 33,360		$ 41,730		$ 50,360	

NOTES:
(1) Based upon a retail sales price of $.79 per dozen donuts and $.15 per cup of coffee
(2) The payroll estimates show $6500 for the services of the Franchise Owner for actual work performed. Payroll is based upon a selling period from 6 AM to 1 AM and has been calculated using an assumed wage rate of $1.40 per hour.
(3) The rent figure does not include real estate taxes and represents an estimate based upon past experience but is subject to a wide variation in each instance depending upon individual location and circumstances.
(4) Taxes are estimated and will vary widely depending on the specific locale.
(5) After first year weekly service fee increased to 4.9%.

18

McDonald's Hamburgers

You've seen the signs. A big "McDonald's Hamburgers" in white letters fastened to a red wedge riding two thirds of the way up a massive yellow arc. And the cars. Scores of them most of the time, parked or inching back into traffic or onto the lot while several scrubbed young men take orders, passing a ton of beef over the counter in an average week.

Any way you look at it, McDonald's is big business. There are now over 1,100 McDonald's hamburger restaurants, and their number is still growing. The company grossed $266 million in 1967 and close to $300 million in 1968. The chain has served over 4 billion hamburgers, and they are going at a rate of over 2 million a day.

Unless you count Uncle Sam, McDonald's is the nation's largest buyer of hamburger beef. In 1967 alone, McDonald's bought about 60 million pounds of hamburger, 55 million dozen buns, 150 million pounds of potatoes, 3.5 million pounds of cheese, 10 million pounds of fish, 2 million gallons of ketchup, and 1.2 million gallons of pickles. What's more, McDonald's is Coca-Cola Company's largest single customer for Coke syrup.

That's the general picture. Where would you fit into this scene? McDonald's, widely regarded as perhaps the most desirable franchise in the nation today, does not issue its licenses lightly. There is a waiting list. One man who recently became a McDonald's dealer waited a year before a store was available. What's more, he had to leave his native Chicago and move to upstate New York to take the franchise.

McDonald's says frankly that it makes a determined effort to weed out applicants who appear to have bad work habits. And the initial investment—a cool $53,000, more than the average man saves in a lifetime—tends to discourage misfits and those with marginal work records.

McDonald's, like every other franchise company, is always interested in promising talent. Here's an indication of where the company has found some of its successful dealers. Among the men behind the counter are a golf pro, a chief steward knighted by the Swedish government, a retired Air Force colonel, a controller of a company, a former undersecretary of labor in the Truman administration, lawyers, dentists, a member of the Virginia house of representatives, advertising account executives, a Navy commander, and a research chemist.

McDonald's also has many men from more ordinary backgrounds. One franchise dealer, Frank Yud, is a fifty-four-year-old former railway postal clerk who put most of his life savings into a McDonald's stand. He was trusted with the operation of a store that McDonald's had operated with a manager for several years without notable success. (Like everybody else, McDonald's finds it much harder to make a profit when a man lacks the profit incentive.) It is now being operated at a substantial profit.

Frank Yud and his wife, Elizabeth, work together. Frank spends fifty-five to sixty hours a week at the stand—which is open twelve hours a day normally and an extra hour, until midnight, on weekends—and his wife does the books at home. He usually starts his day at 7:30 A.M., three and a half hours before the opening of business. While his maintenance man hoses down the parking lot and hauls potatoes out of the basement, he is getting the front counter ready, preparing the stove, sinks, and the milk-shake machine, as well as hanging out clean shirts and aprons for his employees. He is at the counter at 11 A.M. and stays there until 7 P.M. waiting on trade, making milk shakes, frying potatoes, wrapping hamburgers, and supervising his crew of at least four employees.

Frank hopes to pay off the mortgage on his equipment in three to five years, and at present is taking a salary of $1,000 a month. He pays his wife $100 a month for taking care of the bookkeeping and for pitching in behind the counter in a pinch. Frank is just getting started, but has "turned the corner" to profitable operations after less than a year in business. His profit, while meager, is over and above his salary and mortgage payments. One of the first items on the agenda when profits improve: a raise for his loyal and hard-working wife.

Frank devotes a great deal of his time to breaking in new employees because they don't stay long. Employee turnover averages 300 percent a year, but McDonald's says this turnover reflects unusual local circumstances—not the national picture, which is "more favorable." Some employees are lazy, others eat too much, and the good ones can do better than $1.65 an hour. (There is no tipping, as you may know.) Mr. Yud undoubtedly hopes someday that he can spend less time behind the counter—perhaps hiring managers and moving into the big time as owner of several McDonald's stores. Others have done it, and a few are millionaires.

But before we go further, let's look at the first McDonald's store. If you had driven into that restaurant some thirteen years ago, you'd have found Ray A. Kroc behind the counter turning out a hamburger, milk shake, and french fries in about fifty seconds.

Kroc, now board chairman, had an idea that if he could turn out hamburgers on an assembly-line basis—like so many Model-T cars—he could lure the nation's burgeoning eat-out family trade. Turning the burgers out the way Detroit turns out cars, Ray Kroc was able to slice the price to meet the needs of economy-minded families.

Rigid standards kept quality up, and "no frills" self-service paved the way for success. The formula, refined and modified, is essentially just as it was when Kroc wore the peaked cap. Kroc is a demon on cleanliness and never visits a dealer without checking for waste paper and picking up any litter he might see.

Kroc says that the secret of his success is in "finding something the public wants, something basic and simple, something that can be sold in volume and sold fast. What could be more natural than meat and potatoes—and that's what we're selling at McDonald's."

But why has McDonald's been so successful at selling something that has long been an American favorite—something that had been merchandised effectively long before those golden arches began dotting the highways? Mr. Kroc answers: "Science."

You'd never think there was a science to making and serving a hamburger. But McDonald's has reduced it to a science. "After determining that the hamburger was American's most popular single food item," Kroc says, "we worked out the precise formula of making hamburger to the public's liking, from the exact size to the catsup and mustard proportions. In applying science to the hamburger, we did not forget the most important factor of all—taste."

McDonald's leaves nothing to the caprice of the man at the grill. Everything from the size of the bun (diameter 3¾ inches) to how much onion goes on a burger (¼ ounce) is precisely spelled out in a confidential eighty-four-page specifications book. The company designed special equipment to speed hamburger making and a mechanical device that sprays an exact portion of mustard or ketchup on each burger. "We put the hamburger on an assembly line without losing any of the delicious flavor Americans want in a burger, and we came up with a formula that has given us the greatest growth in the history of the restaurant business."

So successful has McDonald's been that the company owns or controls about $100 million worth of real estate. McDonald's owns or controls the land and building, and they are in turn leased or subleased to the operators.

Where does McDonald's buy their properties? Out on the

Inside view of a McDonald's stand

highway where the tourists pass like so many fireflies on a summer night? Not at all. McDonald's likes to settle into a community because it believes its profits are heavily rooted in local family trade.

So McDonald's pays less attention to the traffic count, an index of transient trade, than to signs of a solid, substantial family neighborhood. The company looks for churches, schools, shopping centers, and plenty of nearby residential streets. McDonald's units draw as much as 90 percent of their business from local families.

The company offers its dealers "supervision in depth," which includes not only site selection but engineering and construction. It has its own real estate, engineering, and construction departments, staffed by experts.

McDonald's looks for large sites. Most units are located on lots of not less than 23,000 square feet, with paved parking space for 50 cars, and each building has an area varying from 1,200 to 1,500 square feet.

McDonald's units not only look alike, but have identical equipment, fixtures, supplies, and food. The company does not buy or sell any of these things; it sets the standards and negotiates the contracts, but the operators buy everything themselves— locally in most cases.

McDonald's menu is standard and quite limited. That's one of the keys to the company's success, specialization—concentrating on turning out a few things fast.

Until 1965 McDonald's sold nothing beyond hamburgers, cheeseburgers, french fries, milk shakes, coffee, milk, hot chocolate, and soft drinks. In 1965, in the first menu change in the company's history, a fish sandwich was added—an instant success.

One of McDonald's greatest assets is quality control. You know how it is to inch up to a strange restaurant when you are on the road. You have no way of knowing until you are actually inside and looking at your platter whether you have found a good place or not.

How do you get controlled quality when you sell hamburgers by the million? You have to work at it. Every motorist who has stopped at a McDonald's stand knows the company does work at it. What to buy, how to prepare it, how to serve it—all these things are rigidly prescribed in detail and closely checked by the company.

Every unit has to purchase fresh food every day. You are unlikely to get a stale hamburger or french fry at McDonald's. Dealers are required to chuck the french fries after seven minutes and the hamburgers after fifteen.

If you were to get a McDonald's store, you would have to attend the company school before they ever let you tie on an apron. The school, in Elk Grove, near Chicago, lasts two and a half weeks and covers everything you can think of—standards, procedures, specifications used in the chain, food preparation, maintenance of equipment, purchasing, hiring and firing, quality control, and on-the-job training in an actual unit.

But schooling is just part of the story. The company works closely with the men in the field, helping them with everything from advertising and promotion to operations and quality control.

To make its vast system operate more effectively, McDonald's divides responsibility into five areas, each with a director, an advertising manager, and an administrative staff. Regional headquarters are Boston for the East, Washington, D.C., for Mid-Atlantic, Atlanta for the South, Columbus for the Mideast, Chicago for the Midwest, and Los Angeles for the West. The regional offices function as a kind of liaison between the national office and the units at the community level.

McDonald's maintains that not only is the company getting bigger through more and more units, but that sales are increasing too, and not just because there are more units. Each year the stores do more business than before, McDonald's says. The average unit grossed nearly $300,000 in 1967.

If you're not a joiner, think twice about applying for a McDonald's franchise. It's McDonald's policy for its dealers to support local causes and participate in community activities.

Why all this activity? Because McDonald's is keyed to the local family trade. To be involved with the community is to build the business. For example, dealers are to buy locally wherever possible. Standards are set nationally and rigidly enforced, but that doesn't change the buying policy. The beef is bought from local butchers. By buying beef this way McDonald's can be sure that the meat will be fresh.

McDonald's banks locally too and has an even greater effect on the community financial scene that this might suggest. The company estimates that each new unit means at least twenty-five jobs in the community.

"Everything about the unique McDonald's operation—from its prices scaled to family budgets, to the speed and convenience of service, to the rigidly enforced standards of quality and cleanliness, to the wholesome atmosphere—is planned with the local family trade in mind."

Here's how McDonald's describes its franchise:

It guarantees your right to the nationally famous McDonald's name. This gives you an advantage in sales and advertising and of starting off with signs and special printed paper containers. It provides for your primary training in the company's training school in Illinois. There you will receive both classroom instruction and actual operating experience, conducted by a staff of McDonald's specialists. The company also furnishes you with its "proven formulas, records, and system of operation."

Approximately $53,000 of initial capital is required. This is for the McDonald's fees, equipment, supplies, and so on. The initial franchise fee is $10,000. A service fee of 2.8 percent of the gross volume is paid semimonthly to McDonald's System, Inc. Two deposits totaling $4,000 are paid when you register. The deposits are applied to the fees charged by the company when you accept a specific location.

McDonald's adds that you will be in business for yourself and yet enjoy all the advantages that only a "great organization can command. Visit one of our units and see for yourself how alive it is." If you are interested and can qualify for a McDonald's franchise, the company will be pleased to arrange a personal interview.

Here's the breakdown of the $53,000 cash requirement:

FRANCHISING

$2,500. Site-Development fee. Selection and analysis of location and inspection of parking area and building during construction.

$10,000. License fee. Exclusive license, assistance in obtaining local supplies, and opening unit.

$15,000. Security deposit against the lease.

$2,500. Cash down on approximate $11,500 net cost (including installation) of arches, signs, and neon work.

$10,000. Cash down on approximate $45,000 net cost (including installation) of food-service equipment, including roast-beef equipment, which may not be required immediately.

$13,000. Approximate cash requirement for miscellaneous equipment, landscaping, and opening expenses. Cost of miscellaneous equipment varies depending on optional items and terms of purchase.

The product inventory—food, paper, and condiments which are needed to open the unit—costs approximately $8,300. Usually these items are not paid for until after the unit is in operation.

McDonald's says that this is merely an estimate. The balance due on the food-service equipment, signs, and arches (approximately $44,000) is usually financed. A loan must be secured on the dealer's own credit from an independent financial source. McDonald's neither lends money nor guarantees the obligations of its operators.

Suitable sites for a McDonald's operation are provided exclusively by McDonald's Corporation. This company is constantly at work securing desirable locations, which they provide to operators, complete with a McDonald's building and hard-surfaced parking lot, on the basis of a twenty-year lease with rent equal to 8 percent of annual gross sales (which averaged nearly $300,000 in 1967).

There is a great deal of confusion about franchise-company fees that often leads to misunderstandings. McDonald's in an unusual step explains precisely what the dealer gets for the 2.8 percent fee paid to McDonald's System, Inc.:

1. McDonald's System, Inc., negotiates volume contracts with all purveyors and suppliers. These contracts are based on high

quality and low prices. McDonald's System, Inc., makes all items available to the individual operator at the exact price of the contract. The overall advantage of this centralized buying power reflects a saving to the operator of approximately 4 percent of his gross, of which he is paying only 2.8 percent.

2. Upon the granting of a license to a new McDonald's operator, arrangements are made for the new operator to spend at least fourteen days in training and indoctrination into the business. A trained McDonald's consultant is sent to each unit at opening for no less than three days. He will take charge of the opening of the unit, assist in training the employees and generally oversee the opening to assure greatest efficiency.

3. McDonald's has a fully proven and tested system that enables an operator to sell the limited number of food items at a price well below market on a highly profitable basis. The average McDonald's unit operates on a food and supply cost of approximately 40 percent, which provides an average gross profit margin of about 60 percent.

4. The standards of high quality are maintained throughout all the operating units by virtue of centralized buying and periodic inspections and consultations.

5. McDonald's System, Inc., is available for consultation with all operators and acts as a clearing house for information. We advise each operator of new ideas, improved methods, and aid him to guard against pitfalls of trial and error.

6. All the advantages of brand identification, uniformity of color scheme, menu, and service are inherent in the McDonald's System. McDonald's also maintains six regional offices and a research and development laboratory in addition to the home office in Chicago.

7. Each McDonald's operator can benefit by his affiliation with experts in the specialized food field who provide tested and proven operating procedures for greatest efficiency and lowest operating overhead; who outline policies for the best interests of the McDonald's operators, which policies are designed to promote and protect each operator as well as the public interest and who provide personalized assistance and guidance.

Executives of McDonald's would not make available figures on profit margins or sample profit-and-loss statements. They refused on the perfectly reasonable grounds that profits vary greatly depending upon a man's ability and they consider profit-and-loss statements as confidential. However they are available for review by prospective operators during interviews.

McDonald's is considered one of the hottest franchises available today, and profits for the successful are substantial. *Business Week* reported in mid-1968: "The average annual revenue of a McDonald's store is $300,000, about five times the average for all drive-in restaurants, and it turns a pretax profit of between 12 percent and 15 percent. . . . Generally an owner can pay back his investment in three to five years."

19

International House of Pancakes

The International House of Pancakes is the first of more than a dozen franchise companies owned and operated by International Industries, Inc. The others include: in International's foods group, Copper Penny coffee shops, Orange Julius fast-service outlets, Wil Wright's Ice Cream Shoppes, and the Original House of Pies, which are deluxe dessert-oriented coffee shops; in the company's retail group, House of Nine, shops specializing in petite and junior-sized clothes for women, and United Rent-All marts; in education, Sawyer Business Colleges, which provide training in secretarial and clerical skills, United Colleges for medical and dental assistants, and the Institute for University Studies, which offers college-level home-study courses; and in International's service group, First National Credit Bureau, a credit-reporting and collection operation, and AIMS International, which provides marketing materials and services to a franchised network of 2,500 realtors.

Al Lapin, Jr., the dynamic president of International Industries, has also served as president of the International Franchise Association.

One cannot help be impressed by the organization of these

various franchise companies. Lapin is convinced that many franchise companies have expanded too fast, causing problems of logistics and leading the companies into eventual stagnation. Since franchise companies ordinarily get a major part of their profits through initial fees, the incentive to build quickly is strong indeed.

But International Industries, with sixteen different companies, has been able to expand at the rate most conducive to success. For example, International adds pancake houses at a rate of just thirty a year—a fairly slow rate of expansion for the franchise industry. Meanwhile, the company expands in the other fields at the most appropriate rate for each of them.

A look at the House of Pancake setup will provide some insight into the International Industries empire. Perhaps the most useful service offered by the organization is the meticulously detailed bookkeeping that the parent company conducts on behalf of its dealers. Not only does the company check the dealer's figures for appropriate spending levels, it also compares the figures with those from earlier periods for signs of growth and with those of other pancake houses. All this information is offered to the dealer to help him understand what is going on in his business so that he can make the right decision.

First he makes out a transmittal sheet—a weekly summary of how much business he has done, his purchases, sales, overhead and operating expenses, labor cost, food costs broken down into meats, flour, etc.

Four days after this is sent to headquarters, the restaurant owner gets back a computerized profit-and-loss statement for the week, and percentage costs of labor, food, etc., against sales. There is a comparison with what he has been doing and what others in his region are doing with their International House of Pancakes. He gets a comparison with what he did in the corresponding week a year ago and figures showing what he did in the following week or two last year so that he can gauge how much food he should purchase. This helps him buy economically and avoid over- or under-ordering. Thus holiday purchases, for example, can be anticipated.

International's central computer in North Hollywood, California, works out all the store owner's taxes and even arranges to pay his power and light bill. International Industries gets a consolidated invoice from General Mills for all its restaurants. The company looks at the owner's transmittal sheets and bills him for his proportionate amount. Needless to say, International gets a considerable discount for volume and an additional break on the price of the flour because only one bill is required. This cost saving is of paramount importance, because basically the menu consists of all kinds of pancakes. Further central-purchasing economies result through other billings to International that are in turn prorated among the individual stores.

International Industries' advertising program is unique. International owns Continental Media Services, which has a film library of full-length motion pictures. These films are sold to television stations with a proviso that advertising time is bought at one third the normal cost. The dealer pays for only 1 percent of advertising done by the company. In similar barter arrangements, International buys pages in the *Reader's Digest* through advertisers who would like to have some of the television-advertising credits International has accumulated through its film barter. Through this sophisticated barter technique, International once got a $250,000 magazine-record-television promotion for its franchisees on a national basis at a cost of less than $50,000. To augment the barter program, International's sixteen companies back their franchisees with an extensive normal media advertising program.

In addition to the advertising fee, the dealer pays International 5.2 percent of his gross revenues for yearly services, including bookkeeping. International also makes a profit on supplies—crested china and paper books—and on pancake mixes created to International's formula by General Mills. However, the company says that the profit is modest on these items and does not account for substantial earnings for the company.

The franchise fee for a House of Pancakes is $45,000, of which the operator pays $25,000 in cash. (International doesn't care where you get it, whether from your brother-in-law, granny, or rich wife.) The other $20,000 is paid off over four years— it's financed by International—at a rate of $5,000 a year at

6.5 percent interest. You are paying for a turnkey operation. Just unlock the door, flip the light switch, and you are ready to start serving customers.

International estimates that a properly run House of Pancakes should have annual gross sales of $250,000 with a 10 percent profit, including the owner's draw. Thus, the owner should make at least $25,000. Income will remain about the same for the first four years, while he is paying off his franchise financing charges. After that, he should net an additional $5,000, since he is no longer paying off his loan. If he has built his business to a larger gross, then, of course, that 10 percent profit can mean much more.

Before he gets a store, he will have to undergo eight weeks of intensive training in the North Hollywood foods-division school.

The owner leases his building from International, which in turn leases from a real-estate investor. His rental expense should not exceed 10 percent of his gross revenues.

The International Pancakes owner will be only a memory to his wife during the first six months, for he will be working twelve to fourteen hours a day seven days a week. He'll have to adjust his social life more or less permanently because 35 to 40 percent of his business is done on weekends.

Once he learns the system, he will be able to go on a less arduous schedule. He will be in the restaurant for the breakfast, lunch, and dinner hours but will be able to play golf in between if he wishes. The degree to which he trains his personnel will determine how much free time he will have. He is given extensive instruction in this at the company's training school.

If the owner wants a vacation, International will supply a store supervisor for a week at a rate of $50 a day. The same arrangements can be made should he become ill.

An International Pancake House is not a family setup. Ordinarily there will be nineteen or twenty employees.

International obviously has a big investment in a man once his store is opened, and as a result the company assesses a big penalty for anyone who quits during the first year of operation. He will forfeit $10,000 if he quits during that period.

At its school International gives the franchisee motel money, the use of a car, and about $70 to $75 salary, out of which he buys his food. (If International washes the man out, he owes them nothing.)

During the last week of training, International brings the franchisee's wife in so that she can become familiar with the management and with the role her husband will be playing.

That role is usually a new one for him. International does not want people with food experience because the company would have to help him unlearn habits that do not square with their successful methods.

He is, of course, taught food preparation and quality control. (There are twenty-one pancake specialties among eighty-four food items.) He learns to be a busboy and a cook because he may have to take over those functions in an emergency. The store must remain open at all costs. He is also given extensive training in store maintenance, since this is viewed as one of the most important factors in its success.

International, like many other leading franchise companies, has a national insurance program that is available to all its owners. This is important in an age of riots and rising crime rates. Some lesser franchises do not offer such programs, and this is a decided drawback because the owner may not be able to get necessary insurance on his own. International's program includes protection against such remote eventualities as boiler blowup as well as theft, water, and fire damage and employee liability. Through mass purchasing, the insurance is available at lower rates.

What kind of a man is International likely to choose? The company's average owner is thirty-eight; he has two children and another on the way; and like as not he came from a job where he felt he had reached his peak. He sees his friends getting better jobs and he becomes dissatisfied. By joining International, "he's not buying a guarantee of success, but an insurance policy against failure. He knows that he is going with someone who can give him guidance and an assist in operating profitably," the company states.

International considers the choice of a site to be the single most important detail in a dealer's success. "We don't give figures, but we consider density of population; we look for a high social-economic level. A good 70 percent of the business will come from people living within a three-mile radius of the restaurant. We're not so anxious to get the transient trade as some others. We look for certain numbers of professional people who tend to eat out often.

"As for location, we look for a corner by the traffic light on the going-to-work side of the street. The reason is that we know that the husband on his way to work, an the wife on the way to shopping will decide to go to the House of Pancakes fairly frequently as a result. We are interested in travelers, but we're not competing with fast-food service outlets. We're competing with the wife who is deciding whether to eat out or at home."

The term of the International House of Pancakes license is fifteen years with renewal options. After the first fifteen years International expects to charge $1,000 additional each year for the use of the name during the first five years of renewal. Should the owner die, International will provide a buyer, and any profits go to the widow.

As for the competition, International feels that its pancake mixes give its owners an edge. "We think our pancakes are a lot better than others. Having a product that is exclusive will insulate you against the competition."

International has one woman franchisee, but prefers to steer women into the House of Nine. Retirees simply wouldn't have the stamina. International franchisees represent virtually every racial and ethnic group.

International says that money isn't necessarily a stopper for those who cannot afford the down payment. Some who qualify as good potential dealers are brought into a junior franchise program. They act as managers and when they build up sufficient capital, they are allowed to buy a franchise.

Like many another franchise company, International does not want investors. "All dealers must run their businesses. What's more, we want a good home environment. The problems and stresses over the first six months can wreck a man's home. That's why we bring the wife out to California."

20

Kentucky Fried Chicken

Colonel Sanders, the man who began the Kentucky Fried Chicken franchise, is perhaps the only major franchise founder who is a well-known movie and television personality as well. It all started on a plain dining-room table in the colonel's gas station in Corbin, Kentucky, during the Depression years.

The colonel put the table in the station because he recognized a demand for good food that was not being met. His fried chicken soon established his reputation as a cook, and it wasn't long before he had a 150-seat dining room catering to his growing clientele. In time he franchised his idea, traveling thousands of miles to popularize his product with restaurant owners everywhere. He has built his Kentucky Fried Chicken idea into a world-wide empire of more than 2,000 restaurants and carry-out stores.

His recipe was developed, he says, over twenty-five years of experimenting in his own restaurant. In his cooking method the chicken is cooked all the way through to the bone, "retaining all the flavor and natural juices." The special process, which he later patented, and his seasoning of eleven different spices and herbs was named Kentucky Fried Chicken to distinguish it from other Southern-fried chicken, which, in the colonel's opinion, had been brought into disrepute by restaurants with no consideration for quality.

The recipe was perfected in 1955, when the colonel was sixty-five. He took his car, his chicken cooker, his idea, and, in true Kentucky-colonel style—white suit, string tie, silver-handled cane, and his now famous mustache and goatee—began traveling about the country offering his Kentucky Fried Chicken formula to restaurant operators. The idea grew popular, and the concept of the "take home" store, introduced later, proved to be so successful that it now represents the major share of the volume done by the 1,400 outlets spread around the globe.

In March 1964 Colonel Sanders sold his business for $2 million plus a $40,000 yearly salary as adviser and public relations consultant to the new owners. He now serves as the company's ambassador of good will, spreading the name Kentucky Fried Chicken on national television and radio programs, in magazines and newspaper articles, and even in feature films, including a Jerry Lewis movie, "The Big Mouth."

The Kentucky Fried Chicken dealer pays 1 percent of his gross sales for this advertising program, which the company describes "as extensive as any advertising program can be." Kentucky Fried Chicken chips in another $1 million at present, over and above what it collects from its dealers.

To become a Kentucky Fried Chicken take-home dealer, you would need $22,600 in cash, which includes the franchise fee of $3,000. Once in operation, you would make regular payments to the company at the rate of 3 percent of gross sales. You would have to buy your paper goods, secret seasoning mix, and equipment from Kentucky Fried Chicken, which makes a profit on these items too.

The $22,600 does not pay for everything. Rather, that investment represents the minimum cash and includes a 25 percent down payment—$7,000—for equipment. In addition, you would have to pay $688.33 for thirty-six months for the remaining cost of the equipment.

Stores must be built according to Kentucky Fried Chicken

specifications. Your store will be the familiar square shape with red-striped pagoda roof and soaring sign topped by a bucket of chicken and the colonel's famous visage.

Kentucky Fried Chicken asks you to build the store yourself or to get an investor to do it for you. The company says that a real-estate man should be able to find you an investor and that you should pay no more than 5 percent of your gross sales or 10 percent of land value plus 12 percent of the cost of improvements. You may find that you can do better than that. If you pay a great deal more than the recommended 22 percent maximum, you will have trouble making anticipated profits.

While you must find an appropriate location, Kentucky Fried Chicken must approve it. You will have an exclusive franchise within a radius of 1½ miles of your store or. an area with a population of 20,000, whichever is less. The company adds, "It is not our policy to grant extensive territory as this can be detrimental to a franchising company, unless it is applied to a performance schedule."

As for profits, the company says that dealers ordinarily net 15 percent of their gross sales and that some do better. Good management can easily produce 18 percent. The company says it is common for take-home stores to average $30,000 a month in gross sales, or $360,000 a year. At 15 percent that would bring net profits of $54,000. The company uses the testimonial of Marshall Scott of Kirkwood, Missouri, who showed a first-year gross of $150,000 and profits of about 20 percent—a net of $30,000.

On the other hand, Kentucky, like most other reputable franchise companies, does not guarantee profits to anyone. A spokesman says, "[Our franchise] has proven so successful that we have never had a franchisee fail, nor have we ever been in a court of law with a franchisee. We are one big happy family."

The company also franchises Kentucky Roast Beef stores, where sandwiches and milk shakes are the staples. The same profit potential exists for these stores, according to the company experience.

New franchised dealers spend five days at a school in a Kentucky Fried Chicken take-home store. The future dealer ob-

serves and participates in every function of the operation from the time the door is opened in the morning until it is closed at night. "The course includes seventeen hours in the classroom, fifteen in the kitchen, and five hours for touring other Kentucky Fried Chicken outlets in the area."

The company trains the franchisees in cooking chicken, making gravy, potatoes, and salads, operating all necessary equipment, and in maintenance and sanitation. The course also includes detailed instruction on such management functions as accounting, sales, advertising, catering, and purchasing.

A typical franchisee is thirty-five to forty-five years of age and a family man. He has a high school education or better, and is a hard worker.

The stores are seven-day-a-week operations, and the dealer must either work that long or provide adequate management. The fact that many dealers have several stores suggests that managers can be trained successfully.

Dealers who expect to take vacations will have to train people who can take over the management of the store, because it should be open 365 days a year. The stores should have from six to ten employees, which rules out a strictly family operation.

Should the dealer die, the heirs may sell the franchise, but only to a person approved by Kentucky Fried Chicken. The contract runs for twenty years and contains no renewal options (although there is the understanding that the store will continue to be operated by the dealer thereafter). The dealer is also permitted to sell his store, so long as his buyer has the blessing of the company.

Colonel Sanders explains his philosophy in this tribute to hard work and excellence:

"It is comparatively easy to prosper by trickery, the violation of confidence, oppression of the weak . . . sharp practices, cutting corners—all of those methods that we are so prone to palliate and condone as 'business shrewdness.'

"It is difficult to prosper by the keeping of promises, the deliverance of value in goods, in services and in deeds—and in the meeting of so-called 'shrewdness' with sound merit and good ethics.

"The easy way is efficacious and speedy—the hard way arduous and long. But, as the clock ticks, the easy way becomes harder and the hard way becomes easier.

"And as the calendar records the years, it becomes increasingly evident that the easy way rests hazardously upon shifting sands, whereas the hard way builds solidly a foundation of confidence that cannot be swept away."

The sample profit-and-loss statement on page 156 was prepared by Kentucky Fried Chicken and shows the kind of expenses and the profits a man can expect from an average operation:

KENTUCKY FRIED CHICKEN—TAKE-HOME LOCATION
Statement of operations for month of September 1967
and for year ending September 30, 1967

	Sept. 1967	Percent	Oct. 1, 1966, to Sept. 30, 1967	Percent
Income				
Sales	$27,700.78	100.00	$301,209.52	100.00
Cash variation	80.01	.29	(1,217.63)	(.40)
Total net income	$27,780.79	100.29	$299,991.89	99.80
Cost of sales				
Beginning food inventory	1,180.74		657.30	
Food purchases	10,465.67		115,893.51	
Total	$11,646.41		$116,550.81	
Less ending food inventory	1,083.33		1,083.33	
Total cost of sales	$10,563.08	38.13	$115,467.48	38.33
Gross profit	$17,217.71	62.16	$184,524.41	61.27
Operating expenses				
Paper supplies	$ 1,530.70	5.53	$ 13,892.66	4.60
Freight	74.65	.27	1,083.93	.36
Linen service	239.71	.87	1,859.98	.62
Other supplies	438.38	1.58	3,681.91	1.22
Gross salaries—direct	4,047.61	14.62	44,394.22	14.73
Gross salaries—Gen. Mgr.	174.80	.63	4,169.81	1.38
Gross salaries—commissary	633.18	2.29	4,715.47	1.57
Repair and maintenance	397.55	1.43	5,088.67	1.69
Advertising promotion	936.50	3.37	11,527.84	3.82
Coupon advertising	322.20	1.16	894.24	.30
Service vehicle expenses	69.20	.25	799.55	.27
Bad checks	(15.49)	(.05)	117.74	.04
Audit and legal	56.37	.20	1,634.92	.54
Miscellaneous expenses	121.43	.44	1,009.47	.34
Rent facilities	309.75	1.12	3,733.93	1.24
Rent equipment	8.91	.03	15.14	.01
Utilities	462.58	1.67	4,659.57	1.54
Royalties	831.02	3.00	9,036.28	3.00
Training salaries	—	—	—	—
Insurance	93.47	.34	1,230.23	.41
Interest	—	—	—	—
Travel expense	72.85	.26	656.50	.22
Payroll taxes	223.89	.81	2,304.14	.77
Business tax and licenses	3.50	.01	200.00	.07
Depreciation	751.04	2.71	8,423.70	2.80
Total expenses	$11,783.80	42.54	$125,129.90	41.54
Net operating profit	$ 5,433.91	19.62	$ 59,394.51	19.73
Other income and expenses				
Gain (or loss) on sale of capital assets			(6.07)	(.01)
Vending-machine income			198.68	.06
Net profit	$ 5,433.91	19.62	$ 59,587.12	19.78

21

Burger King

When one company does so well that its name practically becomes synonymous with its line of business, it is natural to believe that any other company in the field will be a poor second. But in hamburgers, that is not so.

McDonald's is one of the top opportunities available in franchising today, and its name is on the lips of every child who watches television. Remember, though, that hamburgers are the best-loved food in America. There is plenty of room for competition. Both Burger King and Burger Chef are excellent franchises and should not be overlooked in a search for opportunities in this field.

We've already written about Burger Chef, so let's look at Burger King. Burger King, a Miami organization now owned by Pillsbury (the flour company), has over 300 restaurants and is therefore not overly worried about the appeal of rival organizations.

In the words of one of its top officials, the company's aim is "a record of 100 percent success, and we work to make all franchisees make money."

The appeal of Burger King is different from that of Mc-Donald's. Basically McDonald's is a carry-out store—there are rarely more than a few seats for customers. They usually take their purchases with them or eat in their car. Burger King, which also offers fast service, provides extended seating for customers in its self-serve restaurants. Thus it provides the appeal of speed and the comfort of a period away from the car.

McDonald's looks for profit in rapid turnover and concentrates in a seventeen-cent hamburger and a low-priced cheeseburger. Burger King features the Whopper, a king-sized broiled hamburger on a big toasted bun served with tomatoes, lettuce, pickles, onions, ketchup, and mayonnaise. It is advertised as a meal in itself, and it costs considerably more than a hamburger unadorned —forty-five cents.

To become a Burger King man, you must purchase a fully equipped restaurant, which will cost $69,750 plus any sales or use taxes on the equipment as required under state law. Burger King will finance half of that sum, or $34,875, and you will need about $40,000 in cash to cover the balance and working-capital needs. A $6,975 down payment is required upon approval of the application.

Burger King supplies all equipment, personal property, and signs needed for the operation of the restaurant, including such items as office supplies and equipment, tools, and maintenance and cleaning supplies. The company's own design and engineering personnel will draw up the architectural plans and supervise the construction of the distinctive Burger King building. The land and building are subleased to the franchise owner. At present annual rentals average $18,000 to $22,000.

If possible, Burger King will find a site in the city of the man's choice. The company's real-estate department chooses the location based on thorough surveys of the area. The company insists on a minimum population of 40,000 within a two-mile radius. Burger King considers heavy industrial, well-traveled commercial, and shopping-center areas to be desirable.

While Burger King franchises on a single-store basis, the man who proves himself able to manage more stores—which includes

Inside a Burger King

the ability to train managers—will be considered for additional units.

Burger King licensees are given complete training in a four-week course at the company's "Whopper College." Training fees are included in the franchise price. Room and board are available at a "very equitable group rate" through an arrangement with a local motel. After the formal training, he gets two weeks' training in his own store. Prior to entering the company school, the new owner will have been assigned to work in a Burger King store for two weeks.

When the store is about to open, Burger King will assist the owner in hiring and training the store staff. One or more Burger King people will be in the store during the first two weeks to make sure the man's new staff are functioning within the system.

Burger King hires and pays $200 toward the services of an accountant for the first two months of operation and expects the licensee to provide similar service thereafter.

Shortly after Burger King became part of Pillsbury, the company hired a top Madison Avenue agency to extend its advertising program on a national basis. The company believes that television is the most effective way to communicate with people and is now advertising via national television.

The owner of a Burger King store pays the company 4 percent of gross sales to cover the costs of advertising. He also pays about a 2.9 percent royalty to the company. The original franchise price includes a $1,000 allowance for the grand-opening advertising campaign.

About $5,000 of your $40,000 cash investment will be needed for inventory, utility deposits, change fund, insurance premiums, first month's rent, and local sales or use taxes on equipment. Your initial deposit of $6,975 is applied toward the purchase of equipment once your license is in effect.

Burger King says that you should net from 10 to 17 percent of gross sales. The company states that "generally, Burger King stores average between $200,000 and $350,000 a year in sales, with some exceptional units exceeding $400,000." The company also adds that a yearly net profit of 100 percent of original cash investment—normally $40,000—has been produced in a large percentage of cases.

What kind of man does Burger King draw into its business? The average Burger King man is between thirty-five and forty years of age. He is married and has children. He is a college graduate with above-average intelligence. He is personable and congenial, and knows how to direct his initiative properly.

In a game in which long hours are usually required, the Burger King schedule is inviting. The company says that the average single-store operator works eight to ten hours a day and has an assistant manager to handle the store when he is not there. It's twelve months a year, though. The operator may take a vacation provided "proper management" is available during his absence.

During the rush hours there will be ten to fifteen employees in the store. Regular full-time employees will number eight to ten.

Burger King licensees may sell their franchises, but Burger King, in line with industry practice, must approve the buyer.

If the licensed owner should die, his heirs are entitled to continue running the unit or to sell to someone approved by Burger King. The term of the license agreement is fifteen years. No renewal option is provided, but renewal is anticipated on the basis of continued satisfaction on both sides.

Burger King believes that its franchise is strong enough to withstand direct competition. "We have in many instances located Burger Kings directly adjacent to main competitors where market potential warranted with no threat to sales. Burger King deals in quality and fast service, which precludes threats of failures due to area competition."

Burger King is looking for healthy restaurant operators— men able to withstand the pressures, both mental and physical, of running a Burger King restaurant for the full term of the license agreement.

"There is no prejudice whatever toward minority groups. We simply require that a prospective licensee be intelligent and possess the personality traits necessary for a successful operation."

22

$$\boxed{\textit{Dairy Queen}}$$

Dick Johnson is a six-foot Illinoisian of Swedish extraction whose natural Midwestern reserve hasn't kept him from developing a prosperous Dairy Queen business over the past fifteen years.

He got into the retail business naturally enough. His parents ran a grocery business in Galesburg, not too many miles from Urbana, where Dick Johnson leases a Dairy Queen soft-ice-cream store from Gilbert Stein. Dick's success has been substantial. Although he doesn't own the Urbana store, he has since opened two stores in Champaign, Urbana's twin city. Dick owns the right to develop Dairy Queen throughout the city of Champaign. Eventually he hopes to buy the Urbana franchise from Stein.

Dick's success with Dairy Queen has come about somewhat differently from the norm. More usually, a man leases a store from a franchise owner and pays the owner rent in an amount tied to the volume of business he does. He pays more than he would if he were the franchise holder because the owner supplies equipment and the franchise right in addition to the store

162

itself. He might, for example, pay the store owner $32 a can for soft-ice-cream mix that costs the store owner $16 a can.

What usually happens is that once the man who leases the store saves up enough capital, he gives up his lease and opens a Dairy Queen of his own. Subleasing is a good way to start a business that promises substantial profits before you have enough money to buy a franchise outright.

Dick Johnson is in his forties. He is personable, unmarried, and well suited to a business that calls for considerable physical activity during the rush hours between 7 and 10 P.M. There is a certain amount of tension in this business—"stress and strain," as Dick calls it.

But Dick is accustomed to it. He see no reason why a man could not "spend his normal working span in a Dairy Queen store." He finds the executives and others in the Dairy Queen organization attractive and says that Dairy Queen draws "good quality people" into the business. He knows many other dealers from the annual conventions, which are usually held in some warm-weather spot during the winter months when a large number of Dairy Queens close down.

Like many franchise companies, Dairy Queen is an organization in a state of change. In times past the company was strictly a specialist in soft ice cream, and is still regarded as the leader in this field. Now, however, many stores have added a brazier, where hamburgers, cheeseburgers, and french fries are prepared. This addition has brought gradual change to the system under which dealers pay royalties to the organization. The franchise fee is a flat $5,000, a one-time charge. A store with a brazier now pays a license fee equal to 4 percent of gross annual sales. Soft-ice-cream stores pay an average of 30 cents a gallon for the ice-cream mix —a royalty rather than a percentage of gross sales.

Many Dairy Queen men prefer the relative simplicity of the soft-ice-cream business. The bill of fare lists no hamburgers or french fries, just variations on the ice-cream theme—such Dairy Queen specialties as banana splits, royal treats, and fiesta sundaes.

Soft-ice-cream dealers treasure their November 15 to March 15 annual vacations, and may take trailers south to sojourn away from the cold. They say the Florida landscape is fairly punctuated with vacationing soft-ice-cream store operators.

A soft-ice-cream store can be a Mom and Pop operation, especially if there is a teenager or other relative in the picture.

One Dairy Queen operator who fled a successful but demanding diner business comments: "I was supposed to be working twelve to fourteen hours a day in the diner. But when the night man didn't come, I had to work his shift and then my own again —thirty-six hours without a break at times. When my father-in-law died, there was just too much to do."

Dairy Queen suits this man to a T because it is a single-product operation requiring little outside help. "I'm no longer at the mercy of the griddle man and the chef. Dairy Queen is a business a family can operate if they aren't too fussy about a few extra hours."

Needless to say, this Dairy Queen operator has no intention of adding a brazier because it would bring back the problems he faced in the diner. He is perhaps somewhat less ambitious than many Dairy Queen operators.

Profits from a straight Dairy Queen operation normally run to $12,000 for the first year of operation, $15,000 for the second, and $18,000 for the third, the company says. In a store with a brazier they run closer to $15,000 in the first year, $22,500 in the second, and $35,000 in the fifth, but it's a year-round operation.

The Dairy Queen organization ordinarily buys or leases the lot and building, often approving a location chosen by a prospective dealer. The company then leases the store to the operator. Dairy Queen says that it strives to hold facility rentals at not more than 7 percent of sales.

The "Red Barn" Dairy Queen outlets are models of efficiency, especially when compared with old-fashioned facilities. The walls are smooth Formica-like material and are thus easy to keep clean. Dairy Queen freezers used to have hoppers through which the mix was poured. A new system pumps liquid mix from a refrigerated cooler directly into the freezing chamber. As one dealer puts it, "You just stick a hollow rod into the mix can and the machine does the rest."

Dairy Queen also makes record keeping easy for the dealer,

offering bookkeeping services for a "nominal fee" not to exceed
$15 a month.

Advertising support comes on three levels. The national program calls for an expenditure of $2 million in 1969 in network
television, with the average dealer's contribution between $100
and $200 for the year. A substantial portion of the $2 million
comes from revenues from supply purchases by Dairy Queen
dealers.

Dairy Queen says that all gross profits arising out of supplies
sales are used in marketing programs aimed at increasing store
sales and profits.

Dairy Queen has territory operators who spend $3 million on
regional advertising. The dealer pays at least half the cost of these
programs and up to 80 percent. In addition, the dealer must buy
local advertising, of which the territory operator pays 10 to 33⅓
percent of the cost.

As a Dairy Queen dealer, you needn't buy your supplies from
the company, but the company insists that supplies meet Dairy
Queen standards.

How much capital will you need to become a Dairy Queen
licensee? Count up your net worth—the value of your equity in
your house and your savings, securities, etc. It should total $25,000
or the company is unlikely to consider you a serious candidate
for any of the many retail-unit franchises it now has available in
all parts of the United States and Canada.

This wouldn't stop you if a relative wanted to stake you, nor
would it keep you from leasing a store from a franchise holder as
said before.

Dairy Queen states: "You can open a store for as little as one-
third cash down, with full financing of the balance arranged
directly through Dairy Queen's self-liquidating mortgage terms
(higher payments in high-volume sales months—low payments
for the balance of the year)."

As for cash, you'll need $10,000 to $15,000 to open a soft-ice-
cream store, and $15,000 to $25,000 to open a store with a brazier.
You will spend two weeks at one of Dairy Queen's training centers. In addition, Dairy Queen supervisors spend the first four to
seven days in your store helping you get used to the idea of

actually running the business. Periodic visits by field personnel follow. You'll have to pay for your own meals while training, but transportation, room, and training fee are all included as part of the $5,000 franchise fee. Refresher courses, which last one week, are available for $250 tuition.

Dairy Queen is looking for self-starters with above-average ambition—men with a strong desire to own their own businesses.

Your store may be in a small town, or it may be in a major shopping center. The company wants a minimum population of 6,000 in the vicinity, demands a lot having a minimum of 17,000 square feet, and wants a good percentage of middle-class people, with single-family dwellings predominating. The location should be in a place where people drive during their leisure. Territories are exclusive.

Some good Dairy Queen operators get by with spending a minimum of thirty-five hours a week on the job. But if an operator cannot find good people to assist him, he might spend up to seventy hours a week at the store—seven days a week. Some get by with working five or six days—they're the good managers, the ones who also work the shortest hours.

While the dealer in soft ice cream may treasure his three or four months off—assuming he's in a northern zone where the weather is too cold to beckon customers in the winter—the man with a brazier in the store will be open eleven or twelve months, especially in the warm climates. In a year-round operation, the store owner's vacation may be limited to two weeks.

Dairy Queen quite naturally prefers stores with braziers, for gross revenues and profits to the dealer are greater for the investment and labor expended.

While the "soft serve" store can be operated by five to eight people, thus making it basically a Mom and Pop operation for some storekeepers, a brazier requires between eight and twenty employees. Dairy Queen does not consider Mom and Pop adequate to operate a brazier store.

The Dairy Queen owner is permitted to sell his franchise—with the company's approval—and the heirs of the owner may sell the interest in the store under the same circumstances.

Dairy Queen franchises run for twenty years, and the franchise is automatically renewable for five-year periods unless either party indicates in writing before the end of the period that he has no intention of continuing the arrangement.

Anyone who qualifies will be eligible for a franchise without regard to age, marital status, or race. Retirees are welcome.

Dairy Queen is a major national franchise with 3,780 units, including 565 with the brazier food line. In addition, there are 400 units in Canada, Mexico, Australia, Guam, Panama, the Philippines, the West Indies, Iceland, and Spain.

Dairy Queen sums up its marketing strategy: "We want consumers to think of Dairy Queen as the place where they can get quality products at a value while having a pleasant experience."

Or as John Greenley, who operates a soft-serve Dairy Queen in northern New Jersey, puts it: "We try for a mixed crowd. I don't want to discourage the teenagers—just those who are unruly. If they're unruly, I make it quite obvious that I won't tolerate it. When they find horsing around is not permitted they soon find a place where they are more welcome. We have a great deal of family trade. They are the backbone of the Dairy Queen business."

DAIRY QUEEN
Profit-and-Loss Statements
(Representing high average)

Sales	Soft Serve *	%	Soft Serve with brazier †	%
Soft serve	$49,140	85%	$ 53,570	30%
Brazier food	—	—	107,140	60%
Soft drinks	3,469	6%	8,930	5%
Mr. Misty	5,203	9%	8,930	5%
Total	$57,812	100%	$178,570	100%
Cost of goods sold	21,969	38%	78,570	44%
Gross profit	$35,843	62%	$100,000	56%
Operating expenses				
Labor	7,515	13%	30,350	17%
Rent	4,047	7%	12,500	7%
Utilities	1,734	3%	7,140	4%
Advertising	1,734	3%	5,360	3%
Cleaning and sanitation	138	↑	400	↑
Conventions/meetings	350		600	
Donations	30		50	
Insurance	350		700	
Laundry	150	4%	250	5%
Legal/accounting	300		500	
Repairs/maintenance	300		500	
Telephone/telegraph	250		350	
Taxes/licenses	400		1,960	
Miscellaneous	45	↓	60	↓
Total operating expense	17,343	30%	60,720	36%
Net operating profit	$18,500	32%	$39,200	22%
(Prior to depreciation and federal income tax)				

* Sells soft serve, soft drinks, Mr. Misty, limited food menu
† Sells soft serve, soft drinks, Mr. Misty, brazier food line

23

Shakey's

In an age of increasing leisure, people are looking for places to have fun. For toe-tapping pleasure and genuine relaxation, there is nothing like a visit to a music parlor where you can listen to old tunes while someone else does the cooking. Music parlors, however, are not too common these days. It's a long time since every gathering place had its upright and a man in shirtsleeves and suspenders tickling the keyboard.

Yes, even though there's a decided demand for it, this sort of place is hard to find in an age of electronic music. Lots of people remember the rinky-dink piano with affection and would like to know where to find it.

Shakey's Pizza is bringing it all back. A piano and banjo player are a regular part of the scene in every Shakey's pizza parlor. The company says: "It is a well-proven fact that we offer a fun-filled environment for the entire family as well as offering a high-quality pizza product. The musicians are a necessary adjunct to Shakey's fun atmosphere."

Straw boaters and string ties help to create a sense of informality and fun that builds traffic for the Shakey's dealer.

Shakey's also touts the "exotic flavor" of their aged Italian cheese, herbs, oils, and spices and Shakey's "secret sauce" that brings cars from miles away.

Shakey's is looking for reliable people with respectable credit ratings. The company says that their successful dealers come from all kinds of backgrounds, age groups, and educational levels. They are looking for people with a great deal of common sense, willingness to accept advice, and the abiilty to meet and deal with people.

Shakey's Pizza Parlors generally earn $20,000 to $50,000 a year for their owners, and some even more.

If you decide to open a Shakey's and you rent your building, approximately $35,000 will pay for everything and also provide you with $5,000 in working capital. By financing the equipment you will be able to reduce the cash outlay, probably to $15,000. The cash requirement for the lease—which will vary from case to case—is not included in these figures.

Shakey's gets an initial franchise fee of $10,500 and a royalty of 5 percent on gross monthly food sales. There is no fee on beverage sales. Pizza represents about 70 percent of total sales in most parlors.

For those dealers who lease their land and building, Shakey's says that landlords generally require the tenant's personal net worth to equal the cost of the land and building. The cost of building a Shakey's—they are all similar in appearance but differ in size and layout to meet local needs—ranges from $50,000 to $80,000. This can be reduced if an appropriate building is available for remodeling along Shakey's lines. Shakey's does not guarantee leases because this would add to the charges the company makes. Occupancy costs should not exceed 8 percent of anticipated gross revenue.

If the dealer plans to put up his building himself, he must get his plans from Shakey's. Fees for the plans range from $250 to $350 for eight sets. The dealer employs an architect to prepare a plot plan showing the building location, driveways, parking layout, sign location, and modifications to the plans necessary to meet local building codes.

Shakey's own staff will conduct a market survey and site analysis

A grand opening of a Shakey's Pizza Parlor

to determine the best possible location. A fee of up to $300 is charged for this service. The parlor will probably be in a middle-class community of 75,000 to 150,000 people. Shakey's tend to be most successful in such communities.

Some Shakey's hopefuls who have not been able to present sufficient net worth to cover the costs have been accepted nevertheless. A potential dealer is put in contact with investors seeking working partners for their Shakey's parlors or the dealer is referred to land developers who will build a Shakey's on the strength of the franchise and their faith in the future owner.

As a Shakey's dealer, you and key employees will receive three weeks' training. There is no charge for the training, but you will have to pay your travel costs to St. Louis and your room and board. The management training school emphasizes operating and management methods and pays particular attention to food quality control. The regional offices are staffed by trained specialists who keep in contact with the owner after he opens his store to assist him in maintaining the highest standards of food quality and service.

Shakey's believes that one of the most important services the company offers the dealer is "continuous supervision and assistance after your business is established. In addition to field staff, the home office in Burlingame, California, is staffed with specialists in accounting, advertising, promotion, real estate, systems, and procedures."

Shakey's Pizza is nationally advertised on radio and television and in magazines. The dealers pay 1 percent of their gross food sales into a national advertising fund, and Shakey's adds to this fund from its own revenues. In addition, the dealer is expected to spend a minimum of 3 percent of his gross food sales to advertise in his own area.

Running a Shakey's is a full-time proposition, particularly in the beginning. Initially, the owner will have to devote seven days a week to the operation. The amount of time he spends on the job once he is rolling depends on his ability to develop management talent. The parlors are open year-round.

The smaller parlors can be run almost as family enterprises with a minimum of part-time help.

Should the dealer decide to sell his franchise, he is free to do so, but Shakey's must accept the buyer. Shakey's has no death clause in its contract, but says that it is very cooperative in settling such matters. The term of the license is twenty years, and Shakey's expects to renegotiate renewals at the end of that term.

Shakey's has many sites available. If you're interested in a Shakey's the company suggests you visit one of the more than 300 dealers coast to coast for a reading on the company.

SHAKEY'S PIZZA

Profit Potential

| | FIRST FISCAL YEAR | | MONTH OF FEBRUARY | | | | | |
| | Pacific Coast | | Southwest | | Midwest | | Central Plains | |
	Amount	%	Amount	%	Amount	%	Amount	%
Food and beverage sales	$274,622	100.0	$17,651	100.0	$24,111	100.0	$30,962	100.0
Cost of food and beverage	90,866	33.1	5,426	30.7	7,929	32.9	10,277	33.2
Gross margin	183,756	66.9	12,225	69.3	16,182	67.1	20,685	66.8
Operating expenses:								
Salaries (including musicians and janitorial)	62,253	22.7	3,744	21.2	5,952	24.7	7,090	22.9
Advertising	14,840	5.4	835	4.7	1,026	4.3	1,390	4.5
Rent	11,458	4.2	1,075	6.1	1,063	4.4	916	2.9
Franchise payments	11,915	4.3	659	3.7	807	3.3	1,048	3.4
Taxes (including payroll taxes and licenses)	4,928	1.8	648	3.7	397	1.6	640	2.1
Other expenses	22,894	8.3	1,957	11.1	1,845	7.7	2,880	9.3
Total costs and expenses	128,288	46.7	8,918	50.5	11,090	46.0	13,964	45.1
Net income from operations	$55,468	20.2	$3,307	18.8	$5,092	21.1	$6,721	21.7

24

Mr. Steak

Mr. Steak is a nationwide group of restaurants offering six varieties of steak (mostly sirloin) priced at $1.39 to $3.79. The restaurants also serve a steak-and-lobster combination plate for $3.99, shrimp or chicken platters, and sandwiches. Every dinner includes a tossed green salad, "ranch house" toast, and a choice of potato or cottage cheese.

Mr. Steak uses place mats to lure prospective owners. As he is eating in a Mr. Steak restaurant, the customer sees a reprint of an ad about Mr. Steak. There is a Denver post-office box number in the ad for those who might want more information.

A score of the company's customers write each day. This brings a response from an area representative. He doesn't try to sell him on the idea. Quite the contrary. He works very hard to discourage the prospect, telling him about the blood, sweat, and tears that go into making a restaurant a success.

If the prospect is not discouraged by this prophet of doom, he is asked to fill out a number of forms and to take a physical examination. The results are sent to company headquarters in Denver, and a two-week investigation of the prospect's character and credit is undertaken. If the executives there think the man is a good prospect they ask him to come to Denver and bring his wife if possible. (They want to be sure she understands what he is getting into.) The company does not furnish the fare. The prospect is expected to pay that himself. (This is a common device used by franchise companies to weed out those who are merely curious.)

The company tells their man that if he aspires to run several Mr. Steak restaurants he should forget it. Mr. Steak is not a several-unit proposition. Each unit has its own investor-manager. It is necessary to work twelve to fourteen hours a day six days a week to make a go of it.

The company examines the potential franchisee for character, morality, intelligence, physical condition, and experience. It does not seek men with experience in running restaurants, but prefers to train them in that area themselves.

However, business experience of other sorts is highly respected. Jim Mather, a World War II pilot, and commercial artist, and the founder of Mr. Steak, says: "Year in and year out, we find our best investor-managers are people who have been in business— usually a small business—for themselves. Our best men generally have come from three former occupations: service-station owner or manager, grocery-store owner or manager, or farmer."

If the man survives the Denver experience, he's a true candidate for a new store. Usually, the money for the new business—$40,000 or more, of which the owner-manager must put up at least $5,200 —comes from financial backers.

The investor-manager will get perhaps 15 percent of the stock in the enterprise—it depends on the size of his cash investment— but Mr. Steak has an option on the stock in case it feels that things are not working out.

Meanwhile the site-location people will be busy. When a site is located and leased, a store is put up according to specific plans. All Mr. Steak restaurants are similar.

Each restaurant costs at least $75,000 and will accommodate 128 diners. The stores are prudently designed so that they may easily be converted to retail outlets or professional space in case things don't work out. (It hasn't happened yet.)

The company arranges for the construction, after which it sends a truck from Denver loaded with some 25,000 items to furnish the store—glasses, dishes, silver, pots and pans, napkins, sink, mechanical dishwasher—you name it. It's a turnkey operation when the job is completed: the owner fires the boiler and he is in business.

Meanwhile the new owner is being trained in Denver. After classroom instruction from 8 to 11 A.M. the students are shunted to one of Denver's several Mr. Steak restaurants to handle the rush-hour crowds. There is more classroom time afterward, then back to the restaurant for the evening meal. After clean-up it is about 11 P.M. This continues six days each week for at least four weeks. The men are trained in every job in the restaurant. They wash dishes, act as busboys, waiters, cooks, and managers.

Is the man now ready to begin business on his own? Not really. When he opens his store he will be assisted by a team from the home office that will help him hire, arrange for the purchase of supplies locally, and so forth. The training team stays for three weeks, then they give a dinner for local celebrities. The man is now in business for himself.

Each week the dealer pays Mr. Steak a royalty of from 4.5 to 7 percent of his gross volume. The higher the volume, the higher the percentage. Accounting services—including a weekly profit-and-loss statement, balance sheet, and a bound printout of the general ledger—are included in this fee.

Mr. Steak's advertising program is national in scope, but the company concentrates on local media. The advertising copy and layout are prepared in Denver, and the owner-managers must use this material. Newspaper mats are furnished free. There is a small charge for television films, radio tapes, billboard paper and other promotional items. An advertising calendar is prepared on a quarterly basis for each of the franchisees that indicates the advertising that is running nationally and tells how to follow up on the local level.

Mr. Steak requests that the owner set aside "3 percent of his gross for advertising and under the contract. Of that, we escrow ½ of 1 percent for national advertising."

Mr. Steak negotiates national contracts for almost all food and nonfood products and offers them to the owner-managers at a price equal to or lower than those of local suppliers. The company takes a small markup on these items, but the idea behind it is to assure the organization of a competitive edge in the local market. The profit involved is minor, as Mr. Steak depends for its profits on franchise sales and service fees.

Mr. Steak does not try to project profits because they vary with local circumstances. The company makes "no promises to anyone. However, for the most part, our operations are profitable from the fifth week of operation and we expect a return of over 25 percent per year."

Here's a profile Mr. Steak gives of the ideal investor-manager.

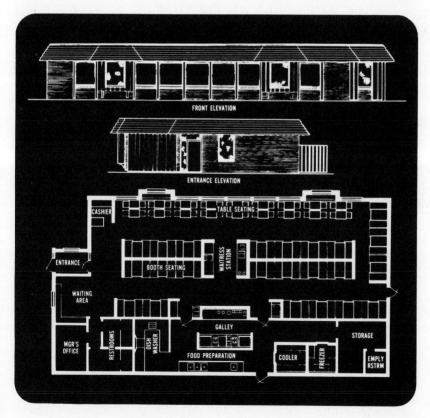

Interior and exterior plan design for a Mr. Steak building

"He would be between the ages of thirty-five and forty-five, married, with children, and with a minimum of a high school education, preferably a college degree. Experience and maturity we feel can make up for lack of academic education, depending upon his reaction to his experience. He should be a self-starter, and some of the ingredients we would like to see in him are character, truthfulness, hopefully a strong faith in his God and himself, persistence, dependability, stability, integrity, and moderation.

"Physically, he should be slim, trim, well groomed, and able to maintain the strain of a twelve-working-hour day, which we ask to be backed up on our own form by a physical examination by his physician."

Mr. Steak shops are set up in communities of 50,000 to 100,000 people, and there will be only one Mr. Steak in any franchised area.

Wherever the man settles, Mr. Steak does nothing to encourage him to think he will have it easy.

"He is told that this is a twelve-to-fourteen-hour-a-day job on his feet, and for the most part, moving. For the first six months he will probably not receive a day off. When he feels he has the restaurant under control he figures his lowest volume day for the week and that is the day he chooses for his day off.

"He is told that in our opinion the restaurant will never make the money when he is gone as when he is present.

"This is a twelve-month-a-year business and he is instructed that he might as well forget the idea of a two-week vacation per year. We feel that this is being honest with him, in that no matter how well a trained and local a crew he may have, the business still does not make the profit when he is gone as it does when he is there. He should arrange for frequent shorter vacations. He is not allowed to hire a manager and be only a supervisor."

The average Mr. Steak restaurant would have about twenty-five employees—it is by no means a business to be managed as a family enterprise. There are, however, several husband and wife teams. In such cases, Mr. Steak insists that the husband be the dominant member of the team.

Nonoperating members of the Mr. Steak dealers-investment group are free to sell their stock at any time. The investor-man-

ager may not sell his stock unless he owns more than the 15 percent minimum required. (Incidentally, by buying the stock of his
fellow shareholders, he can increase his stake in the business as
time goes on).

The Mr. Steak franchise is a lifetime property right. The man
can sell, but both the buyer and his wife must go to Denver for
acceptance. Mr. Steak has no intention of making a profit on the
resale of a Mr. Steak restaurant. "We feel it belongs to him as long
as he is operating within the realm of the agreement and according to our system."

Mr. Steak has territories available, mostly in heavily populated
areas.

MR. STEAK

Profit-and-Loss Statement for One Restaurant

Fiscal Year Income	One Week's Operations		16 Weeks' Operations	
Food services	$6,701.87–	102.2	$112,152.47–	102.1
Cash over and short	.86	.0	18.13	.0
Sales Tax Vendor Fees	.00	.0	60.80	.1
Sales tax debit	196.67	3.0	3,293.39	3.0
Counter sales	29.07	.4	216.26	.2
Misc. income	21.23	.3	738.15	.7
TOTAL GROSS INCOME	6,556.36	99.9	109,856.16	100.1
Food costs				
Food purchases	2,993.57	45.7	46,192.54	42.0
Inventory	.00	.0	47.14	.0
Employee meals	80.25	1.2	1,318.50	1.2
NET PURCHASES	2,913.32	44.5	44,921.18	40.8
GROSS PROFIT	3,643.04	55.4	64,934.98	59.3
Labor costs				
Payroll	1,114.07	17.0	18,316.50	16.7
Employee meals	80.25	1.2	1,318.50	1.2
Payroll taxes	52.37	.8	906.33	.8
TOTAL LABOR	1,246.69	19.0	20,541.33	18.7
GROSS PROFIT	2,396.35	36.4	44,393.65	40.6
Other direct				
Laundry and uniforms	17.63	.3	901.97	.8
Paper goods	.00	.0	755.48	.7
Service fees	458.95	7.0	7,689.93	7.0
Freight	.00	.0	25.87	.0
Restaurant supply and service	.00	.0	83.96	.1
China-glass-silver	.00	.0	487.71	.4

Fiscal Year Income	One Week's Operations		16 Weeks' Operations	
Janitorial supply	8.42	.1	502.82	.5
Kitchen supply service	12.94	.2	239.79	.2
TOTAL OTHER DIRECT	497.94	2.6	10,687.52	9.7
GROSS PROFIT	1,898.41	28.8	33,706.12	30.9
Operating expenses				
Advertising	165.00	2.5	1,415.36	1.3
Automobile	23.54	.4	547.28	.5
Contributions	.00	.0	15.00	.0
Dues and subscriptions	.00	.0	50.00	.0
Insurance—general	48.06	.7	786.43	.7
Manager's salary	175.00	2.7	2,850.00	2.6
Manager incentive bonus	.00	.0	1,887.00	1.7
Misc. supplies	.00	.0	2.32	.0
Office supplies	2.90	.0	57.20	.1
Outside services, labor	.00	.0	52.66	.0
Taxes and licenses	30.27	.5	738.57	.7
Telephone	6.00	.1	93.71	.1
Trash removal	8.07	.1	164.95	.2
TOTAL OPERATING	458.84	7.0	8,661.14	7.9
GROSS PROFIT	1,439.57	21.8	25,044.98	23.0
Maintenance and equipment				
Equipment rental	168.47	2.6	2,711.49	2.5
Maintenance and repair	.00	.0	287.12	.3
TOTAL MAINTENANCE AND EQUIPMENT	168.47	2.6	2,998.61	2.8
GROSS PROFIT	1,271.10	19.2	22,046.37	20.2
Occupancy expense				
Rent	346.15	5.3	5,637.30	5.1
Utilities	105.00	1.6	1,503.25	1.4
TOTAL OCCUPANCY	451.15	6.9	7,140.55	6.5
NET PROFIT	819.95	12.3	14,905.82	13.7

25

Arby Restaurants

At a time when franchise companies are springing up like crocuses in the spring, it is interesting to look at one with origins stretching back half a century.

The Arby's Roast Beef restaurant franchise is run by two brothers, the third generation of a family that has operated in the restaurant field since 1919. Leroy and Forrest Raffel (Raffel Brothers equals R. B.'s equals Arby's) were raised in their father's hotel in New Castle, Pennsylvania, the base of a sixteen-hotel-and-restaurant chain in Pennsylvania and Ohio. Forrest and Leroy never deviated from the course set by the family decades earlier.

Forrest went to Cornell University's School of Hotel and Restaurant Administration and then held management positions in hotels and restaurants in several states. Leroy went to one of the nation's top preparatory schools for executives, the Wharton School of Finance and Commerce of the University of Pennsylvania.

In 1949 the two brothers purchased a restaurant-equipment firm, which they renamed Raffel Brothers, and the company became one of the nation's leading contract and food-service consulting firms. They have designed and installed hundreds of food-service operations in schools, hospitals, public institutions, hotels, and restaurants. They designed and equipped six restaurants that line the Ohio Turnpike and set up the mammoth flight kitchen serving all airlines flying into the Greater Pittsburgh Airport. Their experience includes a wide variety of other food facilities and, as a result, they have become one of the nation's truly expert designers of specialized food units.

If you were to become an Arby's Roast Beef restaurant owner, you would be working with experts whose talents for restaurant design and maintenance are probably second to none. In their brochure the company confidently cites figures compiled by the top authority in the field to show Arby's superiority to other eating establishments. The figures are from Horwath & Horwath, certified public accountants—and the only major accounting concern specializing in restaurant and hotel accounting.

Arby's notes that 75 percent of the 500,000 or more restaurants in the nation gross less than $50,000 a year and adds that it is its policy to issue franchises for locations that have been "exhaustively researched to insure minimum gross sales of $200,000 a year."

Net profits on a restaurant grossing $200,000 would be $21,880 a year. On a location grossing $250,000, the owner could expect to make $36,400; on a $300,000 operation he would net $45,605, and on a $350,000 gross, he would make $58,360—all based on a fifty-two week operation. Arby's says that the harder a man works and the more time he puts in, the more successful he will be.

Arby's says that it has done so well for its franchise owners that the word spreads that they have a good thing going. As a result, Arby's finds it is not necessary to advertise for new owners —they simply come to Arby's and seek the franchise themselves.

As is usual for a restaurant operation, the price of admission is high. The total investment is $65,000, of which $35,000 must be cash. Arby's will finance the rest.

Once the show is on the road, the franchise company will get a royalty and service fee equal to 3 percent of gross sales. Arby's furnishes advertising materials, for which the dealer pays a prorated charge. He also pays for his advertising in local media.

The basic advertising approach is a simple one. The company offers a quality roast-beef sandwich, "a meal in itself," served in a pleasing atmosphere.

Arby's will put you in a location either in a major shopping area or on a busy intersection. The company selects the site and signs a lease with the owner, then subleases the land and building to the dealer. He is given an exclusive Arby's territory within a two-mile radius.

Arby's conducts a seventeen-day training school at no cost to the new owner other than for his room and board. The new assistant manager and staff are also entitled to attend the school. The company teaches food preparation, how to advertise and merchandise the product, and controls and techniques for maintaining top quality. Arby's notes that lack of business experience is the "hidden rock that wrecks most small businesses. Our operating manuals, training, and on-going counsel are a revelation in simplicity and completeness. We have converted principles of business success experiences to simple language and practices and easily understood tools.

"We provide rigorous and revealing insight in how to build with people—how to select, how to recruit, how to induct, how to train, how to supervise—in short, teaching you the skills of building and keeping [the quality of] people in your business as high and excellent as your food quality."

Arby's believes the new owner should be deeply involved in the initial steps of getting underway. "It is our policy that the new member of the Arby's family will play an important role in the new construction and equipment scheduling and follow-up from the day ground is broken to the happy occasion of opening-day ceremonies."

Arby's says that it is difficult to define the type of man the company takes other than that most are college educated. Arby's does not take women franchisees or retirees.

An Arby's restaurant cannot be run as a family proposition. The owner will need ten to twenty employees.

Should the time come that the Arby's restaurant owner wants to sell his franchise he is permitted to do so, but Arby's must agree to his choice of a buyer.

ARBY'S ROAST BEEF RESTAURANT
Statement of estimated operation
based on estimated sales as indicated *

	Annual sales of $200,000.00		Annual sales of $350,000.00	
	Amount	Percent	Amount	Percent
SALES				
Food	$162,000.00	81.00%	$283,500.00	81.00%
Beverages	38,000.00	19.00	66,500.00	19.00
Total sales	$200,000.00	100.00%	$350,000.00	100.00%
COST OF SALES				
Food	$ 74,520.00	46.00%	$130,410.00	46.00%
Beverages	10,260.00	27.00	17,955.00	27.00
Combined costs	$ 84,780.00	42.39%	$148,365.00	42.39%
Gross profit on sales	$115,220.00	57.61%	$201,635.00	57.61%
OPERATING EXPENSES				
Paper supplies	$ 7,000.00	3.50%	$ 12,250.00	3.50%
Salaries and wages	32,000.00	16.00	44,000.00	12.43
Employees' meals	1,800.00	.90	3,500.00	1.00
Payroll taxes	4,150.00	2.08	5,350.00	1.53
Other taxes	1,000.00	.50	1,400.00	.40
Insurance	900.00	.45	1,050.00	.30
Utilities and telephone	4,040.00	2.02	5,670.00	1.62
Supplies	2,400.00	1.20	4.795.00	1.37
Office expenses	300.00	.15	490.00	.14
Advertising and promotion	8,000.00	4.00	14,000.00	4.00
Repairs and maintenance	1,500.00	.75	2,000.00	.57
Laundry and uniforms	1,840.00	.92	3,220.00	.92
Rubbish removal	720.00	.36	1,260.00	.36
Rent	13,500.00	6.75	24,500.00	7.00
Professional fees	600.00	.30	910.00	.26
Royalty fees	6,000.00	3.00	10,500.00	3.00
Sign rental	1,800.00	.90	1,800.00	.51
Miscellaneous	500.00	.25	1,125.00	.32
Totals	$ 88,050.00	44.03%	$137,820.00	39.37%
Cash operating profit	$ 27,170.00	13.59%	$ 63,815.00	18.24%
Interest expense	$ 1,690.00	.85%	$ 1,755.00	.50%
Depreciation	3,600.00	1.80	3,700.00	1.06
Total other expenses	$ 5,290.00	2.65%	$ 5,455.00	1.56%
Net Profit—before income taxes	$ 21,880.00	10.94%	$ 58,360.00	16.53%

* All anticipated costs and expenses have been considered as realistically as possible. Some figures may vary depending on local conditions, individual management, and unpredictable circumstances.

26

One Hour Martinizing

A major reason for franchising's appeal is that it offers opportunities for men with limited educational backgrounds. It enables them to become their own bosses, to enter the professional management class and reach top income levels.

It is perhaps surprising, then, that One Hour Martinizing dry cleaning appeals not only to men of limited educational background, but also to men with college educations. One young college man spent just six months working for someone else after he graduated. Working that short time as a salesman, he came in contact with numerous small business owners and was soon convinced that a small business could bring an ambitious man high financial rewards—college degree or no college degree.

He investigated a number of business opportunities, decided he would like to have a franchising company behind him, and finally chose One Hour Martinizing as the best opportunity. He concluded that Martinizing offered the greatest potential for growth with the smallest initial investment of the available choices. He liked the stability of an established company—

Martinizing began business in 1949—and he was sold on the idea of offering dry cleaning on a cash-and-carry basis. Martinizing features one-hour cleaning at no extra charge.

Within ten years, this franchisee had followed the path of other Martinizing franchisees in establishing a multiple-store operation. His personal income was averaging $9,300 a month, a far cry from the $15,000 net a franchisee makes in the average Martinizing store (in addition to the $5,000 minimum salary most franchisees take). In 1966, this extraordinary young man did a volume of $560,000 in four stores and earned profits of $112,000. Martinizing promises much less than that, of course. The company says that new Martinizing dry-cleaning plants should break even within the first six months.

"However, 99 out of 100 will definitely be in the black by the end of the first year. The second year will show a growth of 25 to 50 percent over the first year, and by the fifth year the gross profit will start to flatten out. Since the business operates on a budget, the net profit will run fairly constant. A figure of 20 to 25 percent is (normally) experienced."

A profile of Martinizing franchisees would reveal a married man thirty-five to forty-four years of age who has had previous managerial or owner experience in running a small business. The company looks for self-starters with more than average ability to look after details. Successful Martinizing men are generally worth $50,000 to $60,000, and are usually found in locations east of the Mississippi.

To become a dealer, an individual must have a net worth equal to the cost of a Martinizing plant—if it is to be financed by Martin. (Martin, incidentally, is in the business of selling the dry-cleaning equipment, and that's where its profits come from.) In other words, a $30,000 plant would require a $30,000 net worth. In addition, 40 percent of the purchase price is required in cash, so for a $30,000 standard Martinizing package the franchisee would have to put up $12,000. Financing is arranged through Martin or through local banks.

Beyond that, Martin charges $1,000 for the first three years for a franchise—$333 a year. After the third year the franchise-renewal cost is $400 a year. This fee is not a royalty, but is used

toward the national advertising program. Bookkeeping services are set up without further charge at the local level by the store's sales representative.

Martin adds to the funds produced by the renewal fees to pay for its extensive advertising program—one of the slickest in the industry, which includes full-color ads in *Holiday, Life, Esquire,* and *Glamour* magazines. This national program is supplemented by local and regional programs—leaflets, posters, and so forth. Local radio is used extensively.

Martin does not sell supplies to its franchisees; they are generally obtained locally.

A prospective franchisee spends two to three weeks in a training plant, followed by additional assistance in his own store. There is no charge for training, and it is conducted in the area, so there is no expenditure for room and board.

A local sales representative of the company will choose the franchisee's location following a thorough investigation. Martin states that territories cannot be made exclusive because of federal law. However, Martin says that the company's advertising program has thus far been successful against all competition.

Franchises are available to anyone who qualifies financially and who has, in the company's words, "the ability and proper character." Locations for new stores are available throughout the country.

One of the attractions of a Martinizing franchise is that the owner does not have to be on hand every minute. The business can be handled by managers. In the beginning the store owner will generally work six days a week. After several years, however, he will have others on the scene and will have considerable leisure—or he can become a "management" man running multiple holdings.

On the average he will begin with three employees, and rarely will even a large store have as many as fifteen employees. Some stores in small towns are operated on a Mom and Pop basis, but Martinizing is a year-round business, so Mom and Pop might have to schedule separate or at least short vacations.

Martin discourages the purchase of locations. Franchisees ordinarily lease their stores. Martin has plans for prefab buildings that can be built by the franchisee or by a landowner who wants to work with Martin.

The franchisee can sell his business at any time, but the new owner must be approved by Martin, along with financing arrangements if required.

27

Culligan Soft-Water Service

This is a pollution-conscious age, a time when the nation has become deeply concerned about the condition of our physical environment. But let Culligan dramatize the story:

"Without water, life would be insupportable. Without water, we would cease to exist. Water is the master component of the body, and the function of every living cell is dependent on it. Water showers its countless blessings on man and beast alike. It insures our food supply and tempers our climate [but] in its natural state, water is often unsuitable to human purposes. On its long journey from the heavens to everyday use, water picks up minerals that harden it, acids that make it corrosive, objectionable tastes and odors that make it unpalatable."

And that's where Culligan and its hundreds of dealers come in, offering water-conditioning services all over the nation. Culligan is one of the nation's oldest franchise companies. In 1937 the company set up a dealership in Wheaton, Illinois, and it still exists under the original management, a tribute to Culligan's ability to maintain long-term arrangements on satisfactory terms. Culligan had only one product at the time, a 9-inch diameter, 42-inch-high service unit that was installed in a customer's home and exchanged for a freshly regenerated unit once a month.

Culligan provides a franchise that offers a good living for a family business, or a five-figure income for a man who wishes to enter the business in a big way. Traditionally, Culligan has appealed to men with an appreciation for mechanical devices. In the old days, many a Culligan man was a former iceman looking for a way to continue to service his route. Having discovered that mechanical ability is not enough, Culligan wants men with a high school education or better. The most successful dealers— those who aggressively seek the big rewards—have more than a passing knowledge of business management. A dealer must have considerable sales ability as well. He must be a self-starter, a pusher, and must make himself well known in the community. He must be a joiner of sorts with membership in church, PTA, Chamber of Commerce, and other community affairs. He must become known as The Culligan Man.

Most of the successful dealers range in age from twenty-five to fifty and are married with children.

Culligan has found that it is easy to find men who can handle a small dealership—minimum capital requirements are $15,000— but not so easy to find men who can grow with the enterprise.

Culligan would like to see its dealers reach the highest rewards in the business, but finds that many of them like to settle into a relatively small enterprise. In a small community a man and his wife might earn $20,000 a year, including salary and profits. But there is much more for the man who can handle a larger business. The average dealer makes considerably more than that; by serving 1,000 to 1,200 customers who rent the Culligan equipment and others buying, say, $5,000 worth of equipment a month, he would make about $13,000 net income plus the salary he would pay himself—in this case about $15,000 a year.

It is not uncommon, however, for a dealer to serve 2,000 rental accounts at a profit of $1 a month per account. Gross sales would add another $10,000 a month. In this setup the owner would earn $24,000 after taxes plus his salary of $15,000 to $20,000. So you can see that Culligan offers a variety of opportunities for men of differing ambitions and energies.

Culligan has a variety of franchise agreements, differing primarily according to whether the services are directed to private or industrial consumers. The two are kept separate because of differing market requirements.

Culligan has no fee, royalty, or other charge on its consumer franchises, but levies a 5 percent royalty on gross sales for water-service franchises serving industry.

Dealers must agree to participate in a national advertising program, and their total contribution pays for half the cost of the program. The dealer advisory council determines the amount of participation, which is limited to 1 percent of the dealer's gross income. In 1968 the charge was 0.4 percent.

Culligan is famous for its award-winning television commercials, written around the theme "Hey Culligan Man!" The company also offers a wide variety of full-page ads in leading national magazines and conducts considerable local advertising and sales promotion activities. The company asks the rhetorical question, "Can you find any dealer organization that has a greater, more comprehensive availability of promotion material?"

Culligan's profits arise primarily from the sale of new products, although it does sell replacement parts at a profit. The company will finance the new equipment that the dealer will be renting to customers, but the dealer must arrange financing with local banks for customers who wish to buy the equipment. When a

Video picture of the now highly recognizable Culligan Man TV commercial

dealer sells his business to a new man, he usually arranges the financing for his successor.

New dealers are usually trained at company expense. The dealer gets four weeks of direct training: one week in North-brook, Illinois, the company headquarters; one week with an established dealer; one week of sales training in the field; and one week of technical-service seminars, which are held in various places throughout the United States. The dealer pays his own room, board, and travel expenses.

The dealer looks for an area that he likes and seeks a franchise there if available. The population may be as few as 10,000 people, but some franchise areas are as large as 1 million. The company's favored range is 50,000 to 100,000. While Culligan cannot give exclusive franchises because of a Federal Trade Commission ruling, the effect of this F.T.C. consent decree is such that dealers retain virtually exclusive rights in their respective territories.

The dealer is expected to provide his own building facilities, either through leasing or by direct ownership. The company supplies floor plans indicating what kind of facilities the dealer will need to accommodate his business.

Culligan dealers are in a year-round business, since service cannot be neglected for extended periods. Most dealers work a five-day week, but sales work is necessary in the evenings and can be very productive on Saturdays.

It takes one service man for each 500 customers, and thus it is clear that a family business is going to be fairly limited in terms of income potential. However, many Culligan dealers operate on a family basis, especially in rural areas.

Should the dealer die, his heirs can sell the business subject to Culligan approval. The term of the franchise is perpetual, although each party has the right of cancellation after ninety days' notice.

The company is actively seeking new dealers, but warns that this is a man's business. It is not a business particularly adapted to quick profit and thus appeals to younger men who want to build their equity over a period of years. Every dealer must meet the necessary capital requirements and show ability to cope with the problems of building a new business.

Robert Schwerin, who has the Culligan Soft-Water Service in Union, New Jersey, got into the business right after World War II. He lived in Pittsburgh, where water pollution has long been an environmental problem. Sold on the Culligan idea, he became partners with another man, Mr. Nelson, who knew the New Jersey market. The two men were Culligan dealers in Union for twenty-two years until Nelson retired. Schwerin, who has a Bachelor of Science degree from Carnegie Tech, finds that he is basically an administrator and manager, and his business is large enough that he can keep away from the mechanical end.

CULLIGAN

Profit-and-Loss Statement for the year ended December 31

Income from sales and services
Service sales		$105,226.57
Soap and salt sales		1,324.31
Installation fees		4,017.55
Domestic and industrial sales		4,679.23
Sales, other		1,840.13
		$117,087.79
Less discounts allowed		725.28
NET SALES AND SERVICES		$116,362.51

Cost of sales and services
Resale merchandise:			
Inventory 1/1/__	$ 568.16		
Add purchases	3,923.64		
	4,491.80		
Less inventory, 12/31/__	1,307.36		
Cost of resale merchandise sold		$ 3,184.44	
Portable service costs			
Salaries	24,927.95		
Plant supplies, salt and mineral	5,834.12		
Gas and oil	3,735.05		
Truck tires and repairs	2,506.82		
Water	2,896.91		
Plant repairs and maintenance	542.47		
Heat, light, and power	686.59		
Freight	848.15		
Installation supplies	735.41		
Depreciation	12,493.08		
Equipment maintenance	153.00		
Uniforms	150.34		
Total portable services costs		55,509.89	
Total cost of sales and services			58,694.33
GROSS PROFIT			$ 57,668.18

General and administrative expenses

Salaries	15,289.09	
Payroll taxes	2,340.77	
Insurance	2,553.53	
Group insurance	1,988.27	
Travel, entertainment, and promotion	1,611.97	
Dues and subscriptions	116.02	
Taxes and licenses	901.83	
Telephone	789.76	
Office expense	548.92	
Commissions	744.43	
Organization expense	306.84	
Advertising and contributions	2,760.68	
Postage	1,175.52	
Depreciation, office furniture	80.04	
Miscellaneous expense	376.19	
Bad debts	382.32	
Interest expense	7,934.60	
Legal and accounting	225.63	
Automobile expense	532.49	
Total general and administrative expense		$ 40,658.90

NET PROFIT FROM OPERATIONS $ 17,009.28

Other income

Discounts earned	$ 404.97	
Miscellaneous	155.02	
Total other income		559.99

NET PROFIT BEFORE PROVISION FOR INCOME TAXES $ 17,569.27

PROVISION FOR INCOME TAXES $ 900.00

NET PROFIT TRANSFERRED TO RETAINED EARNINGS $ 16,669.27

28

Mary Carter Paint Company

Read about Mary Carter Paint Company, see what the company's franchise dealers have to say about the business, and it quickly becomes clear that Mary Carter is the A & P of the paint business.

Like the A & P, Mary Carter is a no-frills, cash-and-carry operation. Like the A & P, Mary Carter does not put on the dog. Dealers stack paint cans on the floor and minimize their expenditures for costly fixtures. The whole operation is geared to the cost-conscious consumer; specifically, the thrifty man who believes in do-it-yourself.

But while the A & P is locked in a monumental struggle with other supermarket giants in a bid for profits, Mary Carter is able to undersell the competition by as much as 50 percent and still offer dealers profits ranging from 17 to 22 percent of gross sales.

Here is the story of how Mary Carter manages to do this and why it has become a major success in franchising. Larry Lehner, vice president in charge of sales, tells how Mary Carter revolutionized the business. Selling paint on a cash-and-carry basis was simply unheard of when Mary Carter began its program. The company shrewdly evaluated the nation's express highway system and concluded that it could offer its dealers a decided edge by servicing their inventory needs through its own fleet of trucks. With plants in Florida, Texas, and California, Mary Carter is able to express paints weekly to all dealers. The deliveries are made without a charge to the dealer.

By buying raw materials in quantity from such leading companies as DuPont, Cyanamid, Alcoa, and National Lead, Mary Carter is able to effect significant savings.

Mary Carter uses its trucks to produce still another saving in both money and time. Conscious of the fact that late deliveries of raw materials can halt production lines, the company sends its trucks to fetch paint-making materials for its factories. The company says that these transport efficiencies save many thousands of dollars in basic costs, enormous freight expenses and, of course, time.

The dealer can work with minimum inventory, for he knows there'll be another company truck in the driveway in a week. The costly business of buying through jobbers and distributors is eliminated. He gets everything direct from the factory without express freight charges. What's more, he pays no royalty fees. Nor is there a franchise fee when he becomes a dealer.

The plain "factory outlet" appearance of Mary Carter stores keeps fixture costs down to about 5 percent of the dealer's invested capital. This means customers do not expect credit, deliveries, or special discounts. "Thrifty do-it-yourselfers prefer top quality and cash savings to fancy fixtures and special services," Mary Carter states.

And yet for all of that, Mary Carter still offers the dealer profits on a par with more service-conscious franchises.

A Mary Carter store can be operated by one man. The franchise is ideal for a family, for it is normally an 8 A.M. to 5 P.M. operation, six days a week, twelve months a year.

Mary Carter anticipates that in his first year of business, the dealer will earn $8,000 to $10,000, $11,000 to $13,000 in the second year, and $15,000 to $20,000 in the fifth year.

Here are a list of expenses involved in starting a Mary Carter paint store: $6,000 to cover inventory (which may be sold by the end of the first week), a $2,000 reserve for advertising, and $2,000 for working capital. That's a total investment of $10,000. What's more, Mary Carter will chip in several gallons of paint free of charge so that you can refurbish your store before the grand opening. The company does not lease or sublease stores to dealers but will assist them in making lease arrangements.

Of the $6,000 inventory cost, 85 percent will be used to buy paint and varnish, and the balance goes for colorants, painting accessories, and sundry merchandise. But if you can't raise the necessary cash, Mary Carter will try to help financially.

Mary Carter makes its profits from the sale of paint to the dealer. As stated, there are no franchise fees or royalties.

The company's factory-trained specialists will survey the community in which you intend to do business and recommend the best possible site—if you haven't already picked one.

Before you open your dealership, you will undergo training for a week at a Mary Carter training store in your area. The company will pay your expenses—up to $15 a day—and will take care of any transportation expenses.

Your Mary Carter district manager will stay with you during the grand-opening week and assist you at your store. Before the grand opening, the company will supply advertising material—newspaper display mats, copy for radio commercials, and copy and art for television spots—all free of charge. The grand opening usually lasts three days, customarily Thursday, Friday, and Saturday.

Mary Carter says that your advertising costs will run to 10 percent of annual purchases from the company. You will pay half of this under a 50-50 plan sponsored by the company. The company also pays half the expense of signs erected outside the store up to $200 total cost.

Mary Carter dealers average forty years of age and many have had some college. The company says they are quite intelligent and have a great deal of enthusiasm; they are self-starters; they are married and have children. Mary Carter also takes retirees and widows.

Many Mary Carter paint store men find that they can cope

with more than one store. The company's distributorship program can provide the ambitious with additional income.

"In addition to profits realized on his own franchise, a top distributor can earn from $10,000 to $15,000 additional annually. He gets this additional income in rebates occurring from sales by his subdealers and by his own pilot store or stores. Such distributors realize total profits, then, from $25,000 to $40,000 annually.

"The program enables our dealers to expand operations with financial help from the company—up to $4,000 is offered by the company as an inducement to distributors in launching new retail outlets.

"The $4,000 is repayable over four-month periods on the basis of 25 percent of the unpaid balance. As new subdealers are started, the distributor may continue to renew his credit with the company, always to a maximum of $4,000.

Many subdealerships are established as departments in existing retail businesses, such as flooring or hardware stores or other non-paint outlets. They must start with an initial Mary Carter inventory of at least $1,500.

Once the distributor dealer has the company's permission, he is free to seek prospective subdealers in a particular city or town and to pursue his own agreements with them. The advantages to the subdealer are that his investment is small; he gets advice from an established dealer and frequent service visits; and he benefits from dealer advertising in the community.

In the final analysis, of course, Mary Carter would be a useless franchise without top-quality products. The company takes pride in its quality control and in its practice of perfecting paint products specially adapted to regional climatic conditions.

"A wide choice of Mary Carter paint products is available to franchise dealers located in extremely varied climates, from Florida to Oregon. Samples of each day's production from all Mary Carter production centers are exactingly tested to make absolutely certain that Mary Carter's high quality standards are steadfastly maintained."

Like many leading franchise companies, Mary Carter is conscious of the need for continued training. Company sales-training experts conduct seminars in dealers' areas at least once annually,

Display inside a Mary Carter Paint shop

and the company sponsors annual one-day conventions in principal cities throughout the country. The company has a publication to keep dealers informed on developments in the industry, and numerous bulletins on new products, sales promotions, and other information flow out of the Tampa, Florida, headquarters. Dealers are given a say in company policy through a ten-member dealer advisory board, composed of nonsalaried dealers representing the various regions.

The company lists some additional pluses:

Mary Carter exclusive franchise contracts assure the dealer of all the Mary Carter business in his city or area. That's one of the main reasons a Mary Carter store increases in value the longer it is established.

Mary Carter stores turn over their inventory approximately ten times a year. "Your investment is therefore returned frequently—not frozen as in a high-overhead type of retail operation.

"There is minimum bookkeeping. Hours are fixed by the dealer to suit his and his community's needs. Most successful dealers work fifty to fifty-five hours a week.

"Mary Carter expresses its confidence in you by guaranteeing your inventory investment. If, for any reason, you should decide to discontinue your business, Mary Carter will help you sell it or purchase your inventory less a small handling charge. The contract is renewable yearly with a thirty-day notice clause for cancellation by either side. The company will not cancel without cause. There is no death clause.

"Steady profits are assured because you are doing business on a cash-and-carry basis. No discounts. No collection problems, no bad debts. Most new territories at present are in the Midwest and Southwest."

Here are comments from two successful Mary Carter dealers. Fred Montinari of Indiana, Pennsylvania, says: "What attracted me to Mary Carter Paint were three very important facts: fine product, coop advertising, and the regular business hours. I am starting my fourth year . . . and am very seriously considering opening another store next year."

And from Howell Crowder of Prichard, Alabama: "I started

with a small investment in one store and grew into a chain-store operation in a protected area. My business has grown from a $30,000 year for one store to almost a $100,000 year for each store."

All of this appears to add up to profits for the 1,200 franchised dealerships from coast to coast. On page 206 are figures from Mary Carter showing volume of business and net profit figures for a number of the company's stores.

The question is, then, is Mary Carter for you? There is no doubt that many franchise businesses are more likely to succeed in the hands of dealers who are experienced businessmen. They often require extensive bookkeeping procedures plus long experience in dealing with the public. But Larry Lehner states the case clearly when he indicates this isn't true of Mary Carter dealers:

"The majority of our franchise dealers have never been in business or have ever sold to the American public prior to becoming one of our franchisees. Consequently, we have found that they all expected a turnkey operation and were most receptive to a package franchise program that included training, direction, and guidance from the day they signed the franchise agreement."

MARY CARTER PAINT STORES

For the year ending December 31, 1965

	Main Street Jacksonville	Jensen Drive Houston	E. Warren (Victor) Detroit	De Kalb Avenue Atlanta
Sales	$99,557.00	$63,061.00	$103,675.00	$47,997.00
Cost of Sales	69,690.00	44,143.00	72,573.00	33,598.00
Gross Profit	29,867.00	18,918.00	31,102.00	14,399.00
Operating Expenses:				
Salaries	—	—	—	—
Rent	2,820.00	2,700.00	3,641.00	1,020.00
Advertising	4,480.00	2,838.00	4,665.00	2,160.00
Utilities	1,116.00	605.00	993.00	310.00
Telephone	200.00	213.00	142.00	253.00
Depreciation	292.00	234.00	278.00	196.00
Taxes & Licenses	300.00	167.00	600.00	257.00
Miscellaneous	850.00	637.00	650.00	470.00
Total	10,058.00	7,394.00	10,969.00	4,666.00
Net Profit	$19,809.00	$11,524.00	$20,133.00	$9,733.00

29

Manpower

Manpower, a company that provides temporary office help at low cost, has just observed its twentieth anniversary. At twenty, the company finds itself with more than 550 offices in thirty-four countries on six continents. Sales have surpassed $150 million a year, and the company now provides a wide variety of office, industrial, sales and technical workers to business, industry, and government—a far cry from the company's modest beginnings.

The beginning was typical of new enterprises, barely managing to continue as tough day after tough day stretched into weeks and months. Before the first year was over, the founder, Elmer L. Winter, now president, and Aaron Scheinfeld, now chairman of the board, seriously considered giving up. Their first two offices, opened simultaneously in Chicago and Milwaukee, gave few signs of viability. But drive and ambition carried the day, and the two men overcame their initial setbacks. Soon they were on their way to success. Their success formula, based on service, has been passed along to their franchise dealers, who own six out of every ten Manpower offices.

It costs about $15,000 to get into the Manpower business. The charge for the franchise itself is $4,500 in the smaller cities throughout the United States where Manpower franchises are still available. Manpower says that the franchisee will need about $10,000, representing working capital and his franchise fee, to open an office in a small city.

"This amount is used as operating capital until such time as the business begins to generate its own capital through profits plowed back into the business and to supply the individual franchisee with personal funds during the initial stages when the Manpower office has not yet begun to return a sufficient amount for this purpose," the company states. Manpower will co-sign loans of established Manpower franchisees who need additional capital to finance continued growth.

The company charges a royalty based on a sliding schedule figured on gross sales. The fee ranges from 5 to 6 percent, depending on total sales volume.

Franchised dealers are not required to buy their supplies from Manpower; the company says supplies are not a profit item. However, they are available. The company maintains a fully stocked warehouse of various types of supplies and equipment, at prices reflecting mass-purchase discounts, needed to operate the franchise.

There is no separate charge for Manpower's advertising program. National advertising is placed through the company's own agency at no cost to franchisees. If you believe you can do better by advertising in local media at your own expense you are free to do so, so long as the advertising copy is approved by Manpower.

How much can you make as a franchised Manpower licensee? Manpower says that the profit potential varies directly with the size of the business community and the amount of effort put in by the franchisee.

Daryl W. Motte, vice president, states: "It would be almost impossible to predict what profit a given franchisee can expect without naming a specific city. Generally speaking, we consider the first-year goal to be to break even and go into the black before the end of that year. The second- and succeeding-year profit potentials will then depend upon the total potential in each indi-

Manpower uses this photograph as a basic identification feature in its advertising and promotion.

vidual market for temporary help services. All I can say is that our franchisees have been quite successful. Many are enjoying above-average incomes, ranging from $20,000 to $50,000 a year, with some earning even more than the upper range would indicate."

Manpower conducts a training school at its home office in Milwaukee every five or six weeks. The course lasts for five and a half days including evenings. Manpower says that the time is "crammed full" with information on how to operate a Manpower office. No charge, but the dealer pays room, board, and transportation, however.

This is followed by on-site training after the Manpower licensee opens his office, and there are field seminars after that to help him learn more about the business. The new man gets a set of manuals detailing every aspect of the business. His regional manager is available for discussion by telephone and by personal visit as necessary.

Manpower says that a typical licensee is a married man thirty-five to fifty. He has two or three children ranging in age from five to twenty.

"Most often he will be a college graduate, but that is not a requirement." His intelligence ranges from average to above average and he is described as a man with drive with a definite orientation toward personal sales work. He should have some business experience, but not necessarily in the personnel field.

Unlike most other leading franchise companies, Manpower does not dictate the franchisee's location. This is not of prime importance in the Manpower business, so long as he picks a site in an "acceptable" part of town near the center.

As a rule, neither the Manpower franchisee nor the company itself owns the building in which the business is conducted. Offices are usually leased from the building owners, and few are built specifically for use as a Manpower office. The central downtown offices may be supplemented with suboffices in the surrounding suburban areas if necessary.

Normally the Manpower franchisee has an exclusive territory encompassing at least one full county and sometimes several counties, depending on the total area covered. "We are currently selling franchises in cities of approximately 30,000 and upwards," Mr. Motte says. He goes on to tell of a somewhat demanding vocation.

"Manpower is not a particularly easy business, and requires a good deal of time and attention. Almost all Manpower offices are open from 8 A.M. to 6 P.M., five days a week and a half-day on Saturdays. It is seldom necessary for the franchisee to work any longer than these hours, and Sunday work is almost unheard of, except under very special circumstances. We are a service company, however, and stand ready to serve our customers on holidays, nights, and Sundays if need be.

"It is not necessary for the franchisee personally to work twelve months out of the year. If he has developed a good staff, he can take time off for a personal vacation, but the business itself does operate year-round. It is not a seasonal business.

"In the smaller communities, a local staff of two people and one part-timer is normally adequate. This can be the franchisee and his wife, plus the part-time helper. As the business grows, however, his need for a permanent staff will, of course, increase.

"In larger cities the staff may range as high as twenty or twenty-five employees, and in the really major markets such as New York City (a company-owned branch) the local staff numbers in excess of eighty people."

Mr. Motte explains that the franchise agreement has a death clause, called a successorship amendment. (Manpower has been a leader in providing excellent license agreements stated in clear language understandable to the layman as well as to his lawyer.)

The successorship agreement gives the man's heirs the right to continue operating, to sell, or to put in a new manager among a number of options they may choose. It also provides for the renewal of his license agreement on a five-year basis, which right continues indefinitely. The basic Manpower agreement is for a term of thirty years. The Manpower franchisee is free to sell his franchise at any time and may ask any price the market will bring. He may keep the proceeds with the exception of a "very small fee" to Manpower for the purpose of processing the new buyer. Manpower does exercise the right to approve the purchaser.

Manpower is looking primarily for young people but does not rule out individuals because of age. "We are primarily interested in a good and reasonable chance of success on the part of the franchisee," they say.

30

Blake Drafting Schools

Education is being stressed as never before, and the best evidence of this is the fact that as a nation, we are spending $50 billion a year on schooling. As our society grows increasingly complex, every college dropout and unskilled high school graduate becomes aware that the best jobs go to the people with occupational skills.

This is an age of technology and while drafting may seem an old talent, it is still in the forefront of the skills needed to meet the problems of today. The U.S. Department of Labor says that within the next ten years industry will need 42 percent more draftsmen than are needed today, whereas the demand for most other occupational skills will rise only 23 percent. If these figures seem high, remember that every building and bulldozer, every causeway and couch, every rocket, radio, motor, and motel has come from a draftsman's drawing board.

The Blake Drafting Schools teach mechanical and electronic drafting and blueprint reading, plus such related subjects as the use of instruments, lettering, projection, tracings, and perspective drawing. Even a bright high school dropout can make the grade.

Sound like a job for a skilled draftsman? You'll have them, but they'll be working for you. Blake recruits the drafting teachers, who must have at least five years' experience, and promises to get you as many as you need. You won't need any drafting skill at all; your job is that of administrator.

Your time will be occupied getting students. Blake wants management men, not teachers, as its dealers. "Our franchisees come from all walks of life, some married, some not married, but they all have one thing in common, the ability to manage, as well as the desire to succeed."

The company is looking for personable men, men who can talk well and impress educators and guidance counselors. Your job will be to advertise the school by newspaper, direct mail, radio and television, and to select students out of the ranks of those who reply. Your advertising program must produce enough leads to fill sixty positions at the drafting tables in your school two or more times a day.

Prospective students will come to the school to be interviewed. It's your job to convince them that drafting school will help them meet their aspirations. You will be doing a great deal of public relations work as well, meeting with school guidance counselors and local, state, and federal rehabilitation and man-power officials. You will meet with the press hoping to interest reporters in your star students. Horatio Alger stories are common among Blake Drafting School graduates. You'll be asked to speak at men's clubs and fraternal organizations to present to parents the opportunities to be found in drafting.

"That's the kind of a business it is. It will cost you quite a bit to open a Blake school, but the rewards are unusually high and the hours relatively short. Blake Drafting School dealers work about forty-eight hours in a five-and-one-half-day week.

The Blake franchise fee is $29,500. This pays for the complete package, including sixty drafting setups, adding machine, typewriter, executive office with desk and chair, a furnished and decorated reception area with secretarial desk, and other equipment. You'll need $15,000 in working capital on top of the $29,500. Of this capital investment, you will need $30,000 in cash. Blake can arrange bank financing for the remainder.

Students being advised at a Blake Drafting School

Actually the Blake schools are a new venture of a company that has set up more than 100 schools to teach people to become computer programmers, the Electronic Computer Programming Institute. The dealers in that now-filled organization make high profits, company officials say, and add that profits in Blake schools are also high. They estimate first-year profit potential, including salary if you pay yourself one, of $53,700 and second-year potential of $92,050.

The rewards come after 6 percent payments to Blake out of the school's gross receipts. The franchised dealer must also make a 2-percent-of-gross contribution to the company's national advertising and public relations activities.

We have already indicated that advertising is very important to the Blake operation because it is advertising that attracts most of the students. Each school is responsible for local advertising, and the budget will depend on local advertising rates. During the course of training, the dealer gets intensive advertising orientation and is taught how to use his advertising dollar most efficiently. He is also taught how to mix media advertising with direct mail, so as to establish an efficient advertising-sales relationship.

While the dealer may purchase all supplies apart from textbooks wherever he pleases, Blake believes that its own package cannot be matched at the price. This is because the company passes along quantity discounts to the dealer. On the other hand, Blake insists that textbooks and related instruction materials be purchased from the company so to maintain quality and uniformity of instruction.

A dealer undergoes training at a company-operated school, where he is trained in all the managerial functions of both office and classroom. He is not charged for this training program and does not pay for room and board at the school.

The company states that from the moment an individual becomes a Blake Drafting School man, he is assisted in every aspect of his business until his school is actually operating with students.

"This means that a Blake executive is responsible for researching and selecting the dealer's location as well as negotiating his

BLAKE DRAFTING SCHOOL

1st-Year Projection

Income

Tuition sales		$150,000
less attrition (uncollectible)	15,000	$135,000
Supply Sales	1,500	$136,500

Expenses

Instruction	21,000	
Rent	10,000	
Insurance	2,000	
Telephone	3,000	
Office personnel	5,000	
Advertising	12,000	
Royalty and advertising fund	10,800	
Payroll taxes	4,000	
Professional fees	3,000	
Enrollment costs	12,000	82,800
PROFIT		**$ 53,700**

2nd-Year Projection

Income

Tuition sales		$225,000
less attrition (uncollectible)	22,500	$202,500
Supply Sales	2,250	$204,750

Expenses

Instruction	31,500	
Rent	10,000	
Insurance	2,000	
Telephone	4,000	
Office personnel	5,000	
Advertising	18,000	
Royalty and advertising fund	16,200	
Payroll taxes	5,000	
Professional fees	3,000	
Enrollment costs	18,000	112,700
PROFIT		**$ 92,050**

lease; we plan and lay out space, work with him on the selection of furnishings and color coordination. We then assist him in the hiring of all his technical and operating personnel, scheduling of his initial advertising to coincide with the completion of his training. A Blake executive is responsible for every detail so that when the franchised dealer completes his training, he is ready to walk into his fully furnished school, all of his personnel will be there and trained and his advertising will commence," the company states.

Each school needs from three to six employees. The school can be run as a family enterprise—if the man and wife possess the requisite managerial abilities. The franchisee will not be involved in a major real-estate construction program, as schools are located in existing buildings.

The dealer is free to sell his franchise to a buyer approved by the home office. The approval is predicated on the same qualifications demanded of any new franchise owner.

Blake has many available franchise opportunities.

31

General Business Services

Many shopkeepers have an appalling lack of knowledge about paperwork. Ask your barber what he knows about accounting and he'll probably say, "Next to nothing." If he's typical, he probably doesn't even know elementary bookkeeping. He may have no idea where his money goes or how wisely he is spending it. He may be paying three times as much as he should for telephone service, or he may have unproductive partners who are costing him money.

When tax time comes around, he may be at the mercy of the system, a system that becomes more complicated with each passing year. He may pay far more tax than he should. He may file late because he did not anticipate the deadline and may have to pay a fine. He may not know enough about payroll taxes to avoid a fat penalty or even disaster through a whopper of a bill for back taxes. Every year hundreds of businesses go under because taxes were allowed to slide until they became so burdensome the business could not raise the money to pay them.

If this sounds like a dismal story, it is meant to. Bernard S. Browning was aware of the plight of the small businessman and

219

found the situation made to order for a new business. Along with
C. E. Gaw and others, he set up General Business Services, Inc.,
to serve the small unsophisticated businessman, the man who runs
a family enterprise or one employing no more than ten people. It
is a vast market, and General Business Services has grown in six
years into one of the major franchise companies by servicing it.

Bernard Browning was a brilliant student. He enrolled at
Missouri State on a scholarship at the age of fifteen. Later he
went to the Harvard Business School, mecca for America's executive elite, and took his Master's degree. He continued his training
at various universities and eventually served on the faculty of
American University in Washington, D.C., where he lectured on
marketing.

Meanwhile he began serving in the U.S. Naval Reserve, having
been an apprentice seaman during World War II. He rose to the
rank of captain, the youngest man in the reserve ever to be
selected for that rank.

Mr. Browning relates the activities of men who hold a General
Business Service franchise:

"Typically, our area directors are on the move. The director
spends most of his time calling on business and professional men.
Some of the people he sees as prospects, and he attempts to sell
them our services. If the prospect becomes a client, he instructs
him on a start-up call in how to use our system. Depending upon
the client's needs, our area director will set up the kind of system
that will work best for him.

"If the client has never been in business before, he may need
basic instruction in the use and preparation of profit-and-loss
statements. If he has been in business or knows something about
accounting, he will be more interested in knowing what operating
ratios he should be working against.

"We establish guidelines for different expense items. He may
find that his gross profit is too low, or that his net is too low, or
that his expenses are out of line. He'll help the client with his
tax forms, federal, state and local. As he progresses he will find
that he faces the same problems again and again and will soon
become quite knowledgeable on dozens of procedural matters
that perplex the businessman who faces the problem only once.

General Business Services helps the small-business man with accounting and other business problems.

Our area director needn't be an accountant. We have a backup staff of highly professional people who offer the client the detailed technical help that our area directors couldn't expect to handle.

"He'll be thoroughly trained to handle every problem he needs to solve. We have a training institute of seven days, which includes classroom work and then six days of on-the-job field training. And the learning process is continual. Our men are constantly learning.

"We can take a man from virtually any background and teach him what he needs to know. With our backup staff, the area director needs to know barely 10 percent of what his client requires. His basic skill is one of public relations."

Men who hold area directorships with General Business Services enter the business without fees or royalties. The company does get paid for support services, and that's where it makes its profits.

The initial investment required for a General Business Services franchise is $7,500, which covers everything but working capital. The company urges the dealer to hold aside enough money to cover his living expenses for about ninety days, just in case for one reason or another he is unable to work. The company does not provide financing, primarily because of the modest investment.

The company says that first-year profit potential normally ranges from $10,000 to $15,000. The second-year profit potential should be $15,000 to $20,000, and for the fifth year, $35,000.

After the man is trained, he will attend monthly group training sessions and periodic seminars held in his region. In addition, he gets a 500-page operations manual providing all instructions necessary for operating the franchise. The company maintains a lending library for personal professional development. Thirty regional directors throughout the country are available on a continuing basis to provide training as needed. All training is free.

Profiling the successful GBS man, he is forty-three, married, and either has a Master's degree or has done some graduate work. He has approximately fifteen years of business experience and has earned an average salary of $16,500 before he joined General Business Services. He is strong on public relations, is thorough and ambitious.

The company strives to locate each man in an area with business potential the equal of every other franchisee. Exclusive rights are given each man in his area. For the first two years he will have to work more than forty hours a week. Once his clientele is established, however, his income will be more dependent upon automatic renewals and his work week can be cut substantially. During the first two years he will have to work twelve months a year to establish his clientele. He can work less, however, if he is content to draw out his success.

This is a one-man business for those who want it that way, but many franchisees add employees to build an organization and reach full success.

There are no buildings associated with the franchise, which helps explain why the investment is so small. Men with General Business Services quickly become acquainted with certified public accountants in their areas and pass clients along to a CPA when they get too large for ease of handling by GBS. CPA's, for their part, are one of the best sources of prospects for GBS.

Many General Business Services men have sold their franchises at a substantial capital gain. The parent company reserves the right to approve the buyer, but says that it has yet to veto a potential purchaser. Under the contract, the heirs of a deceased franchise holder have the right to sell the business or to continue operating it in the same manner as the original owner.

While there are franchises available in all states, many communities are taken. Competition has not been a problem. The franchisee needs only 5 percent of his market for an income well in excess of $30,000 a year.

General Business Services says that it makes no restrictions on people who may have the franchise so long as they are qualified. As of 1968 there were over 400 franchised men operating in forty-five states.

GENERAL BUSINESS SERVICES AREA DIRECTORSHIP

Profit-and-Loss Statement

Sales	$40,000	
Cost of sales (Payments to national organization for systems and technical support services)	15,000	
GROSS PROFIT		$25,000
OPERATING EXPENSES		
Payroll	—	
Rent	—	
Franchise fees	—	
Advertising	900	
Freight	—	
Store supplies	—	
Office supplies	50	
Utilities	—	
Telephone	420	
Postage	480	
Repair, maintenance	—	
Insurance	—	
Legal, auditing	—	
Depreciation	—	
Dues and subscriptions	25	
Taxes—state and local		
Taxes—payroll	—	
Travel—entertainment	250	
Auto expense	600	
Miscellaneous rents	—	
Miscellaneous expense	80	
TOTAL OPERATING EXPENSES		2,805
NET PROFIT (before owner's draw)		22,195

OTHER INCOME (From overrides on Associates. Supplementary services provided to clients represent an additional source of income but may not be included in a particular Area Directorship.)

32

A to Z Rentals

Frank P. Branz, a former filling-station operator and truck-rental man, settled into a A to Z rental business between two thriving towns just west of Cleveland, Lorain and Elyria, Ohio. He and his wife operate the business with the help of their teen-age son, who also attends high school. Mr. Branz has managed to make A to Z's profit projections each year in his busy location.

Lorain and Elyria are six miles apart, and the area between them is building up constantly. The nearest other A to Z rental stores are quite a few miles away, in Sandusky and North Holmstead.

Frank has kept the store open seven days a week, but will be closing it on Sundays now that he is well established. Sold on the rental business, he can think of no disadvantage in the set-up, although he concedes that a person "up in years" might not want to handle the heavy equipment lines offered by many A to Z rental centers.

But there's no problem there. While A to Z likes its centers to carry a full line, dealers often start with a relatively small inventory—$22,500 worth of tools and equipment. They can build this up in time to a $115,000 inventory.

The centers rent carpenter tools, party and banquet supplies, polishers and sanders, painting equipment, invalid and sickroom equipment, lawn and garden tools, contractors' equipment, concrete-mixing tools, baby equipment and beds, mechanics' hand tools, moving and loading tools, and many other items.

In just a few years, A to Z has gained the respect of leaders in the franchise field. Robert Sheridan, president of Nationwide Industries, Inc., of Chicago, the parent of A to Z, is chairman of the board of governors of the Boston College Center for the Study of Franchise Distribution.

The basis for the popularity of rental centers is, of course, the continuing do-it-yourself boom, which has been largely inspired by rising costs of labor. Americans also have more leisure time these days, and thousands have turned this time to credit by developing handicraft skills. They take pride in their work. It is certainly true that many people become so skilled that they can do work that previously only the most skilled (and most profit-minded) professionals could do. And do it better. For example, while a householder usually removes the switch plates when he paints his walls, many professional painters will paint right over them to save a few minutes.

Many customers of rental centers are particularly concerned about the appearance of their homes. They are likely to appreciate the availability of top-quality tools that they could not afford to buy for an occasional project. Remember that nearly 63 percent of American families own their own homes and that "puttering" is a national pasttime.

While tool rental is no doubt the specialty of A to Z, the company is constantly on the alert for new sources of profit for its dealers. Medicare has poured money into hospitals, nursing homes, and into the hands of individuals. A to Z has thus urged owners to carry wheelchairs and other convalescent and invalid equipment. In yet another specialty, A to Z says it has become the largest source of camping and outdoor recreational equipment.

Worried about the possibility that homeowners will prefer to buy a low-cost tool? A to Z says that customers prefer to rent, because most homes built in the past twenty years lack storage space. Basements are far less common today than they were in the days when nearly everyone burned coal.

Even the professional turns to rental equipment to meet his needs during peak periods. Contractors, caterers, independent store operators, route-owning deliverymen are part of the trade for A to Z owners.

We've already seen what one A to Z owner is like. What about the others? A to Z says its owners run the gamut, including a transit-company owner, a contract negotiator for the U.S. Department of Defense, a retired Air Force officer, and a marketing man for a national soap company. There is an ex-railroad accountant, a salesman, and even an operator of an independent rental store.

Even blue-collar workers can accumulate the capital needed. The owner must put up $8,750, and he will need an additional $6,000 for working capital. With the $8,750, the dealer can stack his shelves with inventory valued at retail at $35,000. If he has $12,500 he can put $50,000 worth on the floor, and with $18,750 his beginning inventory would be $75,000.

It is understood that A to Z expects owners to gross $1.25 for every dollar of inventory. Thus a $30,000 store should gross $37,500 annually, bringing $15,000 to $16,000 in net profits. Of course, the salary the owner pays himself would be deducted from the net-profit figure to arrive at actual profits.

The idea, of course, is for the dealer to grow. Every profit-and-loss statement shown at the end of this chapter indicates a "recommended growth inventory," which adds one third to one half again to the retail value of the inventory in the second year. The company states, "As an A to Z owner you do not commit all of your resources. If you qualify, we will help finance you to start. And, as you grow and maintain your credit standing, additional dollars are available for expansion purposes."

A to Z has a royalty system that amounts to 5 percent of gross receipts. The company performs bookkeeping services for its owners without cost. Standard forms are given owners to make this job easier for the company. Inventory and control records are maintained by owners.

Dealers provide A to Z with complete monthly records to

enable the company to prepare monthly balance sheets. Dealer audits are paid for by A to Z.

The A to Z advertising program includes such mass-circulation magazines as *Life, Look, Better Homes and Gardens,* and *McCalls,* and A to Z ads are heard on over 200 local radio stations that carry NBC's "Monitor." Local TV stations run A to Z ads on the Johnny Carson "Tonight Show" and the Joey Bishop Show.

Owners must agree to spend at least 8 percent of their gross receipts for promotional materials and other forms of advertising.

A to Z insists owners buy their initial inventory from the company. Items carrying the A to Z brand labels, items made exclusively for A to Z, and items for which A to Z has exclusive distribution rights in the rental trade must also be purchased from the company. The owner must purchase no less than 65 percent of all other equipment from A to Z. However, if an item of equipment is of equal quality and performance and can be obtained for less than A to Z's price in the current catalog, the company allows the switch. (The sale of replacement items accounts for about 15 percent of A to Z's earnings.)

A to Z considers its one-week training program to be an absolute necessity for owners anxious to succeed in the business. New owners receive their training at a classroom in the company's headquarters in Chicago. Some of the work is done on the job—in the company-owned pilot store in Niles, Ohio. A to Z pays the costs of the owner's transportation and lodging.

The company comments: "When you leave the training center you will have learned store operation, inventory control, use of rental contracts, maintenance control procedures, telephone selling, and the planning and use of advertising and publicity materials, with emphasis on merchandising and on your grand-opening procedures."

After the training period the company "stands ready to answer day-to-day questions that come up." Field managers work with owners to help them develop their market.

Like many another franchise company, A to Z has an owner advisory panel to keep the lines of communication open so that there is a steady flow of information going both ways.

A to Z has pioneered in working out a comprehensive insurance program for its owners. This means the owner doesn't
have to shop locally, and very possibly unsuccessfully in a time
of rising crime and violence, for complete insurance coverage.

When the prospective owner comes to A to Z to set up a business, the company analyzes potential sites he may suggest. The
company must approve the site and often picks one out for
owners who have no specific location in mind. The location must
have suitable space and be either a satisfactory existing building
or a land area on which a structure can be built.

A to Z assigns territories on an exclusive basis, with at least
three miles between centers, depending on population density.
A to Z centers are suburban or community oriented, and a territory generally averages 50,000 population.

A to Z does not sell, lease, or sublet premises to franchise
owners. The company's six-man real-estate staff evaluates and
negotiates for center facilities. Leases are arranged for owners
and necessary channels established for franchisees who wish
to construct their own building. In virtually every case A to Z
sets the construction standards the center must meet. The company checks on rental or mortgage payments to make sure they
are in line with what the company believes to be reasonable.

While some areas are franchised completely, there are many
A to Z territories available. To get a franchise near a major
city, the new owner may have to pay a premium. A to Z doesn't
shrink from competition from rival rental companies, but where
there is a strong competitor in the area, the company takes this
into consideration in site selection.

The centers usually open at 8 A.M. and close at 6:30 P.M., relatively short business hours for retail operation. The centers are
open six days a week and some are open Sunday morning.

The franchise agreement calls for a twelve-month year, but
vacations can be arranged if the owner has a good assistant. A
center with a small inventory can be operated by a family two-
some, but when the center grows to a $30,000 inventory it will
require a full-time employee and one part-timer. On the high
side of the scale, a center with an $80,000 inventory that is grow-

ing to a $115,000 inventory will need three full-time employees and one part-timer in addition to the owner.

A to Z welcomes retirees, and the franchise is available for purchase by widows on an investment basis.

A to Z is particularly proud of a recent innovation, its "Reserve it here—Rent it there" camping service, which allows customers to sign for equipment in their local A to Z rental store and pick it up at the store nearest their campsite. The plan reduces rental costs for campers and can cut travel time between home and destination. A heavy trailer, for example, might slow the trip and, incidentally, can be a safety hazard.

A to Z realizes that enterprising Americans have a deep-rooted desire to be their own bosses, but knows that the fear of failure often keeps them from trying their own business.

"An A to Z Rental Center Franchise cuts down the risks . . . offering assurance and support," the company says. "If you fit the standards established for an A to Z Rental Center owner, you will have joined an elite and successful group. You and your family will be on the road toward the twin goals of financial and social importance."

Detailed financial tables follow:

A TO Z RENTAL CENTER PLAN NO. 1

	1st Year Inventory With A to Z Rental, Inc. Financing	2nd Year Inventory With A to Z Rental, Inc. Growth Financing
Original Inventory	$22,500	$30,000
Recommended Growth Inventory	7,500	15,000
Total Inventory	$30,000	$45,000
Income		
A. Rental Income	$36,750	$52,500
B. Merchandise Sales	4,250	5,750
C. Initial Advertising		
Reimbursement	1,000	—
D. Delivery Revenue	720	1,040
E. Total Revenue	$42,720	$59,290
F. Cost of Goods Sold	2,765	3,740
G. Total Gross Profit	$39,955	$55,550
Expenses		
A. Rental Income	$ 1,500*	$ 7,000†
B. Occupancy Cost	6,000	6,000
C. Repair & Maintenance	600	1,500
D. Advertising	3,418	4,743
E. Insurance	788	1,125
F. Supplies	840	1,200
G. Legal & Auditing	150	200
H. Telephone	450	450
I. Taxes	550	720
J. Delivery Costs	720	950
K. Miscellaneous	500	650
L. Time Price Differential	2,455	3,124
M. Royalties	2,136	2,965
N. Freight on Growth Inventory	375	750
O. Sign Lease	372	372
TOTAL EXPENSES	$20,854	$31,749
Income Before Depreciation		
and Taxes	$19,101	$23,801

* One part time employee
† One full time employee and one part time employee

A TO Z RENTAL CENTER PLAN NO. 2

	1st Year Inventory With A to Z Rental, Inc. Financing	2nd Year Inventory With A to Z Rental, Inc. Growth Financing
Original Inventory	$37,500	$ 50,000
Recommended Growth Inventory	12,500	25,000
Total Inventory	$50,000	$ 75,000
Income		
A. Rental Income	$61,250	$ 87,500
B. Merchandise Sales	7,300	11,840
C. Initial Advertising Reimbursement	1,000	—
D. Delivery Revenue	875	1,750
E. Total Revenue	$70,425	$101,090
F. Cost of Goods Sold	4,750	7,695
G. Total Gross Profit	$65,675	$ 93,395
Expenses		
A. Rental Income	$ 7,000*	$ 13,500†
B. Occupancy Cost	7,200	7,200
C. Repair & Maintenance	960	2,330
D. Advertising	5,634	8,087
E. Insurance	1,313	1,875
F. Supplies	1,080	2,165
G. Legal & Auditing	150	200
H. Telephone	550	550
I. Taxes	750	900
J. Delivery Costs	900	1,600
K. Miscellaneous	750	1,000
L. Time Price Differential	3,560	4,675
M. Royalties	3,521	5,055
N. Freight on Growth Inventory	625	1,250
O. Sign Lease	372	372
TOTAL EXPENSES	$34,365	$ 50,759
Income Before Depreciation and Taxes	$31,310	$ 42,636

* One full time employee and one part time employee
† Two full time employees and one part time employee

A TO Z RENTAL CENTER PLAN NO. 3

	1st Year Inventory With A to Z Rental, Inc. Financing	2nd Year Inventory With A to Z Rental, Inc. Growth Financing
Original Inventory	$ 62,500	$ 80,000
Recommended Growth Inventory	17,500	35,000
Total Inventory	$ 80,000	$115,000
Income		
A. Rental Income	$ 99,750	$136,500
B. Merchandise Sales	10,900	16,000
C. Initial Advertising Reimbursement	1,000	–
D. Delivery Revenue	1,310	2,620
E. Total Revenue	$112,960	$155,120
F. Cost of Goods Sold	7,085	10,400
G. Total Gross Profit	$105,875	$144,720
Expenses		
A. Rental Income	$ 15,000*	$ 19,500†
B. Occupancy Cost	9,000	9,000
C. Repair & Maintenance	2,400	3,430
D. Advertising	9,037	12,410
E. Insurance	2,138	2,925
F. Supplies	2,500	3,335
G. Legal & Auditing	200	300
H. Telephone	700	700
I. Taxes	1,000	1,400
J. Delivery Costs	1,200	1,800
K. Miscellaneous	1,200	1,500
L. Time Price Differential	5,302	6,864
M. Royalties	5,648	7,756
N. Freight on Growth Inventory	875	1,750
O. Sign Lease	372	372
TOTAL EXPENSES	$ 56,572	$ 73,042
Income Before Depreciation and Taxes	$ 49,303	$ 71,678

* Two fulltime and two parttime employees
† Three fulltime employees and one parttime employee

33

Convenient Food Mart
— the Superette

While the major supermarket chains are scrambling for small profits on big orders, a relatively new franchised supermarket business is offering its dealers big profits on individual orders small enough to go through the express checkout at the A & P. Sound like a retailer's dream? Maybe. But that's the formula Convenient Food Mart stores have used to compete successfully with the big chains. And Convenient offers virtually the same breadth of selection as the majors—just fewer brands.

You know what it's like to go into the average big supermarket. You're faced with a bewildering array of brand names, as many as 8,000 individual items or more. There are the popular nationally advertised brands as well as the store's own brands.

No doubt this duplication is in part responsible for bringing grocery carts to the checkout counter brim-full. But it doesn't necessarily lead to high profits. The supermarket manager is conscious of his competitors' prices, and must pare his profits to pennies per item. The big supermarkets must move warehouses full of goods to make modest profits. In 1968, leading supermarket chains earned an average of one cent on the dollar.

Meanwhile delicatessens and small stores skim big profits off the top by offering late hours and other conveniences in a relatively small market. These stores are usually limited to walk-in trade, as they can offer little parking space in their congested locations. And this in a nation that travels by car. This leaves a massive convenience market to someone else. And Convenient Food Mart is moving in to fill the gap.

Convenient Food Mart stores try for "selection without duplication." Their shelves carry an average of 4,000 items, about half of the stock carried by the bigger chain supermarkets. The size of the store makes it physically impossible to carry several brands of one item. You'll find one primary brand and a secondary brand. Even the second-line brand is a well-known brand.

What's more, Convenient stresses short shopping stints—seven-minute shopping, the ads say. (Compare that with the time you spend in the checkout line alone at a busy chain market.) Convenient Mart goes for a smaller average sale. Their $1.25 sales slip is peanuts against the $6 average or better that the large supermarket tallies up.

Convenient's profits come not so much from the basic items as from nonstaple items that are bought largely on impulse. Convenient says that men often buy for their wives and when they do, they do two seemingly contradictory things: they buy on impulse but are also quality-conscious. They're more likely to walk out with the bigger markup items, raising the profitability of the store.

This is not to say that there are no bargains in the Convenient Mart stores. Quite the contrary. The company maintains that its staples are indeed competitively priced.

Let's take a look at the history of this company for an insight into how the plan can work for you. Convenient Food Mart, Inc., is an Illinois corporation that was organized and chartered on May 28, 1958. The founders were the Meadowmoor Dairies, a division of Scot Lad Foods, Inc., and Bresler Ice Cream Company. The plan was to set up a nationwide group of superettes or bantam supermarkets to provide individuals from all walks of life with an opportunity to own a business providing above-average income.

Not all of the profits come from the food store itself. While the

Convenient Food Mart store dominates the scene, there are frequently several other stores operated at the same location. For instance, there might be a barber shop, a laundromat, drugstore, hardware store, dry cleaner, and several other outlets—all providing additional traffic for the Food Mart franchisee. In short, the company is creating small neighborhood shopping centers, which build substantial traffic for all of the stores in the complex.

The company's place in this is described as follows. Through the Bresler interests in real estate and construction, sites are purchased, stores built, and rentals established that will yield an adequate return on invested capital. Sometimes the centers are built by wealthy individuals in the community who agree to build the stores according to company plans. The company then leases the stores from the investors. Each of these centers is then sublet to a franchised operator for fifteen years. (There are provisions in the lease providing for two five-year renewals.)

Many who sign up with Convenient will want to limit themselves to the Food Mart alone—and the company will accept operators who wish to do this as Food Mart franchisees. As such, they will not be involved financially or operationally in the satellite stores. A considerable investment is involved even so, but the company is prepared to help the dealer raise the necessary capital.

A typical store investment, apart from the rental fees, would come to $12,000 in groceries and other inventory and another $36,500 for equipment and equipment installation. That's a total capital commitment of $48,500.

Convenient Food Mart lists the following cash requirements:

Insurance, licenses, and initial rent (approx.)	$1,100
Operating cash	1,000*
Franchise fee	1,500
Architectural and building plans	2,000
Deposit on grocery stock	2,500
Deposit on equipment, signs, etc.	3,650
Rent security deposit (subject to change)	3,600†
Total cash requirement	$15,350

* Operating cash is returned to the store owner on opening day.
† The rental security deposit is refunded at the end of the lease payments.

A Convenient Food Mart center, which includes other small-business activities. Note another franchise operation.

Convenient Food Mart arranges all financing for its franchised dealers, with average financing terms running from five to seven years based on the company's evaluation of the dealer's "credit and financial stability."

As a Food Mart store operator, you are entitled to Convenient's discounts from merchandise suppliers. The company contracts for merchandise on behalf of all dealers at cost and obtains bulk prices for the dealers. As the company puts it, "These costs, because of our past growth pattern, are always very competitively priced at all levels. The operator receives full benefits of any discounts, allowances, cooperative and merchandise earnings."

The new dealer pays a one-time franchise fee of $1,500 and another $2,000 for a location search, development, and construction supervision. He pays a further 1 percent of his gross volume for the use of the franchise.

When the owner enters the store to do business, he will find that it is complete in every respect, including fixtures, cash registers, adding machine, right down to the little hanging lanterns that provide a "friendly colonial air" in an efficient contemporary setting.

But before the new dealer takes over his store, he receives full-time training in a Convenient Food Mart store for six weeks. The parent organization pays its franchise trainees $100 a week as part of its franchising program. Operators are assigned to training stations near their homes, so there is no room-and-board expense.

In his management training, the dealer-to-be learns stock control, inventory analysis, the value and use of merchandising aids, and how to coordinate pricing and promotions with all major suppliers.

Modern electronic accounting equipment processes the store owner's daily activity report and furnishes him with detailed profit-and-loss statements, comparative percentages, analysis of profit items, payroll records, and so forth. It prepares the forms and checks for state and local sales taxes, withholding and other payroll taxes he must pay.

The Food Mart system uses a direct advertising approach, bulk-mailing up to 3,000 full-page newspaper-type ads to families in the immediate vicinity of each store at two-week intervals throughout the year. There is, Food Mart says, no wasted circulation, as each recipient of the mailed circular is a potential customer.

Since franchise areas vary in size and scope, some areas are additionally serviced by TV and/or radio advertising or supplemented by newspaper advertisements. However the advertising is handled, whatever the approach, dealers contribute 1 percent of their gross sales to the parent company for this service.

What profit can the franchised Convenient Food Mart dealer hope for? The company says profits usually range up to $25,000 but can go even higher. "In some areas profits have been as high as $15,000 in the first year and in others as high as $46,000. Sometimes there is an advantage in developing a location seemingly prematurely—in an area where a major housing development is imminent in order to obtain an advantageous low rental." The company says this procedure has paid off handsomely in areas where it has been followed.

If all of this sounds interesting, perhaps a Convenient Food Mart store is for you. Here's the company's appraisal of its kind of man. As a group, the age range is from thirty to fifty. Operators represent moderate income levels and they are men with a "strong sense of thrift," which has made it possible for them to accumulate enough money to buy a relatively high-cash franchise. They place a high value on the idea of being their own boss and are reaching out for some of the comforts of life that were denied them in work-a-day jobs.

The company continues the profile: "They're willing to make sacrifices to achieve their personal goals. For the most part, they are high school graduates and a few have college credits. A number have been in semimanagerial positions such as supervisors, foremen, salesmen, or management trainees. As a group, they are best described as eager learners, personable, self-starters, and highly motivated to reach success."

Convenient insists that its "sophisticated team" of site selectors have been able to negotiate leases and build stores on desirable sites virtually without failures.

"A high-density population is always the first and foremost

consideration" in site selection, the company says, and this helps guarantee success. In crowded city areas where vacant land is unavailable, the company often rehabilitates existing structures.

"Mushrooming suburban areas too small to support full-scale supermarkets provide ideal conditions for CFM development. To be adjacent to an apartment complex or family dwellings where there is a minimum of 700 to 800 families and where no competitive stores exist is considered an ideal setup."

Stress on the name "Convenient" is by no means accidental. Not only is the store location chosen for convenience to a number of people, it is also kept open for the same reason. A Food Mart owner is faced with hours stretching from 9 A.M. to midnight 365 days a year. No man could meet that schedule alone, and that is the way the company intends it. The company stresses that the franchised dealer will have sufficient earnings to employ the necessary personnel to run the store for the hours he doesn't choose to work himself.

The normal work week for the boss, who pays attention to management details primarily, is fifty hours or more. Often two partners will divide the work week into two fifty-two-hour segments with regularly scheduled time off to suit their convenience. They add part-time cashiers or stock clerks to help out, but by and large they need no other help beyond what they are able to give to the business themselves. This partner setup allows skillful managers substantial leisure time for vacations and holidays.

If a man chooses to go it alone, he will need an assistant manager and three or four part-time employees. Another partnership arrangement—the familiar Mom and Pop idea—doesn't allow the team to split the holiday and vacation schedule the way unrelated partners can, but it does offer a way to run the business successfully. Teenage children often spell Mom and Dad to give them more leisure time.

One family in the business has five teenagers, and as a result needs no outside help. Mom and Dad have set up a regular schedule of brief duty for each member of the family to supplement their own forty-five-hour stints.

Should an owner wish to sell his store he is free to do so to a buyer the company approves—a man who is both morally and financially qualified. The heirs of an owner who dies have the right to sell.

The franchise license is for the duration of the lease or sublease, normally for fifteen to twenty years, with renewal options, which vary from lease to lease, for additional five-year periods.

Territories are exclusive and are controlled by independent regional franchisers who have been granted exclusive regional areas in which to establish and sell stores to owner-operators. As of 1969, there were about forty regional franchises and nearly 400 stores, including those under construction. They dot several sections of the nation.

Convenient thinks there may be thousands of opportunities left, certainly hundreds.

The company says that it does not restrict its franchise in any way. A qualified potential dealer can have a franchise no matter what his walk of life. This includes widows and retirees who are financially and physically qualified and who can withstand a thorough investigation of personal and business responsibility, integrity, and moral character.

The company says that they are "not an emulator, a look-alike, or a follower. CFM has found the pinnacle and intends to keep its perch."

CONVENIENT FOOD MARTS

Profit-and-Loss Statement *

	Amount	Percent
Sales (less taxes)	$441,285	100.00
Cost of sales	359,689	81.51
Gross profit	81,596	18.49
Earned rebates and other income	7,842	1.78
TOTAL GROSS PROFIT	89,438	20.27
Expenses		
Store wages	20,539	4.06
Franchise fee	4,413	1.00
Service charge	8,826	2.00
Laundry	240	.05
Outside services	746	.17
Rent	6,546	1.49
Utilities	4,612	1.05
Telephone	274	.06
Maintenance	1,548	.35
Licenses	240	.05
General taxes	1,513	.35
Payroll taxes	1,801	.41
Store supplies	2,624	.59
Office supplies	218	.05
Depreciation	3,009	.68
Legal and professional	67	.02
Interest	2,036	.46
Insurance	936	.21
Advertising	4,413	1.00
Promotional advertising	75	.02
Miscellaneous	146	.03
Cash short (or over)	103	.02
Bad checks	448	.10
Officers' life insurance	133	.03
NET EXPENSE	$ 65,506	14.85
Wages drawn by owner	8,000	1.81
Net profit after draw	15,932	3.61
TOTAL INCOME	$ 23,932	5.42

* This statement represents true figures of an average Ohio Convenient Food Mart store which gives a reasonable expected figure for future stores in this area with the services and advantages of the O.C.F.M. formula.

34

ServiceMaster

Julian Simms, Jr., a young Afro-American with an eye for excellence, had learned carpet installation from his father and he was good at it. As a high school football player, Julian had learned to appreciate active competition and team spirit.

But fifteen years in the carpet trade convinced him that he was equal to a bigger challenge. He wanted to be in business on his own. One day while he was laying carpet for a customer in a new home, he noticed that the used carpeting from the old house was so clean it seemed almost new.

He had the same experience again and again. It wasn't long before this ambitious man was able to learn that the best cleaning results always came from the same people, franchised dealers for ServiceMaster.

He investigated ServiceMaster by paying a visit to the company office in his native Corpus Christi, Texas. He discovered that ServiceMaster had a franchise plan. But, even though his background in carpeting seemed to qualify him uniquely for the opportunity, he still had his doubts. He learned that, as much as anything, ServiceMaster required direct selling. Would he be able to make sales? Could he manage his work? Would he fit in with the company?

Myron Clark, regional director for ServiceMaster, thought so: "We knew we could work out Julian's problems. The single most significant fact for us was his will to succeed. We know that our formula will succeed when properly applied. Julian had a commitment to the course set out for him, and we were sure that he could build a business of his own."

Characteristically, Julian Simms began cautiously, buying a limited-service franchise for carpet and furniture cleaning. The company's regional director arranged partial financing and also counseled Julian personally during the preliminary training period. Another ServiceMaster man, Ron Sardone, showed him how to put selling theories into practice, even accompanying him on first calls to customers' homes.

A dealer needs $5,600 to purchase a standard ServiceMaster franchise. Of this, $1,600 is for his license and training fee. The remainder includes all of the equipment necessary to perform the ServiceMaster services and sufficient supplies and products to accomplish approximately $20,000 to $30,000 of service sales.

In addition to the $5,600, the new franchise owner should have $1,500 to $2,000 to use as working capital. He will also need a vehicle. This can be a station wagon or a panel truck. Beyond that, the ServiceMaster licensee pays a 10 percent fee monthly on gross service sales.

A prospective licensee is given ServiceMaster manuals, which he is encouraged to study while on his present job. After reading the manuals he completes several open-book tests. Following that, he has two weeks of on-the-job training with someone who already holds a franchise.

There is still more training. For three days the man is trained in his home by one of ServiceMaster's traveling regional managers, who instructs him in bookkeeping procedures, sources of business, and other managerial matters. After these three phases of training the new associate attends a six-day "Academy of Service" at ServiceMaster's plant in Downers Grove, Illinois, the company headquarters.

Julian—who was an immediate success—fairly well fits the ideal set forth by the company. The company wants men with at least a high-school education, men who get satisfaction out of rendering service. ServiceMaster wants their men to have a need to achieve and a desire to grow.

"Desire to grow," says Richard A. Armstrong, coordinator of market services, "means he will not be satisfied with his achievements this year. No matter how much he has grown he feels he must do better next year."

"Any man of average intelligence who will follow our program will be successful. Our concern is whether or not he will be motivated to follow the program. Personality inventory tests are given as a part of every interview with prospective licensees. These are scored and compared to norms established by men who are already successful licensees."

The company is looking for full-time people. As James F. Mertes of Houston, Texas, put it: "I am on call twenty-four hours a day, fifty-two solid weeks of the year. I usually arrive at the office about 8:30 or 9 A.M. and leave for home or arrive there at around 7 or 7:30 P.M."

Usually for the first two or three years the franchisee works from his home. This minimizes his investment, and his overhead expenses are almost nil.

"In an average community, a first-year licensee will generally do somewhere in the vicinity of $15,000 in service sales," Mr. Armstrong says.

Julian Simms, by the way, did better than that. In the first year he grossed $18,000 and by mid-1968, his second year in the business, sales had already surpassed first-year figures, so that he expects to double his first year's gross.

Mr. Armstrong said that it is reasonable to presume that the ServiceMaster man will be able to take 70 percent of his first year's gross out of the business because he will be selling and doing the work himself. As he adds employees to his organization, the percentage will go down, but not the dollar income.

ServiceMaster permits franchisees to sell their businesses to any person approved by the company.

ServiceMaster has many available territories. It had approximately 700 licensees in the United States and Canada and another 100 in foreign countries in 1968.

ServiceMaster is no ordinary cleaning service. Men flying the

ServiceMaster banner do the cleaning for many important companies. One ServiceMaster dealer who has a business ranging high into the hundreds of thousands yearly does the cleaning work for a major shipping line. Another services an airline.

Here's a description of the ServiceMaster markets. ServiceMaster does house-wide cleaning either on a one-shot basis or on contract. A program introduced in 1966 enables homemakers to schedule housecleaning help on a year-round basis. The housewife is offered the program on the installment plan. Sometimes she will charge the cost to her account at a store that leases space to a local ServiceMaster licensee.

Among the stores that offer ServiceMaster services are Bloomingdale's, New York City; Higbee's, Cleveland; Carson, Pirie, Scott, Chicago; Dayton's, Minneapolis; Rich's, Atlanta; Joske's, Houston; Duff & Repp, Kansas City; Breuner's, in various cities in California; Woodward & Lathrop, Washington, D.C.; and Sears, Roebuck & Co., in more than 300 markets.

ServiceMaster also offers "post-disaster" service packaged through insurance adjusters with complete "one stop" service for cleaning and restoration of fire- and flood-damaged property. This service includes specialized techniques such as smoke and fuel-oil odor control, deodorizing, furniture refinishng, and carpet reweaving along with the basic ServiceMaster cleaning service.

ServiceMaster has expanded its franchise operation with a program to serve the growing commercial-building maintenance field.

Julian Simms has both home and office accounts. ServiceMaster says that the growth of his young company is based largely on Julian's reputation for beyond-the-ordinary service. His emphasis is on complete customer satisfaction. He still gets a thrill when he is able to salvage carpets that competitors in Corpus Christi could not clean. He lists among his customers the city's leading citizens and firms.

Julian Simms is married and the father of five children. His most enthusiastic assistant is his wife, Selia, who takes an active interest in the business, helping with the telephone and the office work. Last spring she attended a company regional training meeting with her husband.

Julian's early doubts have disappeared. How far will he go in his new career? ServiceMaster believes the prospects are unlimited.

SERVICEMASTER

Profit-and-Loss Statement *

Sales		$131,472.06
Cost of sales		
Beginning inventory	$ 3,394.29	
Costs—material, labor, and franchise fee	84,906.22	
	88,300.51	
Less inventory	4,726.16	83,574.35
GROSS PROFIT		$ 47,897.71
Business expense		
Salaries and wages	$16,070.63	
Rent	1,241.74	
Interest	123.68	
Taxes	1,979.58	
Bad Debts	267.07	
Repairs	68.16	
Depreciation	2,156.70	
Telephone	1,362.91	
Postage	236.53	
Bank charges	28.21	
General expense	1,554.79	
Utilities	167.45	
Freight	193.76	
Insurance	403.91	
Legal and accounting	309.24	
Auto and truck	1,368.33	
Advertising	5,456.97	
Truck lease	1,143.10	
Supplies	466.61	$ 34,599.37
NET OPERATING PROFIT		13,298.34
Add gain on sale of equipment		255.75
NEW PROFIT FOR PERIOD		$ 13,554.09

* This represents a business four years old in a city of 150,000.

35

Aero-Mayflower

The following story is one of many in which a franchise operation was the means by which a man who otherwise might not have come to grips with life's problems found happiness and success.

Four years ago you wouldn't have picked Richard Stoddard as likely to emerge as one of the top half-dozen contract truck drivers for Aero-Mayflower—a respected small-business man earning upward of $20,000 a year.

Not that the Brooklyn-born trucker, who is at once genial and blunt-spoken, didn't have impressive qualities. He had literally carved success out of the mountains of Pennsylvania, descending 700 feet to dig anthracite coal from his own mine near Minersville. And he ran a small trucking business, a barroom and restaurant, as well.

But regrettably, Dick Stoddard was also a spender—a man who couldn't manage money.

"I was blowing it as fast as I could get my hands on it," he said, with a wry smile as he recalled his hell-raising days.

'I once hit a car at the intersection and the guy told me

he had just paid $1,000 for it. I reached into my pocket and said, 'Here it is,' handing him $1,000. I did a lot of other things I'm not particularly proud of either. . . . I knew every crap game from New York City to Miami."

His instability reflected, possibly, his experiences in the Korean conflict, a war which left thousands of G.I.'s confused and unsettled.

As a prisoner of war, he had to eat fish heads or starve. It took him several months of tunneling to escape and make his way back to American lines.

Suffering from malnutrition, Dick Stoddard was sent to Indiana Town Gap, Pa., to convalesce. There he met Clare, an Army nurse, who became his wife and who remained loyal to him over the rough years ahead.

After he recovered, he went to Penn State for a while, worked for the United States Public Health Service and finished three years of sociology at night. But he soon turned to mining and spending.

Dick Stoddard might have passed out of sight were it not for an automobile accident that sent him to a hospital with critical facial injuries that required radical surgery and a long recovery. As he lay there thinking about his life, he grew dissatisfied.

"I had nothing to hold on to," he said. He had nearly exhausted his finances, most of his enterprises were gone and his wife was "pretty disgusted."

There were important family considerations. The Stoddards were well on the way to becoming a family of eight.

At this critical point in his life, two important things happened.

First, he met "a couple of very impressive guys who were with Aero-Mayflower. They showed me what you could do . . . that hard work would bring in good money."

Second, an insurance settlement gave him the capital he needed to get started in the trucking business. The accident was not his fault. He was a passenger. "When the insurance company told me they were going to pay me $7,500, I got an immediate lift—my first in six months."

Dick Stoddard, like thousands of other men who wish to be their own boss but find they can't accomplish it on their own, had found a solidly based franchise company that was willing to supply the necessary management assistance and guidance he so desperately required.

"I really needed the supervision," he said, adding after a thought, "I don't need it any more. But I needed it then."

By joining Mayflower, he drew on the strength of an idea that had been thoroughly tested in the marketplace. He benefited from marketing programs and refinements that were known to work and had been applied successfully to hundreds of other men in Dick Stoddard's position.

He was trained in one of the finest driving schools anywhere, so that he could wheel his 50-foot rig through city traffic without fear.

He was taught Mayflower's principles of management, and he learned how to pack his truck and how to evaluate the condition of goods loaded on his truck—to avoid arguments over damage.

As soon as Mayflower delivered his trailer—the men must supply their own tractors—he began to benefit from the brand identification that is another key feature of franchising.

Mayflower's national advertising program—through magazines and on television—began to go to work for Dick, too.

Mayflower acts as a central clearing office for its 1,500 drivers. Mayflower's agents—the men and women who answer the telephone at local offices and book the business—channel this business to the drivers as they reach the area.

Any driver eager to load his truck can get a run almost anytime at any of the major population centers of the United States.

For instance, if Dick Stoddard expects to arrive in Los Angeles in a day or so, he will have been in touch with the Mayflower agent there—perhaps from the mobile telephone in his truck, which puts him constantly within the beck and call of Mayflower and—equally important to a family man—in touch with his wife.

Checking in with an office near where he unloads, Dick

can arrange for his next trip. Traveling alone, as is customary
—he uses only the bed behind the seat for quick naps if he
is overtired—he also arranges with the local agent to pick
up experienced moving men to unload and load his truck.
The men work in pleasant circumstances for the most part
because Dick's truck is rigged for stereo music.

Dick pays the men himself out of a Mayflower advance
which covers running expenses, and is equal to about one-
fourth of the freight charges. Mayflower does all the billing
work. Mayflower sends the remainder of Dick's pay—he gets
52 percent of the hauling charges—to his home in Minersville to cover the family's living expenses.

Is truck driving a rewarding experience for a man with
three years of college? Evidently so.

Besides Dick, Aero-Mayflower has a number of other well-
educated men who have turned to truck-driving careers.
There is an ex-Air Force Colonel behind the wheel, a former
airline pilot, a lawyer or two, some school teachers and even
a banker. (There is reason to believe that some additional
schoolteachers drive during the peak summer months when
Mayflower adds 300 drivers or so.)

But in addition to the professional men, Mayflower also
has a considerable sprinkling of high-school and even a few
grade-school dropouts. What binds some of these men together in a common profession is, no doubt, their desire to
be on the move.

As Dick says, "I get restless if I don't get to the Coast
every few weeks—just to find out what's going on."

Mayflower's vice president of operations, Charles Hulett,
elaborated on the wanderlust theme, saying:

"Many drivers enjoy what goes with a change of scenery.
Some are avid fishermen and like being able to throw a line
in a mountain trout stream one day and in a quiet pond in
the Midwest a few days later."

"Some drivers try to time their trips so that they can see
major sporting events—bowl games and so forth."

Truck-driving is not, however, an easy job. It is physically demanding, and, strange as it may seem, mentally exhausting, Dick commented.

"You've got to think all the time. That 50-foot rig isn't a car. You've got to think for everybody else, too. Automobile drivers do all kinds of things you're not expecting. These big trucks are complicated and you have almost as many things to check out as an airline pilot. You have to make a safety check for the Interstate Commerce Commission every day on the condition of your truck."

Dick drives and works close to the 60 hours a week he is permitted, and at the end of each day he signs in at a first-class motel—usually a Holiday Inn, a Howard Johnson or a Western Motel.

He rarely carries a passenger, although he once had an apprentice with him for a summer, who eventually bought his own rig. He is not interested in carrying a "gentleman of the road" (read tramp) either for company or for assistance. They're unreliable, he's found, and usually in need of a bath.

It's lonely on the road, but Dick wouldn't think of taking his wife even if she could leave the six children. He doesn't like what other drivers think of women seen in trucks.

Leaving the children is the "worst part" of the job for Dick, but even there, the job has its compensations. For one thing, the driver can live anywhere in the country he chooses and Dick likes Minersville.

For another, loading piecemeal from time to time, he may get more time at home than most men, just as he did recently when he started in Bangor, Me., came down through New Haven and completed his load in the area. He spent six days at home during this period.

It's a pleasure to be in Minersville these days. Dick is a respected member of the community and has one of the biggest incomes. He has, on occasion, put more trucking receipts in the local bank in a week than the cashier earns in a year.

Dick did well with Mayflower from the beginning. The first year he took home $14,000 after all expenses and the next year he made $16,000 or so.

He netted $20,000 in the third year, and this year, on a gross anticipated at $40,000, he should earn about $23,000.

Last year he paid $7,300 for labor, $4,000 for fuel and $500 for oil. His repairs cost $3,000 before he sold his tractor and bought a new one. His new tractor, an air-conditioned General Motors diesel, cost about $17,000 and his tractor payments are running at a rate of $4,800 a year.

He will probably drive his new tractor 350,000 miles before he buys another one. With a new rig he doesn't expect any serious repairs for three or four years.

Tire replacement is not regarded as a serious matter. He spent $1,500 on this item last year and got 15 new ones. This was regarded as unusual, with eight to 10 new tires closer to average.

His tools cost him $1,125 and his insurance 2 percent of his $35,000 gross, or $700. His living expenses run $16 a day while he's on the road.

Dick buys one license plate a year, which costs from $195 to $250. His highway use taxes—to say nothing of taxes on fuel—total $150.

Mayflower supplies the 160 plates, tags and official decals required by the various states and municipalities and they cost about $580 for a truck of the type Dick uses.

He likes his work and plans to stay with it. He makes a better living than most people he knows, but remembering the old days, he remarked: "It's nice to be able to hold my head up."

There you have it then, a success story involving a truck driver—a successful small businessman earning more than $20,000 a year.

Not all Mayflower drivers make that much. The average man earns about $12,500 a year. But Mayflower says that the five-year man who really works at the job should be able to make $17,000 to $20,000 a year easily.

While Dick Stoddard put up $7,500, Mayflower says that all you really need to get a start in this business is $2,000 for a down payment on a cab and another $1,000 to carry you over the beginning, before you begin to make money. You'll have to finance the truck yourself, but Mayflower will be glad to refer any man who needs a banking acquaintance.

Before you start out, you'll go through three weeks of training. (Chances are you'll be in the business for six weeks before you get dispatched. But you can draw an advance as soon as you start operating, which can come within a week or so after you finish training.)

At the training school you will learn to handle a tractor-trailer until it feels as natural to you as the wheel on the family car. Mayflower teaches its men how to load and unload the truck including, the important business of lifting heavy, awkward objects safely.

Mayflower also teaches its drivers how to handle bills of lading and to keep the log required by the Interstate Commerce Commission, which regulates trucking. You'll get an easy-to-keep accounting book for your bookkeeper. Dick pays his Minersville bookkeeper $10 a month.

While you are going through the three weeks' training period, Mayflower will pay you $10 a day, seven days a week. If you're anything like Dick, you may begin to feel as though you are part of a big family. "That's the thing that got me about the company. You're not just a number. You have a personality and you are respected." Dick's automobile injuries make it painful for him to work in the cold, and as often as possible Mayflower gives him Florida runs during the winter months.

Under a company benefits plan, Dick has $120,000 in life insurance. He has joined a retirement fund that the company recommends. The life insurance is part of that, as are monthly checks once he retires. He pays about $77 a month for the package.

While Dick often uses loaders and unloaders, he has no regular employees, so he doesn't have to worry about filing complicated payroll reports to local, state, and federal governments. He pays his loaders in cash and gets a receipt for the amount paid. The loaders are responsible for taking care of their own withholding and social security payments.

You will remember that Dick paid no fee. The price of admission was the cost of his cab. And if he leaves the business, that's all he has to sell. And if that day should come, there'll surely be a buyer because Mayflower needs more men and is involved in a expansion program.

Mayflower is an Equal Opportunity company and raises no barriers to any ambitious man, regardless of the limits of his schooling, so long as he can speak good English.

AERO-MAYFLOWER

Estimated Projection of an Average Year's Income and Expenses For Franchised Truckmen

Gross hauling revenue	$49,617.00	
Truckman's gross hauling income (52%)	25,801.00	
Truckman's gross auxiliary services income	525.00	
TOTAL GROSS INCOME		**$26,326.00**
Less operating expenses		
Workmen's Compensation, comprehensive, bobtail insurance, and bond	$ 225.00	
Insurance—collision (tractor only)	626.00	
Insurance—PL and PD (operating with trailer)	992.34	
Tractor depreciation (original value $9,000)—30%	2,700.00	
Tire expense—tractor and trailer (based on mileage life of 60,000 miles)	451.00	
Fuel—estimate (61,000 average miles at 5 m.p.g.— average 34¢ per gallon—12,000 gallons)	4,148.00	
Labor—estimated (average cost $3.35 per hour— 592 m/hr.)	1,983.20	
Licenses—home state plate	210.00	
Frailer depreciation and maintenance	Mayflower expense	
Furniture handling equipment— depreciation and maintenance	Mayflower expense	
Taxes (property)	Variable	
Supplies—operating and office	Mayflower expense	
Accounting assistance—personal records	35.00	
Accounting—business	Mayflower expense	
Tractor repairs and inspections	664.00	
Advertising	Mayflower expense	
Sales cost	Mayflower expense	
Interstate operating license and permits	Mayflower expense	
Communications costs	Mayflower expense	
Business counselling—full time	Mayflower expense	
Professional movers training—accredited	Mayflower expense	
Miscellaneous expense	1,320.00	
TOTAL ESTIMATED OPERATING EXPENSE		**$13,354.54**
NET PROFIT (before taxes and personal road living expenses only)		**$12,971.46**

PART III

36

Fraud—and How to Spot It

Since the Garden of Eden, there have always been tempt-
ing offers of forbidden fruit, sunken treasures, worthless
gold mines, Brooklyn Bridges, and Grant's Tombs. Human
nature, more than franchising, would seem to be responsible
for the corrupt offer and credulous acceptance of such "get
rich quick" business schemes. Indeed, these deceptive acts
contrast sharply with the customary practices to be found
in franchising. Normally, franchise rights are offered and
accepted in the course of arms-length negotiations conducted by informed parties . . . It seems self-evident that
franchising would not currently represent such a substantial
percentage of our nation's retail sales were it premised to
any substantial degree upon an illusory foundation of illicit
fraud.

*—From a study of deceptive
practices in franchising by the Center for the Study
of Franchise Distribution, Boston College*

If you stick to the mainstream of franchising, seeking out the
best franchise opportunities and carefully investigating their

programs, you're not going to have trouble with deceptive offers.

Nevertheless, you should be aware of danger signs before you start. As you might expect, there are confidence men who are active in the field of franchising. Since so much capital is involved in setting up a business, it's no wonder that the unscrupulous are seeking ways of making fast money at the expense of unwary investors. Fortunately, they are a small minority, but you must be alert to detect them in your quest for the best opportunity for you.

It is not always simple to tell the good franchise opportunity from the shady one. Both use recognized advertising techniques to draw your attention. If anything, the salesmen who work for the crooks are more persuasive. Remember, these men are living by their wits. They must be sharp indeed to fool you and avoid arrest.

How to Spot Fraudulent Schemes

First, then, a few words about fraudulent schemes.

The Postal Inspection Service distributes to local post offices a booklet entitled *Mail Fraud*, which gives considerable attention to the use of the mails to promote fraudulent franchising schemes. It reads in part:

"The success of the franchising industry in the United States —it is the fastest growing system for marketing goods and services—has made it relatively easy for fraudulent promoters to convince their victims that they, too, can achieve financial success as a franchisee.

"The reputable franchiser wants the men and women handling his products to succeed—his profits grow as their sales increase. In contrast, the fraudulent operator strives to exploit franchisees as quickly as possible.

"First, the victim is sold an 'exclusive territory.' If it involves a product, he is next required to purchase a large initial supply from the promoters. Generally, the goods are greatly overpriced and are of poor quality. The victim often finds himself with a large inventory for which there is little or no demand. Products sometimes used in these swindles have been found to be: coffee, confectioneries, cosmetics, greeting cards, hot foods, insurance policies, money orders, paint, phonograph records, plastics, swimming pools, and toys.

"In one case, six promoters sold 'exclusive' sales territories for marketing an 'amazing new liquid plastic coating.' Some $1.5 million was lost by hundreds of victims who paid up to $7,000 each only to find territories overlapping, the product inferior, and the promised earnings mere fiction. The six swindlers were arrested, convicted and sentenced to federal prison terms totaling thirty-two years. Another swindler obtained $750,000 by misrepresenting the sale of franchise territories to market cemetery mausoleums."

The Better Business Bureau reports an alarming increase in the number of schemes and frauds calling themselves franchises:

"Until about 1959–60, we had only a few examples in our franchise file. Now, apparently keeping pace with the reliable section of this growing industry, we record several hundred offers which bilked franchise investors, mostly in the last two or three years. They run the gamut of goods and services, from tire sealants and fire alarms to swap shops and credit cards.

"Twenty-two people are known to have paid a total of $41,000 for vending machines dispensing aspirin in a state whch prohibits the sale of aspirin by machine. (The salesmen had promised profits of 80 percent.)

"Thirty-two investors were bilked of $89,000 in a greeting-card deal. (Salesmen promised profits of up to $50 a day on an investment of $24,000 in greeting cards and vending racks.)

"Two promoters fleeced an Indiana resident out of $15,000 in a radio-equipment deal. (He was led to believe he'd get high-quality, high-performance equipment. It turned out to be shoddy merchandise worth only a fraction of what he paid. His was an 'exclusive' franchise, but only because no one else in the area fell for the scheme.)

"Another group of swindlers took in $75,000 through a merchandising scheme involving the installation of service racks of first-aid supplies in drugstores and other outlets. (Prospective distributors put up a $1,200 bond. Few got any supplies, and none got his money back.)

"One promoter left a trail of $80 cigarette-vending machines among eager investors who paid $250 each for them. Others paid as much as $936 for floor-waxing machines worth no more than $100."

These above examples from the Better Business Bureau obviously deal with cases of outright fraud. But there are many cases of overzealousness that can be damaging to your interests as well.

Every Aamco (transmissions) dealer was hurt by the acts of some of the company's dealers who followed practices deemed reprehensible by the attorneys general in two states. Aamco is presently repairing the damage and has hired skilled investigators to ferret out acts of unscrupulous conduct by members of its franchise network.

Both Minnesota and New York acted against Aamco dealers. The order in Minnesota enjoined Aamco and its dealers from removing auto assemblies unless "reasonably required," adding:

"If the customer desires no further service [his automobile] must be reassembled at no extra cost.

"Low-priced services, such as a $4.50 adjustment, may not be advertised unless the service is performed in good faith.

"Shops may not display 'burned-out parts' to a customer unless the parts actually came from the customer's car."

In New York State, the attorney general sought an injunction against a waffle franchiser who was selling waffle-vending franchises for $7,000 and promising purchasers they would earn up to $700 a week in net profits. The firm also agreed to supply machinery, a "secret Old World recipe for Belgian waffles," and other assistance.

It was alleged that the defendants had been in the waffle business only seven months, did not own or operate waffle stands at World Fairs (as claimed), and had absolutely no experience in the food field. Also that the defendants had no secret waffle recipe of their own, but instead obtained a waffle recipe from a former employee of a company that actually sold waffles at the New York World's Fair.

According to complaints made to the Bureau of Consumer Frauds and Protection in New York State, an immigrant in the

United States less than six months complained he had made a down payment of $1,000 to obtain a franchise. Despite the fact that the immigrant could hardly speak English, the defendants allegedly told him he could run a successful business. When negotiations fell through, the immigrant tried to recover his money. He allegedly was given checks that could not be cleared through the banks because the defendants had insufficient funds.

In another New York case involving a well-known name, a hamburger chain sent prospective franchisees promotional literature and advertisements bearing a television celebrity's picture and signature and implying that he was actively engaged in the management. He was not, and the state stopped the company cold.

As we have already seen, the franchise company with a questionable opportunity uses techniques that are often slick and high-pressure. The salesmen in these and other highly promotional deals often as not will insist on a quick signature on the dotted line to save a "territory" for you.

You must remember that high-pressure tactics are not the tool of the legitimate franchise company. Indeed, some of the best franchise companies have found that their reputation is such that they need not hire salesmen at all. The word spreads by word of mouth.

Once you make contact with a legitimate franchise company, you will find that the company will go slow—until they know you. The company can no more afford to jump into a contract with you than you can with the company. The company will investigate you thoroughly. Meanwhile, you should be investigating the company—talking to licensed dealers to find out how they have fared with the franchise.

Suggestions of the Better Business Bureau

Let's look at a comprehensive list of suggestions offered by the Better Business Bureau for evaluating a franchise opportunity:

Investigate first, using all reliable sources of information that aren't associated with the franchiser. Check the integrity, reputation, future prospects, financial stability, record of success, etc., of the concern offering the franchise . . . the quality, potential, continued demand, competitive pricing, attractiveness, repeat year-round salability, safety and ease of use, compliance with all applicable laws, type and scope of market, etc., of its products . . . services, markets, and claims.

Make sure the territory is fully defined, whether it's an exclusive representation and protected, and is large enough to provide adequate sales potential.

Determine whether profit charts and prospects are based on fact or are hypothetical. Ask for actual accounting records reflecting the experience of a number of franchisees. If large profits are promised, demand corroboration from accounting records embracing a sizable cross-section of outlets, including failures.

Check directly (and on your own) with several franchisees in your general area who've been in business long enough to know whether the franchising company fulfills its commitments, the degree of success they've had, the tenure of their relationships with the parent company, etc. A first-hand account from an adequate sampling of outlets can be most enlightening!

Carefully scrutinize the contract. Determine that every aspect of the franchise agreement is covered to your satisfaction and whether it can—among other things—be renewed, terminated, sold, or transferred. Don't sign any papers or put up any money until you've discussed the entire franchise offering with your lawyer, banker, accountant, and other sources whose primary vested interests lie with you and not the franchiser. This also includes checking with agencies like your Better Business Bureau and industry representatives and franchising associations to be sure the deal is legitimate. Don't accept verbal promises; get everything in writing.

Objectively and critically analyze the value of the franchiser's continuing aid and association in relation to your investment and obligations as a franchisee and as specifically covered in the agreement. Does the franchiser provide training, assistance in opening the outlet, counseling in record keeping and promotion, good quality and locally applicable advertising and sales materials, nationally geared corporate-image support, etc.? Are you committed to purchasing too heavy an inventory at too high a price . . . too high a proportionate cost of local coop advertising? Is the agreement tailored to you and your locale? Are you too limited in the scope and type of operation and services or products you're allowed to offer, etc.?

Finally, check yourself. Find out what are the requirements—energy, health, time, money, enthusiasm—for successfully operating the franchise business and whether you qualify now and in the predictable future. Consider the possibility that some unforeseen circumstances could cause you to lose your entire investment. Could you afford to do so?

A Professional Warning

The International Franchise Association, which attempts to police its own members to see that they meet certain standards, urges prospective franchisees to watch for "franchisers who use exaggerated advertising appeals to attract franchisees . . . royalty payments out of proportion to sales volume . . . too high costs of initial equipment . . . companies which give certain franchisees preferential treatment [although it is considered legitimate to charge initial franchisees less than the later ones, who come in after the name is established] . . . parent companies with a record of business failures . . . franchisers whose real business is in selling franchises only . . . agreements that do not leave you with power to make basic decisions.

37

Professional Assistance You Will Need

Before you are ready to make a decision on a franchise business—whether you are considering a hamburger shop or a personnel agency, a new franchise or an existing business—you will need the assistance of at least two paid professionals and that of a third professional whose role is likely to be that of "interested observer and confidant."

You should retain a lawyer and a certified public accountant, and you should certainly seek the advice of at least one banker. As said before, he may not be able to offer you any money, in the beginning anyway, but his experience with business and businessmen can be invaluable.

So try to find a sympahetic bank officer. Check with members of your family, particularly if you have a relative who is in business. Ask a businessman you know or trade with if he has found a banker whose judgment he respects.

Your Banker

Bankers are like any other specialist. They are not experts on every money subject. We live in a highly specialized world. Some bankers know business lending, and others don't. Some bankers have never made a business loan in their careers, and some do nothing but that.

Once you find your banker, ask him to spend some time with you. Banking is not ordinarily a high-pressure business. The bank officer ought to be able to spare you an hour or so, and his advice will be most helpful. He'll be able to tell you, for example, whether it is cheaper—should the choice present itself —to borrow from the franchise company or from private investors. Let's say you have the option of having private investors build your store or letting the franchise company do it. Perhaps the private investors ask a slightly lower interest rate, but the franchise company offers other pluses.

It may be that the private investors have a clause in their loan agreement that holds you to a long-term payoff: the investors want to assure themselves of the income over a longer period of time than you want to be committed for. These are factors a banker can evaluate even more readily than your accountant.

Where do you find private investors when you need them? Once again, the banker may be able to help. While the bank's regulations may not permit the banker to lend you money directly, he may be able to steer you to someone who would like to invest in a promising business opportunity. Some people can more readily afford to take the risk (at a higher interest rate in many cases).

The banker will know whether you are being asked to pay too much for a franchise, and he can help you in determining whether the franchise company is a good one.

Incidentally, it is wise also to check with the Small Business Administration to see if they would make the loan. The SBA lends money only on situations they believe to be of sufficient value to the dealer. If they say no to your franchise company, it's a bad sign.

All franchise companies of substance have banking connections. Often they will have local connections. The banker may be able to check on the franchise company's credit rating with other bankers. He will certainly have access to Dun & Bradstreet reports and can tell you what D & B has to say about the financial worth of the company and how quickly it pays its bills. He will probably know someone at the Better Business Bureau and

will be able to put your mind at rest on relatively unknown
franchise companies that strike your fancy.

As we indicated, all this service will be free. You will have
learned a lot—if you have found the right banker—and will
have established a contact to be used later. Remember, that no
matter how well you do in business you will need financial assistance from time to time. Once your business is off and running successfully, the banker will begin to consider you a prospective customer for the future.

Your Lawyer

The good franchise companies prefer not to make contracts
with buyers who do not have lawyers. They want you to have
good counsel. They want your lawyer to explain what their
licensing agreement means so that you won't be surprised, and
possibly embittered, later when things don't shape up the way
you thought the agreement said they would.

Your lawyer will be one of your most valued and trusted aides
—if you find the right one. What you need, of course, is a lawyer
who is thoroughly knowledgeable about small business and how
to organize one. Better still, try to get one who has handled a
franchise contract before. While looking into franchises you
have probably met several franchised dealers. Ask them about
their lawyers. If you can't find a lawyer this way, once again
you might try asking local businessmen.

Here's a technique that can prove successful. Ask your banker
to supply the names of one or more lawyers. Ask him which
lawyers the bank uses. Many legal fees are fixed by local bar
associations. You won't necessarily pay more because you are
going to an attorney prominent enough to work for the bank.

Once you have found a promising lawyer, outline the work
and ask him how much he will charge. Take the guesswork out
of this question right at the beginning so that you can plan your
budget.

A study by the Missouri Bar Association a few years ago concluded that one of the major causes of misunderstanding be-

tween lawyers and their clients was the question of fees. Lawyers, it was found, like to have their clients ask in advance what the service is going to cost, but they rarely volunteer the information.

Be frank with your lawyer. If he is well established, he won't take the business just to add to his income. Ask him frankly if he thinks he can help you set up a franchise business. If he says no, ask if he can recommend somebody else.

As a general rule, the best attorney in this sort of situation is the general practice man. He may be active in business himself; he may dabble in politics. He should be a man with wide acquaintances among the town councils. In short, a town operator. Short of ferreting out a lawyer who is a specialist in setting up franchise dealerships, you'll have found the best man.

In the chapters to come we'll talk about the things the lawyer will be doing for you. Remember that it is well worth the money to get good legal advice. You can be guided to the right opportunity and away from any fast operator who may have slipped through your radar net.

Your Accountant

Most successful accountants have business accounts and ordinarily they will be qualified to help you decide on a franchise company. Remember that your accountant will remain one of your closest and most trusted associates, long after the ink is dry on your licensing agreement.

Your accountant can help you analyze an existing business and decide whether the price is right. *After* you go into business he will be invaluable.

Your accountant is trained to analyze costs and revenues and can tell you why the first may be too large and the second too small. There are some good franchise opportunities with companies that do not give much attention to records and bookkeeping. You may find that you'll need an accountaint to help you set up proper books to make up for this lack. For instance, one of the chicken carry-out franchises does not offer more than a few hours' instruction in how to keep books. All the company cares about on the record-keeping side is how many plates and other paper products the dealer uses, because it gets paid on the this basis.

If better records are necessary, your accountant will set up a simplified system to limit the amount of time you will have to spend on your bookkeeping. After he has set up the system, have him come in from time to time to see if you are making as much profit as you should and, equally important, if not, why not?

Here are some types of problems the accountant is qualified to handle. These examples are taken from a publication of the American Institute of Certified Public Accountants.

"Businessman Robinson said that he really ought to be doing all right. His kind of retailing wasn't very complicated. He knew what things cost, and he knew what it took to handle them; then he just had to make a reasonable markup, and he had a selling price. Still, somehow, there didn't seem to be as much margin as there ought to be . . .

"Robinson's certified public accountant, in the course of an audit which included a special analysis of the company's affairs, began to uncover some reasons for the trouble: hidden costs.

"It was not Robinson's habit to buy stock out of town, for example, but he had been doing so quite frequently to fill special orders. That meant "now and then" freight bills, which had been disappearing into overhead instead of being allocated to the cost of goods sold. The profit margin wasn't really what it seemed to be.

"And another thing—Robinson maintained a crew of service-men, whose area had been expanded to get business. Naturally it cost more to send the men farther away from home base; but these costs, too, were being absorbed—and not by the customers. In short, the special orders and the extra service trips looked profitable when sold or billed at the usual rates with the usual margin. A careful analysis of the figures showed that they were not profitable—they were losing money.

"The CPA helped Robinson set up his books so that he could make a proper charge for the special services to his customers.

These charges didn't add much to any single order from any customer, but taken all together, they made a lot of difference to Robinson.

Regular Audits a Good Idea

"Now take a more complicated case—George Brown and his inventory.

"A small wholesaler, Brown had been expanding gradually for ten years or so, but had never bothered to take a physical inventory. It didn't really seem necessary. Every year he estimated his opening and closing inventories at an even $5,000.

"But Brown overlooked one fact. His inventory was growing as his business grew, and so when he carelessly kept his estimate at $5,000 in his tax return, he was mistakenly including amounts which went into building up stocks under 'cost of goods sold.'

"Finally he did take inventory and discovered to his amazement that goods on hand came to something like $52,000. His bookkeeper told him that he faced the prospect of an $18,000 tax bill! Reason: if he reported opening inventory at $5,000 and closing inventory at $52,000 for one year, the $47,000 difference presumably represented income that year.

"In something of a panic, Brown sought the advice of a CPA. The CPA satisfied himself—and the Internal Revenue Service —that no fraud had been involved, and arranged to file amended tax returns for previous years showing a more gradual growth of inventory and recomputing the actual cost of goods sold each year.

"On this basis, with one year of off-setting losses, the total additional tax liability was cut down very substantially.

"This particular story ended more or less happily, but if Brown had not discovered the discrepancy and reported it himself before the Internal Revenue agents did, and if he had not had the advice of a tax expert, he might have found it difficult to prove that he had not intended to defraud the government, and a penalty might have been assessed in addition to the tax.

He decided that a regular audit by a CPA would be a very good idea.

Another Problem Solved

"Tom Brady was president of a small manufacturing company which made furniture and farm wagons. The original business had been farm wagons entirely when it was started by Brady's grandfather many years before. There was still some demand for the wagons, and since they had always been a profitable item, the firm kept right on making them.

"But in this case, too—for different reasons—profits were not what they should have been.

"When his certified public accountant came in to make an annual audit, Brady complained that he didn't seem to be making as much money as he thought he should.

" 'It's going to be difficult to trace your trouble from your books,' the CPA said. 'You don't keep your cost records separate for your different lines, and you probably have a loss somewhere that you don't know about. For example, how do you figure out what to charge for a farm wagon?'

" 'Well,' Brady answered, 'it's really a matter of history. We've always made a profit on wagons, so when the lumber goes up, or when wages go up, I add a reasonable amount to the price to cover the higher costs, and figure that should be about right.'

"But it wasn't as simple as that. When the main business of the firm had been making farm wagons, the prices were right to show a fair profit. But when the volume dropped off, the actual cost of making wagons went up considerably more than the increases in lumber and wages.

"The thing Brady hadn't figured was a proper allocation of his overhead. Making only a few wagons on special order meant disrupting his regular schedules on furniture and took a lot more time and plant space per wagon than it had when they were in larger volume production. The wagons were also using up expensive materials which did not average out the same as the over-all increase in lumber costs for the whole factory.

"So Brady was not making any money at all on wagons—he was losing money on every one he made.

"But, as he said himself, he might have gone on doing it for years if he had not had the advice of a specialist in the analysis of costs.

"Farm wagons, of course, are a specialty. Not many people make them these days. But a lot of small manufacturers do face similar problems when they make several different products, using the same basic raw materials, but selling in different markets to meet different demands. Under such circumstances, finding out the actual cost of each item—and so what its selling price should be—requires special record systems which take a lot of technical skill to install.

"The three examples which have been given—all of them, incidentally, based on actual cases—are typical of problems which certified public accountants can help the small business-man to solve.

"Hidden costs, special tax liabilities, unbalanced inventories, losses in one line eating up profits from another—all of these can create problems in any business, and the solution is not always apparent to the naked eye.

"Every small businessman must be a specialist in several fields; he must know where to buy goods and materials, how to make or merchandise his products, what prices he can charge in the markets which are open to him, and when he must change his lines to suit his customers. In most cases, he doesn't have time to keep up to date on taxes, cost accounting, and efficient record keeping.

"It is surprising, for example, how many businessmen pay more taxes that they really owe. And of course there are many others who fail to set aside funds to cover taxes because they just don't know about them.

"When it comes to these increasing complexities of paper-work, more and more small businessmen are finding that it saves them time and money to turn to a specialist in that field—the certified public accountant."

There you have a roundup of the specialists you will need.

And add an insurance agent if you are thinking of getting into a franchise business where there is no general insurance coverage for all dealers in the system.

38

Your Insurance Needs

Pity the poor merchant in central city. His insurance needs are substantial and his costs are high. Now the threat of riot adds to his problems. Chances are, he cannot get insurance that would limit his loss to a reasonable level in a fire bombing or a holdup. These events are just too common in his neighborhood. No insurance company can afford to take the chance that one or both events, or some equally serious occurrence, won't take place.

The problem is so pressing that Congress is considering subsidies for insurance companies to make it possible for them to offer insurance coverage in problem areas at reasonable prices.

Once again, this is where a good franchise company can help you. You've already seen that franchise companies stress location. The company will try to find a place for your business that will be far enough away from the problem areas so that you can get enough insurance at reasonable cost.

But beyond that, there is a strong trend in the franchising business that is helping more and more dealers solve this burdensome problem: leading franchise companies are setting up insurance programs that will cover their franchised dealers wherever they may be, on a sun-drenched California plain or in the wooded countryside of Connecticut.

Under these programs the dealer is likely to get a long, detailed insurance manual showing the various types of coverage available to him under the company plan. If the dealer is financing equipment or property through the company, he will have to buy insurance to cover possible loss on these term-purchase items. The rest of the insurance may be optional. He will be well advised to take the manual to his lawyer and to his accountant for their advice as to what additional coverage he will need.

A to Z Rentals, Inc., is one of the franchise companies that offers insurance to its dealers. The A to Z insurance guide contains over fifty pages of explanation telling the dealer what each of the different types of coverage means to him. There are also insurance plans available to franchised dealers of McDonald's Hamburgers, Henry's Drive-In Restaurants, Sherwin-Williams Paints, to Standard Oil Company of California service stations, and several others. Ask the franchise companies you are considering whether they have similar programs. If they do not, ask them what help they can give you in getting the insurance you need.

Basic Coverage

Here's a list of the basic coverage you should consider when you get ready to open your doors. If you must find your own insurance, ask your lawyer or accountant if he knows of a good insurance broker. Good insurance men are not too easy to find. Insurance is complicated, and it takes a man of considerable intelligence and drive to learn enough to serve you well.

Fire insurance. Be sure your insurance is sufficient to cover your loss at all times. Values rise with inflation; increase your coverage as necessary.

Inventory insurance. You may not need this. In a doughnut or soft-ice-cream business, for example, there would be little inventory. However, where inventory is a major factor—as in a tool-rental business—be sure your coverage is increased whenever you increase your inventory.

Burglary insurance. This is the general term covering burglary —when criminals *break* in—and thieves and hold-up men who who walk in.

Earnings insurance. This protects profits in case of damage from fire, machinery breakdown, explosion, or water damage, to name a few key risks. The insurance is designed to continue your profits at the usual level during a business suspension. Without this coverage a shutdown in the early months could close your business permanently.

Liability insurance. The owner's liability coverage pays when a person is injured on the premises. It pays for damage to a customer's property too. It goes without saying that you will want similar insurance for your delivery trucks. In this day of spiraling court judgments, you will want the recommended $500,000 coverage for injury to a single accident victim, and $1 million coverage for all those injured in a single accident. Coverage for property damage to others should be at least $50,000. Insure for loss of your vehicles through fire, theft, or collision.

Product-liability insurance. This protects you against suits by customers in case something you sell injures the customer. Food poisoning is a possibility for a restaurant (not yours, of course).

Comprehensive general-liability insurance. This protects you automatically in case the law is changed to make businessmen liable for some things they were not held to account for in the past.

Key-man insurance. If you or a partner dies, this insurance will compensate for the loss of services. In effect, it is life insurance.

Fidelity insurance. Under a blanket bond, you are protected against losses caused by the fraud or dishonesty of your employees.

Workmen's compensation insurance. You will be required by state law to take out workmen's compensation insurance to cover employee loss through injury on the job. Be sure to sign up for it promptly, for this insurance is particularly important just after you open for business. At that time, things may not be in their proper places and employees will not be used to the equipment. Accidents are more likely in the beginning.

Health and accident insurance. You may wish to offer your employees insurance protection against injury or illness when they are off the job.

This, then, is a brief summary of the types of insurance you will be concerned about when you go into business for yourself. Certain risks are more common in some parts of the nation than in others. Your accountant, lawyer, or insurance man will be able to fill you in on these.

39

Buying Another's Franchise— Pros and Cons

At this point you've thought about a lot of different franchise companies; perhaps you've investigated companies in a number of different fields. But let's assume that you've been through the question of which kind of business you want to be in. Let's say, for example, that you have decided you want to be a Dairy Queen man.

What do you do now? Should you hire a builder to construct a new Dairy Queen store, or should you bargain for a structure someone else built and turned into a profitable operation?

Perhaps the latter idea didn't occur to you, but it is one well worth considering. Mind you, buying a store that is already clicking is no way to get around a franchise company's decision not to give you a license. Franchise companies reserve the right to refuse licenses to people who buy businesses from their dealers. We're assuming, then, that the franchise company would like you to join the family. You're just choosing between options.

Let's weigh the matter carefully. A successful business is likely to cost you more money than a business that is not yet established. In the former situation, you're looking at a business that presumably has gotten underway; one that is operating smoothly and at a profit to its owner.

You Pay a Premium

Like as not, the owner isn't going to part with it for what he paid for it. *He* played the pioneer. *He* shoveled that first spadeful of dirt and saw through the construction and opening day. *He* made the painful decision to spend more money on advertising, if that proved necessary to get the public to come to his new store. Clearly, then, you are going to have to pay him for what he has done, for the good will he has built up in the community.

Assuming you do have the necessary cash, the question arises: Can you afford *not* to buy an established store? to risk your stake experimenting with an untried site? Remember that in a new store you would be wrestling with all sorts of problems not strictly related to the matter of establishing a trade.

On the other hand, maybe you won't be able to keep the other man's trade. This is not so important in a Dairy Queen operation as it would be in a business calling for personal attention to customers' needs, as in, say, a rug-cleaning business. A prominent Cleveland attorney, Chester Gordon, who has watched other professional men take up where another left off, says, "You have to prove yourself to every one of the clients the other man served. Just because you bought his practice doesn't mean they will accept you as a substitute."

We've talked about the premium you are likely to pay for an existing business. But it isn't always necessary to pay a high price for a successful business. Sometimes you can find a man who has decided to retire. He wants out now and doesn't plan to wait around for a buyer who will pay top dollar for the business. Be careful, though. Whenever you find a business that is selling for less than it appears to be worth, have your accountant check into the situation carefully. Make sure the profits are really there.

Now, your accountant has looked into the situation and has pronounced it sound. Let's consider a few of the other advantages of buying an established business. For one thing, you may not have to pay the full price for all those essentials it takes to get underway. The equipment may not be the very latest model, but so long as it works efficiently, what's the difference?

You remember how much it took to set up housekeeping. Every single item down to the last measuring spoon had to be bought new. It was a bonanza if your mother-in-law or the girls at the office could pass along kitchen gadgets. In effect, much of your equipment may come virtually as a gift, assuming again that you've run across a man who wants to retire or is leaving the business due to failing health.

You Avoid Mistakes

Here's another thing you'll have going for you: some of his mistakes will have been corrected by the time you arrive on the scene. Chances are, he'll be more than happy to fill you in on the ways he has discovered to operate efficiently. He may have long-standing discount arrangements with local suppliers, for example. It goes without saying that any customers you keep will put you that much ahead.

If you're planning to buy a business in which the product is quality controlled by the franchise company, such as soft ice cream, you won't have to convince the old customers that they are getting the same delicious stuff they've been buying for years.

In an established business you can avoid that long dry period during which you may not make much money—just after you open for business. This advantage will probably be reflected in the price you pay for the business, but the cash register should be ringing for you from the beginning. And you won't need as much working capital to cover expenses while waiting for people to discover your store.

Some Disadvantages of an Existing Business

These are the advantages of buying an existing business. There can be, of course, decided disadvantages. Here are some of those potentially harmful considerations:

The former owner may have had a bad location, one that took massive advertising expenditures to overcome. His profits may have been won at high cost, so high that they are hardly worth having. Only a careful study of his books will reveal this fact. More on that later.

His pleasant smile and gracious manner may mask a nervous stomach. In fact, he may have failed to make a satisfactory living and thus may be desperate to sell to the highest bidder. What appears to be a bargain may on examination be an invitation to disaster.

Look over the equipment and inventory. Is the equipment of generally high quality? Can you fry chicken in those units in the years ahead, or is the equipment on its last legs? Has he charged you an arm and a leg for inventory that you cannot use effectively?

Suppose he's driven away trade. How are your potential customers to know that the snarly old so-and-so isn't there to insult them any more? Experts say that if you do buy an existing business, it may be wise to change the façade so that everybody will realize that the business has changed hands. This is not always possible in a franchise business where the key signs and format are closely regulated. If the business was a success, you won't, of course, have this problem.

Examine the Books Thoroughly

Your accountant should go over the books thoroughly to find out what the business really amounts to. He should examine the inventory to see if it is in salable condition. He should examine service contracts and customer accounts to see whether the business is likely to continue to click along at the present rate and, if you're counting on more income in the years ahead, whether there is reason to believe the business will grow. He should make sure that any money you are supposed to have coming to you is in fact the present owner's to give. The owner may have "sold" his accounts receivable to a collection agency without noting the fact on his books.

In short, make sure you have an expert on your side, an accountant who knows about the problems that arise in small business; one who will know what questions to ask and then will be able to evaluate the answers so to give you an informed opinion as to just what you are buying.

Your lawyer can find out if there are any law suits pending against the business and if there are debts against the business that don't show up on the books. For instance, there may be a second mortgage on the store. Only a trip to court will determine this fact. He'll check the real estate files and other sources of information. If there is a lease with an outsider rather than with the franchise company, your lawyer will be able to examine its terms to make sure it is not subject to early cancellation or that it does not have some other drawback from your point of view.

Your Lawyer Should Check

Your lawyer should make the initial inquiry as to whether the contract between the franchise company and the present owner allows for transfer to a third party. If a transfer is permitted, he should find out if you are acceptable to the franchise company.

Your investment is in jeopardy if you buy a franchised business without clearing it with the franchise company. If they refuse you after you have paid for the business, it may not be easy to get your money back from the seller.

Your lawyer will be going over some of the same ground as your accountant. He should find out if there are judgments against the dealer: whether the city plans to build a road through the site on a condemnation proceeding; whether there are restrictions on the land that would prevent you from carrying out any expansion program.

Check with the banks too, particularly the one where the

dealer does business. You'll quickly find out whether the dealer made it a practice to pay his bills on time. If he has left important suppliers in the lurch or made them wait unduly long for payment, it may be a long time before you can convince them to serve you.

Wrapping it up, then, it is essential that you know what you are buying and what the dealer is selling. It is especially important to know why he is selling. This is a question you should ask everyone you talk to in investigating the business. Ask his creditors, the salesmen who call on him, and any other merchants who might know. The answer to this question will tell you more about the worth of the business than anything else.

40

The Importance of Contracts

At this point, you've seen some franchise companies that look good to you. You've "kicked the tires," so to speak, and they hold air. So it's time to have your experts, especially your lawyer, carefully look over the finalists. To carry the thought a bit further, you might say that in franchising the "engine" of your understanding with the company is your licensing agreement.

Licensing agreements vary. Some are better than others. All else being equal, you may well be able to make your choice among equally good franchise companies on the basis of one company's exceptional licensing agreement. (We're assuming, of course, that you have limited the finalists to mainstream companies—companies with established records of success and solid reputations in their fields; companies that take pride in their ethical standards.)

At any rate, no matter what type of franchise you go into—whether you become a Watkins Products man with chemicals and household aids in the back of your car, or a McDonald's hamburger baron—you will be asked to sign a licensing agreement.

Although the terms of a given agreement will reflect the particular business represented, the general thrust is the same in all franchise contracts. For example, all companies, no matter how diverse their activities, must block out your territory and let you know whether it is yours exclusively or whether it is to be shared with someone else.

Your lawyer will read the contracts, dip his thumbs into his vest pockets, and peer thoughtfully into the distance as he ponders the termination clause, the charges to be made by the franchiser, the obligations of the franchiser to you and yours to him.

Chances are, none of the franchise companies you talk with will want to alter their set agreement substantially. The companies have found it's to their advantage to keep the contract uniform throughout the system. It avoids arguments among dealers and makes things more clear-cut.

Your lawyer will tell you that it is clearly to your advantage to make a contract with a company that spells things out in considerable detail. That way, a difference of opinion between you and the franchise company can be tested against the terms of the contract. This helps avoid needless, and often acrimonious, argument.

You Can Often Expect More from a Good Company

It is fair to say that, generally speaking, the franchise companies will do more for you than their contracts call for—if you're doing a good job for them, of course. The company may not want to commit itself in writing to offer you a delayed-payment privilege if you have trouble getting underway; the company may feel that this ties it down too much. However, the company's attitude is likely to be, "Sure we'll do it for Harry, he's knocking himself out and the future looks promising. Jim can forget it. He's fought us every step of the way and he closes the store to go fishing seven or eight days a month."

It's always helpful to know what's behind contracts, just as it is helpful to know why a particular law was passed.

It is easier, for example, to understand why the oil companies get 27.5 percent of their income free of federal income taxes if you know about the compromise that led to that odd figure. One house of Congress didn't want the oil companies to get more than 25 percent, the other wanted to give the oil companies 30 percent. They compromised the argument at mid-point.

Points the Agreement Should Cover

Let's look at some points franchise agreements should cover. We'll take our cue from Matthew L. Lifflander, who is corporate counsel to Hertz International, Inc., the company whose dealers put you in the driver's seat. Speaking before the American Management Association, Mr. Lifflander told businessmen who were thinking of starting franchise subsidiaries that they would have to answer a number of questions for themselves before they could write meaningful licensing agreements. The points he made, paraphrased here, should help you understand why the agreements are written the way they are.

Exclusive or not? He asked them to consider whether this was desirable. Wouldn't competing dealers offer the dealer stimulating competition, which would build his incentive to produce? Or would it? If the contract is exclusive, will the dealer be permitted to appoint subfranchisees to serve the territory?

The territory. Is it to have a definite border and, if so, what is the meaning of the border? Is it a precise location or address —or for a city, county, state, or larger region? Can the dealer sell to customers outside his territory? Can he advertise outside it?

The customers. Can the licensee sell to anyone at all, or does the franchise company reserve certain classes of customers, such as large national accounts or government business, to itself or to some other class of licensee? (Fuller Brush men, for example, do not ordinarily sell to industrial accounts. These are usually handled by special salesmen who visit only industrial companies.)

The term of the agreement. Shall the term be set for a fixed period, or shall it be indefinite—terminable by mutual agreement or terminable by either party at any time on short notice?

Mr. Lifflander explained that some agreements are "open-end."

"They are intended to provide the greatest flexibility [since they can be terminated on short notice—thirty to ninety days] but in reality, they can be most troublesome. The law books are full of cases that have been argued on the question of whether or not termination in accordance with the language on an open-end franchise agreement was in 'good faith.' "

He said the dealers argued that they were misled into thinking that they could keep the license even though the contract called for termination on short notice, and either sought a money settlement for the loss on their investment or a court order allowing them to keep the license.

Lifflander then covered a key point, one that we'll discuss again later: What ownership rights do you have, and what you are permitted to do with them? For instance, suppose you wanted to sell your business, could you do it under your contract? That is, is the license *personal* or can it be "assigned," as the lawyers put it? What would happen if you died? Would the license go to your estate? Would your estate be able to sell the license back to the company, or would the company get it without any payment whatsoever? Could your lawyers sell it to someone else?

Merchandise. Can you sell items other than those provided by the franchise company? Can you handle products that compete with those you are selling for your franchise company? Is the company going to supply all inventory and supplies to the dealer, or can he get them catch-as-catch-can, wherever he wants to?

Prices. Does the dealer have to pay whatever the franchise company demands for supplies? Can the dealer in turn charge whatever the traffic will bear, or must he charge what the license company tells him to?

Trademarks. If the franchise company has a trademark, how does it keep the dealer from using it after the license expires? How does the company get the dealer to use it properly when the agreement is in effect?

Charges. Will the dealer have to pay an initial franchise fee to the company? A percentage-of-gross charge? An advertising charge or other special assessments? Or will the company take its profits on the sale of its own goods and services to the dealer?

Responsibility. What specific obligations is the franchise company expected to take on, and what does the company expect of the dealer? How will these matters be controlled and audited? How will the company protect itself against liabilities incurred by the licensee?

Restrictions. What controls will the franchise company impose on the dealer? Should it prescribe special forms for record keeping and accounting? Is the dealer required to follow the manuals in detail? Are the manuals or instructions subject to change without notice? How far can the company go in imposing controls? Can the company designate office hours, the banks, insurance companies, advertising agencies the dealers will use, or the amounts to be spent on local advertising? Should the company allow the dealer a voice in advertising and other decisions regarding the entire system, or even with respect to cancellation of other dealers?

Not only do these points let you know what the franchise company was thinking about when it made up the contract, they offer *you* hints as to what to look for in a contract.

Now let's look at licensing agreements from a slightly different point of view. The author had long chats with Daryl Motte, a vice president of Manpower, Inc. His company—the people who find secretaries and other "temporaries" for business and industry—is regarded as very progressive. Its licensing agreements are fair, partly because it periodically calls in a select group of dealers and listens to their suggestions for improving things.

Termination Clauses

Mr. Motte said that the dealer should regard termination clauses with a sharp eye. He indicated that, generally speaking, you will want the longest term your franchise company will give you—five years at least, ten years if possible, and even longer, with options to renew for further years. Manpower's initial contract is one of the longest in the industry, thirty years.

Motte said that the prospective dealer should have his lawyer figure out whether he will be building property rights, for unscrupulous franchise companies occasionally write their agreements with such finesse that the dealer winds up as an agent of the company with a salary. "We, for example, allow dealers to sell their contract to someone else at any time. Some of our ex-dealers have made nice gains in their capital. That's fine from our point of view. Lots of contracts hold that if the dealer quits he has nothing and can sell nothing. We believe that the dealer should be allowed to sell [what he has built up] so long as the company has the right to approve the buyer."

What the Company Will Do—in Writing

Motte agreed that the dealer should know—and have in writing—just what the company plans to do for him and what it is going to cost him to get those favors.

"The dealer shouldn't accept a statement by the company that as a matter of policy it will do certain things. Those certain things should actually be spelled out in the contract. The actual services should be covered in detail so he knows exactly what he is going to get. For example, how much advertising help, and whether he must pay for it in part or get it free, what public relations help he is going to get, what manuals are to be provided, and so forth.

"What supervision is he going to get? He pays his money and he keeps paying. Is someone with responsibility going to come and see him on regular visits and give him help? We say once a year, but in practice visit much more frequently than that. We respond on call too, but that's not in our contract either."

Licensing agreements are likely to be rather general regarding training, Motte warned. The clause in the contract might merely say, "The company will operate and maintain a training school" and agree to train the licensee. He added that Manpower's training-school clause is rather general but that the Manpower school is there anytime a dealer wants to come back or send his staff for further training.

Requirements Should Be Listed

There should be a clear and concise list of requirements of what the dealer must do to maintain the franchise agreement. The Manpower contract is written in layman's language—the "parties of the first part" and "parties of the second part" have been left in the lawyer's lexicon.

Possibly the most unusual innovation in the Manpower contract is the death amendment. Relatively few franchise company contracts cover the point, but what happens in the case of the dealer's death is one of the questions many have asked the International Franchise Association. Motte said that no legitimate franchise company will take over a dealer's business at his death, but that until recently Manpower's contract did not cover the point. Now, after much careful thought and discussion with the select dealers committee, the Manpower contract sets up procedures in the event of a dealer's death. Under the clause, there is an orderly process under which the license can be continued or disposed of by the heirs of the dealer.

Under Manpower's thirty-year license, the dealer is allowed to renew five years at a time, so that in effect a Manpower dealer has a lifetime contract, "assuming he continues to meet our conditions—a condition we regard as reasonable."

Motte summed up his company's attitude toward licensing agreements: "The license agreement must be a fair agreement that benefits both parties. We believe in giving more to our franchisees than the license calls for. We have done this since the beginning. It is our way of helping to perpetuate a way of doing business in which we believe strongly."

These, then, are key points in licensing agreements. You can't expect to become an expert on this complex and sometimes baffling subject. But you are now aware of the sticky points and will know what your lawyer is talking about when he mentions specific clauses in the different agreements. By all means make a careful evaluation before you sign any contract, and do it only with the help of your lawyer.

41

Making Your Final Decision—
Twenty Key Questions

By this time you have probably decided whether a hamburger stand or a soft-ice-cream store, a water softener or a business school is your cup of tea. Chances are, you have narrowed down the choices to two or more franchises in a given category. Thus you are on the verge of making the final choice—if you haven't already done so. But, before you call in your lawyer and notify your bank that you want to withdraw your life savings, you should check off a number of points about the companies in question to see whether they measure up to minimum standards of excellence.

As you may have noticed, each chapter in this book about a specific franchise answered a number of questions about that franchise, for example, how much cash is required, how much of a royalty the company takes from your billings, and the kind of advertising the company does and who pays for it. In all, twenty key questions were considered in virtually every one of these chapters.

Here then is a checklist of the questions that should be answered to your satisfaction before you commit yourself:

1. *What fees, royalties, or other charges does the company take? Are royalties based on gross or net? Does the dealer pay for bookkeeping services, or does the company?*

As a rule, franchise companies make their money through these means: their profit from equipping the licensee with a store and fixtures, and the fee they charge to set you up in business. Almost invariably, they get a royalty based on your sales. Again, almost invariably, this royalty is based on your gross receipts rather than your net profit. Thus, you'll have to pay the royalty even if you don't make any money. Royalties will probably run several percent of your gross, and you should check this percentage against similar franchise royalties—taking into consideration the comparability of other charges made by each of the companies—to be sure they are in line. Know exactly what you are getting for this royalty and for the fee. The fee, for example, may cover training, tuition and even room and board while you're at the school. You may even get a "salary" while you are training, and that too could come out of the fee.

Some franchise companies—relatively few, it would seem—take care of their licensee's bookkeeping for him. He fills out a company form, and the tax work and so forth are taken care of at company offices. Ordinarily, though, you should expect to pay a bookkeeper for this work, unless you do it yourself. One Aero-Mayflower licensee in the small town of Minersville, Pennsylvania, pays a man $10 a month to perform these services. That's Dick Stoddard, of course. Chances are, you would pay two or three times more than that (unless you too live in the hinterlands where charges are low).

2. *What types of advertising does the company do? How extensive is the advertising program? Who pays for it, you or the company? If you must pay, how much?*

Since one of the prime advantages of associating with a franchise company is that you benefit from the use of the company's good name, the amount and type of advertising the company does is of paramount importance to you. Some companies spend a great deal—Shell Oil spends $20 million a year to keep the public aware of its gasoline. Others spend relatively little. A nationally known franchise company will generally spend a big portion of its advertising dollar on national programs. It may buy prime television time, and it will probably take full-page ads in leading magazines. A specialty product company such as Snap-on Tools may advertise in publications most people have never heard of—trade papers that reach the potential market. Where the emphasis is on national advertising, the best companies will also keep the local man alert to good tie-in possibilities. For example, if the Schwinn Bicycle Company advertises a Spyder model bicycle nationally, they'll alert their dealers so that they can feature the bike in their windows with appropriate "copy" indicating this model is the one that's being touted. The company will also supply advertising mats that you can insert in your local paper. Some companies charge several percent of your gross revenues for advertising.

Once again, you should refer to the chapter that covers the kind of franchise you are interested in for an indication of what's to be found in the field. You may find that the company will pay most of the cost, or that you have to pay most. As for local advertising, it is common for the company to share this cost with dealers, but not always. Remember that a television advertising campaign that is not carried on your local channel cannot help you. Weigh this consideration in terms of cost.

3. Must the dealer buy supplies from the company? Is this a profit item for the franchise company?

Years ago, franchise companies insisted that their licensees buy supplies from the company. Now, except in cases in which the dealer is advertising a specific franchised product, for example, International House of Pancakes pancake mix or Shakey's pizza, he is normally free to buy his supplies locally from approved suppliers. The court has ruled that a franchise company can be found guilty of operating in restraint of trade, a violation of federal law, if the company is too restrictive on this score. This doesn't mean that the company is necessarily trying to exact a price from the dealer—although some companies use premium-priced paper plates and the like as a means of charging him for the use of the franchise.

On the other hand, some franchise companies use central billing and purchasing as a means of getting the dealer a better break on supply costs. House of Pancakes buys flour from Pillsbury, for example, and pays Pillsbury directly. The company says this makes it possible for dealers to get the mix at a much more attractive price. Some companies use supply receipts as a means of generating enough money to conduct an advertising program, and they will probably tell you this. By the way, just because a company makes its profit through a charge for cups and plates (a less and less popular approach) doesn't mean it is not playing square. It's just another factor you must evaluate in terms of the attractiveness of the offer.

4. How much capital do you need?

This question is closely related to the next one, *How much cash?* Franchise companies want to be sure that you have sufficient "net worth"—over and above the cash you can raise—to keep going until the business begins to support you. Perhaps you can raise $25,000 through indulgent relatives and close friends but that's it—all you have in the world. The franchise company wants a cushion so that you won't drop out through sheer inability to earn a living while you are getting underway. They've got a big stake in your business, and your success is a contributor to their own. However, most companies soft-pedal this one and set up their financial requirements in such a way that those who can raise the necessary cash will have a built-in cushion against early hardship.

5. How much cash?

Cash requirements vary all over the lot. A Holiday Inn or a Budget Rent-a-Car franchise might require up to a quarter of a million dollars in cash or the equivalent—bank credit could make up a major portion of the "nut." The mainstream fast-food franchises require from a minimum of about $5,000 to a maximum of well over $60,000. Generally speaking, they don't care where you get it—relatives, friends, banks, etc. Check the appropriate chapters to see whether cash investment for the franchise you like is in line with industry standards.

6. *Does the company arrange financing, or does it expect its dealers to arrange financing directly?*
It can be a real plus for you if the company will finance your business, or it can be a disadvantage. Check the rates the company offers you and see whether you can do better by financing through your own bank. In addition to the rate, the company may impose certain conditions that are not in your favor. Your financial adviser or lawyer should be able to help you evaluate the financial implications of the deal.

Many franchise companies—and some very good ones too—do not finance their dealers. In such cases, it's up to you to get your own financing. The franchise company may, on the other hand, take you to its own bank and secure a loan, possibly on better terms than you can get elsewhere. Or, in a few cases, the franchise company may be willing to co-sign a loan at your bank. This practice, it appears, is relatively unpopular with franchise companies.

7. *What are the first- second-, and fifth-year profit potentials?*
This, of course, is a key question. The best franchise companies will not overstate their profit potentials. Some, however, will tell you what their best dealers have made, and you may be lulled into thinking that such rewards are general in the company. Get in touch with franchised dealers for the company and ask them how much they make, being sure to subtract the salary they pay to themselves for a true picture of their returns.

Check with dealers in the area where you are planning to do business and ask the company to identify similar areas so that you can be in touch with dealers who face the kinds of competitive factors you will face. Remember that the best franchise in the world is not so good in an area saturated with similar franchise companies. Ask the dealers whether they think there is room for another franchise in your area. Ask the franchise company this question point-blank and ask for specifics as to how they arrived at their conclusion.

8. *How much training will you get? How much will it cost you? If the training is free, will you get room and board at the training center? Will you be paid to learn?*

Some franchises are relatively easy to operate. Others are more difficult. For example, a restaurant operation calls for a great deal of skill and familiarity with a variety of mechanical and personnel factors. You might say that the longer the bill of fare, the more complex your chore is likely to be. However, several weeks of training are required even for a doughnut stand, because you must be a pretty fair baker to do the job. At least one of the leading doughnut franchises pays a wage to trainees, as does Shell Oil. Most companies do not pay a wage. It is not uncommon for a franchise company to insist that its dealers pay room and board while they are attending the company school. If there is a tuition fee for the training, it should be identified as such. Be careful. Most franchise companies do not charge tuition.

9. *What is the profile of the successful dealer in a particular franchise? Do you fit that profile?*

Is the successful dealer younger than you? Is youth necessary in the business, to work long hours or lift heavy loads? Are the dealers family men? Does the company take the man's wife into consideration? A few franchise companies, realizing that the man's wife is one of the most important factors in his success, make a special effort to bring her into the program so that she will know what to expect. ServiceMaster, for example, has an entire twenty-two page manual called "The First Year of Your New Career as Mrs. ServiceMaster," which will give the wife the whole picture. How well educated is the average dealer? Will you be spotting the others a substantial degree of knowledge? If so, will this be likely to hurt you? The company is likely to give you tests to see if you are qualified, but if not, weigh this factor yourself.

Generally speaking, you'll find that the company itself will weed out those it feels are not qualified. Beware of the franchise company that is so eager to get you to sign on the dotted line that they ask no questions. Their selection approach should be careful and exacting. It's to your advantage that this be so.

10. *Is the franchise available to widows? Relatives? Minority groups?*

There are quite a few franchises that are available to widows, but as a rule they are limited to the obvious ones, such as cosmetics. Often, however, if the dealer's widow had been active in the business, she will be allowed to continue. Retirees who are able-bodied and not too old—mid-forties to early fifties— are usually welcome, especially policemen and servicemen, who usually have enough income and savings to be prime prospects for franchising. Vigorous older men are often welcome. Most top franchisers eagerly seek members of minority groups who have ambition and drive. Check a booklet called "Franchise-Company Data for Equal Opportunity in Business." It is available from the U.S. Department of Commerce, Business and Defense Services Administration, Washington, D.C.

11. *Does the franchise company choose the dealer's location or okay his choice? How does the company settle on a location? Are territories exclusive? If not, why not?*

Most top franchise companies place a great deal of stress on location and use sophisticated (and usually highly secret) means of finding locations. Therefore, the franchised dealer will usually have a choice limited to preselected alternatives. If the franchise company does not place a great deal of emphasis on location, be careful. Ask for details on site location. Did the company consider population both as to size and type, traffic patterns, and the permanence of the roads leading to the location? If the company does not offer exclusive territories, the management should be able to offer convincing proof that exclusivity is not important.

12. *Does the company lease or sublease premises to its dealers? If the dealer is expected to buy the premises, does the company*

help round up a group of investors to participate in the purchase or build the property for the dealer? Does the company specify building plans or supply prefab buildings? Does it specify rental or mortgage expense?

It is common practice for the franchise company to lease the premises to the dealer either directly or indirectly. In a direct lease the company may own the land and the building, and in an indirect lease the company may have gotten local investors to build the building so that the company can lease it and then sublease it to the dealer. A practice that seems to be waning called for the dealer to buy the land and build his own building according to the franchise company's specifications. Dairy Queen for years had many dealers who owned their land and building. This can hurt the dealer, however, if highways are moved or closed for long periods of time. Some gas-station owners have suffered substantial losses in such cases, and station ownership is less popular today than it was some time ago.

Very frequently, the franchise company will expect the dealer to find a group of local investors, such as doctors, businessmen, and other professionals, to build his store. In effect, he must take them into the business as partners. How effective this is depends on how much of a price the dealer must pay the investors for the use of their capital.

The question of cost of a lease or mortgage is a key one. Some years ago it was common for unscrupulous franchise companies to charge such a high rent that the dealer soon found he was working for the company. The franchise company that was truly dishonest would sell such stores again and again, bleeding each man until he had to abandon the franchise. This practice has not been eliminated, but it is decidedly on the wane. Be sure to get convincing evidence of the cost of rent or mortgage, checking this point with other dealers in the company. Also ask your banker to evaluate this charge.

13. *Is the dealer well protected from rival franchise companies?*

This is one of the most difficult questions to evaluate. The franchise company will tell you that, with them behind you, you can't miss. However, franchising is a competitive business and is becoming more so. It is not uncommon to see several hamburger stands within shouting distance of one another. And those shouts, if they could be heard, might be waging a price war. But just because there are several stands in close proximity does not necessarily mean that the dealers can't make out. Insist on a hard-headed analysis of the competitive factors before you commit your money. Again, ask your banker and accountant for help. Talk to one or more of your potential competitors. Sound them out. Find out whether the competitive pinch is too much for them.

14. *Has the franchise company many available territories?*

This question is related to the previous one. If the franchise company is asking you to go into a tight competitive situation and you are convinced it's too risky, ask for an area where your chances are greater. The franchise company may be so well sold that there are no other territories available. If so, perhaps you would be better off in another company or even another industry where the potential hasn't been tapped so fully. Overbuilding is always a temptation, since in most cases profits arise from the sale of equipment.

15. *How many hours a week must you work? Must you work a seven-day week?*

Sixty-hour or longer work weeks are not uncommon, particularly when you are just getting a business underway. If such hours are a factor, once again, be sure your wife is aware of just how little she and the children are going to see of you in the beginning. Some franchises demand extended work weeks throughout their duration. That's okay if you're a demon for work. But if you aren't, look for a franchise that takes you away from home fewer hours. There are quite a few of these. Some dealers find that they can eventually open several stores, several Martinizing outlets, for example, and can work from offices in their own homes. Some restaurants require that the owner-manager be on the premises only for opening, closing, and rush hours; the man can frequently play golf during the day. This is exceptional in the restaurant business, however.

16. *Must you work twelve months a year? If not, how many months?*

Some franchise companies will supply a substitute manager so that their man can get away. Be prepared to pay him. Most expect you to train an assistant who can take over during an absence. Vacations are not the most common plus in franchising, although the soft-ice-cream store offers an almost idyllic existence for the man who likes to spend a leisurely winter in Florida.

17. *How many employees will you need? Can the family handle the business?*

Restaurants usually call for stubstantial hiring, in some cases, more than twenty employees. Such operations—McDonald's is one—call for considerable personnel skill. Indeed, the ability to manage people, the strength and courage necessary to fire, are perhaps the most important essentials in a labor-intensive franchise. If you don't like this kind of thing, steer away from restaurants, inns, and appliance stores, among others. Soft-ice-cream stores, rental agencies, and personal-service franchises are examples of family-type businesses, if they're small operations.

18. *Are you free to sell the franchise? If so, must the franchise company approve the buyer?*

When you have invested in a franchise you usually get a property right that can be sold—franchise company willing. Almost invariably the franchise company will insist on the right of veto over the customer you line up for the business because the company's own interests are at stake too. As a rule, a good franchise company will be able to help you find a buyer if for any reason you must give up the business. Be sure, however, that this point is covered in the contract. On the other hand, if you have a business in which you do not own anything, as in a gas-station franchise, you are not building value in your investment. If you decide to give up the franchise, that's it. The oil company will generally buy your inventory, but you have little else to sell. Some businessmen go into business so that they can build up the trade enough to establish a valuable property right. If this is your goal, make sure that the contract provides you with something to sell.

19. *Has the franchise contract a death clause giving your heirs the right to sell the franchise? What is the term of the license? Has it renewal options? If so, for what term?*

This question is related to question 18. You should try to get a franchise with a progressive company—of which there are many—that permits your heirs to sell the franchise if you should die. This idea is relatively new in the franchise industry, since the big push began so recently that the question hasn't come up too frequently. It is an important one, though. The contract should spell out the rights of your heirs, as your business may be the most important asset you own. Your franchise agreement should be a long-term contract. If it is not, you should make a determined effort to learn whether the company's dealers have questioned the good faith of the company in this respect. Some good franchise companies do not like to give long-term licenses, although they tend to keep their franchised dealers as long as the dealers want to stay. A long-term license (with reasonable clauses permitting revocation for gross misconduct) is a plus. Many licenses carry renewal options, and this is good too. Once again, your lawyer should be able to help you evaluate this factor of the contract.

20. *Does the franchise company have a national insurance contract that will give you the necessary protection to run your business without fear of ruinous loss?*

There is a healthy and growing trend in the franchise field to set up national insurance plans covering the company's licensed dealers. You should look for such a plan, particularly if you are in the restaurant business and particularly if you are in an area where there is considerable crime. Most insurance companies fear the restaurant operator will not clean his grease traps and as a result they will be on the hook for fire damages. In restaurant chains it is therefore essential that either the company supply you with an insurance plan or that you be able to get local coverage before you commit yourself. Crime also scares off local insurance men, because their companies tend to refuse insurance to businesses in areas where robberies and burglaries are rife.

A FINAL CAUTIONARY NOTE: Under no circumstances should you attempt to negotiate a franchise agreement without the assistance of a lawyer skilled in evaluating business contracts. Although many nonspecialists are good at such evaluations, others are not. Get the best man you can find when you sit down with the franchise company to sign on the dotted line.

Remember, as stressed before, this may very well be the most important signature you ever write.

Appendix

Where to Find Information on Specific Franchise Companies

For the very latest information on opportunities being offered in the franchise field, consult the business-opportunities column of your local daily newspaper. Two newspapers that are widely distributed nationally, *The New York Times* and *The Wall Street Journal,* regularly run pages of advertising devoted to franchise opportunities. See particularly *The New York Times* business section on Sundays and *The Wall Street Journal* on Wednesdays. By answering newspaper ads you will receive the kind of information you will need to have about individual companies.

Franchise shows featuring exhibits by franchisors are held annually in every section of the country. At such shows you will be able to talk to representatives of the various companies. A list of cities where these shows are held may be found on page 311.

Since franchising is such a rapidly developing field, it would be impossible in a book of this kind to include a list of companies which would be up to date and accurate. New franchises are being offered every week. Executives change, and headquarters are moved.

The most inclusive list of franchise companies which is regularly updated may be obtained by writing to:

Mr. Rogers Sherwood, Publisher
National Franchise Reports
333 North Michigan Avenue
Chicago, Illinois 60601

Mr. Sherwood, one of the most respected figures in the world of franchising, has been compiling information about franchise companies for many years. He points out that his directory of companies is not compiled critically. He tries to weed out franchises that seem to be spurious, but he also stresses that inclusion in his directory does not represent an endorsement. Neither does the absence of a franchise from his list indicate that the company is not legitimate.

The International Franchise Association is an organization that makes a strong effort to limit its membership to companies that subscribe to a code of ethics (see page 312). Thus, the membership list offers a reasonably accurate indicator of the best of the franchise companies. You may obtain this list by writing to:

International Franchise Association
333 North Michigan Avenue
Chicago, Illinois 60601

You should understand, however, that not all the top companies belong to the IFA. If you do not see a company listed in which you are interested, it does not mean that the company is not a good one. On the other hand, the fact that the company is listed does not mean that it can provide you with an ironclad guarantee of business success.

There are a number of other books which give information on franchising, and several magazines that regularly report on developments in the field and on new franchises. See "Additional Sources for Franchise Information," page 328.

Cities in Which Franchise Shows Are Usually Held

Anaheim, California
Buffalo, New York
Chestnut Hills, Massachusetts
Chicago, Illinois
Cincinnati, Ohio
Cleveland,Ohio
Dallas, Texas
Detroit, Michigan
Denver, Colorado
Des Plaines (Chicago area), Illinois
Hartford (West), Connecticut
Indianapolis, Indiana
Los Angeles, California
Miami Beach, Florida
New York, New York
Omaha, Nebraska
Philadelphia, Pennsylvania
Pittsburgh, Pennsylvania
St. Louis, Missouri
Washington, D.C.

Code of Ethics
International Franchise Association

Adopted 1960

Each Member Company Pledges:

1. To properly and effectively serve the needs of the ultimate user or consumer of the company's products or services.

2. To provide a professional, competitive, and successful program that will establish and maintain a franchising enterprise to distribute the company's products or services.

3. To establish terms of franchise, license contract, or similar agreement completely and clearly set down in print. All terms of said agreement are to be fair to the franchisee and fully understood by him prior to signing. The franchisee shall in all cases be furnished with a complete and accurate signed copy of the agreement. The company shall abide by its franchise agreement in letter and in spirit.

4. To always provide complete information to prospective

franchisees concerning the cost of entering into such business. No company shall minimize, diminish, or in any way disguise or withhold the amount of necessary capital, work, or qualifications necessary to commence and maintain ordinary operations as a franchisee.

5. To advertise or communicate to any person or company, by conversation, correspondence, newspapers, magazines, radio, television, or any other means of communication:

   a. Factual information concerned only with the growth of the company or its number of operating outlets at the time of communication.

   b. Realistic or average yearly net profit projections that can be reasonably expected by franchisees. Reaonsable net profit figures are to be ascertained by using known average figures for comparable cities and/or operations. Overstated or exaggerated figures are to be eliminated.

   c. True and proper representation of all policies, products, and any other important information which has influence on the enterprise.

   d. Ethical consumer advertising, to avoid any misleading claims such as, but not limited to, false comparisons, untrue, unproven, or exaggerated statements, trick photography, or omission of pertinent facts.

6. That all products furnished and sold to franchisees through, by, or upon the recommendation of the company shall be as represented, and manufactured with ingredients or materials of acceptable standards approved by the applicable trade, profession, or industry.

7. That distribution of the company's exclusive franchise products, services, or equipment under more than one name in order to obtain business through more than one outlet in a franchised area, without disclosure to the franchisee, shall be a violation of the spirit and/or letter of the franchising agreement and shall be prohibited.

8. That it shall completely avoid by demonstration and action, and shall encourage its franchisees to avoid, illegal practices of any sort.

9. That it shall respect all contracts, pay all obligations, maintain good credit rating, and in other respects follow the highest standards of business conduct.

10. That it shall not in any way copy or represent the trademark or other distinguishing marks of other companies with intent to mislead the public.

11. That it shall assume the moral obligation to conduct continuing research in its field to increase the knowledge of its franchisees with respect to all phases of their business operation and to assist them in maintaining competitive position, achieving better performance and obtaining maximum profits.

A Sample Contract

Weather-matic Sprinkler Division
Telsco Industries

Dealer Agreement

This agreement entered into this ――――― day of ―――――――――,
19――, by and between the Weather-matic Sprinkler Division of Telsco
Industries, a corporation, hereinafter referred to as Company and

hereinafter referred to as Dealer.

Witnesseth:

Whereas, Company is engaged in the manufacture and sale of turf irrigation equipment consisting of spray heads, valves, rotary sprinklers, con-
trollers, accessories, plastic pipe and fittings, which, when assembled and
installed integrally according to a custom designed plan, constitutes a
weathermatic Turf Irrigation System hereinafter referred to as System, and

Whereas, Company has developed training techniques for teaching the art
of designing, selling, installing and servicing these Systems, and

Whereas, Company has gained a national acceptance for these Systems and
related products, and has developed certain sales programs and sales promotional material for the effective merchandising of its System, and

315

Whereas, Company is also engaged in research and development which has and will continue to result in useful new and improved products from time to time on a continuing basis, and

Whereas, Dealer is anxious to acquire the foregoing facilities and advantages, and Company is willing to grant the full rights to the System and related articles, including use of the Weather-matic trademark, all in a manner prescribed by Company;

Now, Therefore, in consideration of the mutual covenants and understanding set forth hereinafter, and the faithful performance thereof by the respective parties, the Company and Dealer hereby agree as follows:

1. *Appointment:* Company hereby appoints and licenses Dealer as an authorized dealer for the design, sale, installation and service of the System and its related articles manufactured or supplied by Company within the following area:

Dealer hereby accepts such appointment and agrees to use his best efforts to promote and increase the sale of Weather-matic Turf irrigation Systems and related articles manufactured by the Company or products either supplied by the Company or approved by the Company throughout such area and to achieve the market potential determined by Company from time to time.

2. *Number of Dealerships:* Company reserves the right to appoint and license more than one (1) dealer in the geographical area set forth above, depending on potential sales in such area. Potential sales will be determined by the company by the use of the formula set forth in exhibit (A). Dealer shall be allocated potential sales of $300,000. When potential sales in said geographic area reach $600,000 as determined by the use of the aforesaid formula, a second dealer may be appointed and licensed by Company. Additional dealers may be appointed and licensed for each additional $300,000 of potential sales.

If Dealer's sales consisting of total invoicing on new construction work and service for the fifth anniversary year does not reach $150,000 (50% of $300,000 potential) on his fifth anniversary, his allocated potential will be reduced to two hundred percent (200%) of his actual sales during such fifth year. In this event, a second dealer may be appointed and franchised when the remaining potential is equal to $300,000 or more. Additional dealers may be appointed and licensed for each additional $300,000 of potential sales.

3. *Quota of Purchases:* Based on an average material cost of forty percent (40%) of sales, Dealer shall purchase the following amount of Company products:

	Dealer Sales	Quota of Purchases
1st Anniversary year	$30,000	$12,000
2nd Anniversary year	60,000	24,000

3rd Anniversary year	90,000	36,000
4th Anniversary year	120,000	48,000
5th Anniversary year	150,000	60,000

Failure of Dealer to purchase at least seventy-five percent (75%) of the stipulated quota in any of the five anniversary years will constitute sufficient cause for Company to cancel this Dealer's Agreement upon thirty (30) days written notice from Company.

Thereafter, Dealer's annual quota will increase five percent (5%) each year over the previous year's quota.

4. *Terms:* This Agreement shall continue in effect and govern all transactions and relations between the parties hereto for a period of five (5) years from the date hereof and for successive periods of one (1) year thereafter, unless at least ninety (90) days prior to the end of the first five (5) year period or at least ninety (90) days prior to the end of any succeeding one (1) year period, either party hereto shall give the other written notice of his, or its, intention to terminate this Agreement at the end of such five (5) year period, or any succeeding one (1) year period, as the case may be.

5. *Initial Purchase:* In consideration of this Agreement and the mutual covenants herein contained, Dealer has paid Company herewith the sum of Three Thousand Five Hundred dollars ($3,500.00) as listed in exhibit (B), sales promotional material and an initial inventory of Company products to be shipped freight prepaid and allowed promptly upon the execution of this agreement.

6. *Training:* Dealer, and at Dealer's option, members of his staff, shall take a full two (2) week training course at Company headquarters at Dallas, Texas, regardless whether Dealer may have already been active in the turf irrigation business as a contractor handling either Weather-matic or other lines of products. In the event Dealer himself will not participate in the engineering, design, or installation of the Systems, but will only occupy a management position in his company, the requirements that Dealer take such training course may, at the option of Company, be waived and only a member or members of Dealer's staff will be required to take such training course. Dealer will pay for his own travel expense and lodging and/or that of members of his staff.

Training will consist of schools of engineering, estimating, selling, servicing, installation methods and job site inspections, instructions on finances and administration, observation of manufacturing processes and product orientation.

Dealer shall complete the prescribed training course to the satisfaction of Company's examiner and be properly certified before commencing business operations. More than two weeks of training will be required if trainee is not certified within the allotted period of time.

Certification in the form of a diploma will be issued in the name of individuals only, not to companies.

7. *Continuing Assistance:* Training by Company's Regional Sales Manager will continue during the formative stage of the new dealership when in the opinion of the Company it is required at Dealer's place of business without charge. Such training will be extensions of the courses of training previously taken at Company headquarters.

Regional Sales Manager will continue to assist Dealer thereafter without charge. This will include joint sales presentations, staking out jobs, supervision of construction and trouble shooting. This assistance will continue from time to time until Company determines Dealer to be proficient in all aspects of the business. Thereafter, at the option of Company, Company and its Regional Sales Manager will assist, counsel and guide Dealer upon request.

8. *Trademark:*

(a) Dealer hereby acknowledges Company's entire right in and title to the "Weather-matic" trademark as registered in the U. S. Patent Office under numbers 784418, 721781, 614209 and other registrations, either now pending or to be applied for in the future.

(b) Company hereby licenses Dealer to use the Weather-matic trademark in the design, sale, installation and service of Weather-matic Turf Irrigation Systems in the foregoing geographical area by the use of labels, building signs, job signs, posters, literature, printed material, advertising material, etc., which have been provided by Company or in forms prescribed by Company. Company will require and hereby licenses Dealer to use the Company trademark "Weather-matic" in Dealer's Company name or trade style in a manner and form to be approved by Company prior to the use of such company name or trade style by Dealer. Dealer shall not use the trademark in any other form or in any other way unless specifically authorized by Company.

(c) Dealer agrees not to use the Weather-matic trademark in connection with the design, sale, installation or service of turf irrigation systems unless it is done entirely with Company made or Company supplied products or other products approved by Company.

(d) Dealer hereby appoints Company as its sole agent for the limited purpose of listing and renewing the Weather-matic trademark in the classified section (yellow pages) of telephone directories in the foregoing geographical area. Upon receipt of an invoice from Company, Dealer will pay Company fifty percent (50%) of the cost of such advertisement or his, or its, proportionate share if there be more than one Dealer. This does not apply to display type phone directory advertisements which will be placed in the form prescribed by the Company and will be paid for in its entirety by Dealer.

(e) Dealer agrees to assign its phone number and/or relevant telephone directory listings to Company in the event this agreement is cancelled or terminated by either party hereto for any reason whatsoever, and that upon such cancellation or termination, this instrument shall constitute an effective assignment of such number and/or listings.

(f) In the event this agreement is cancelled or terminated by either party, for any reason whatsoever, and with or without cause, Dealer agrees to immediately discontinue the use of the Weather-matic trademark in Dealer's trade style or in any other form and will immediately return to the Company freight prepaid any and all labels, building signs, job signs, posters, literature, printed material, advertising material, or any other articles bearing the Weather-matic trademark.

9. *Prices:* Company will sell its products to Dealer at the list prices shown on exhibit (C). Such prices will be in effect as of the published date thereon but are subject to change without notice. Company shall provide advance notice of price change whenever possible, otherwise accepted orders will be invoiced at prices in effect on date of receipt of order. Company assumes no liability for the reduction of prices insofar as the Dealer's inventory of affected parts or products is concerned. Dealer's discount from published list prices shall be no less than the following schedule:

Weather-matic Sprinkler Equipment	33⅓%
PVC Plastic Pipe	Per Distributor
PVC Fittings	Per Distributor

10. *Master Dealer:* Dealer will be advanced to Master Dealer when Company's Regional Sales Manager has certified that Dealer has met all of the following requirements:

(a) Has learned all aspects of the turf irrigation business and possesses a high degree of skill and knowledge in engineering, selling, installing and servicing, and

(b) Is completely self-sufficient in the business requiring little Company help except occasional counseling, and

(c) Devotes full time to the business, or has a full time department or division devoted to the business if Dealer operates this business as a sideline, and

(d) Has purchased $25,000 or more of Company's sprinkler equipment, at his cost in the past anniversary year exclusive of plastic pipe and fittings.

When certified as a Master Dealer, he will be given a preferential discount which will be negotiated with the distributor.

11. *Conditions of Sale:* Company will sell its products to Dealer under the Conditions of Sale per exhibit (C) attached hereto. Company reserves the right to alter or modify said Conditions of Sale whenever warranted by changing circumstances.

12. *Distributor:* In most cases Dealer will purchase Company products from an Authorized Distributor as directed by Company. In that event the terms of sale shall be those of the Distributor but in no case shall said terms be less favorable than those stated in exhibit (C).

13. *Market Divisions:* The turf irrigation market for Company products is sub-divided into five natural categories defined as follows:

Residential—Private homes, single dwellings, duplexes, apartment houses, and other types of private residential buildings and grounds.

Commercial—Stores, shopping centers, factories, office buildings, motels, hotels, condominiums, putting centers, driving ranges, and other types of commercial buildings and grounds.

Private
Institutions—Churches, nursing homes, cemeteries, senior citizen complexes, private hospitals, private schools, private colleges and other types of private institutions.

Public
Institutions—Public schools, public colleges and universities, public parks, public recreation centers, public hospitals, municipal, county, state, federal and other public funded and public supported projects.

Golf Course—All private and public golf courses.

14. *Sales Rights:*

(a) Company dealers shall have the exclusive right to solicit, promote, sell, install and service the Systems and related Company products in the residential market.

(b) Company dealers shall have the same exclusive right in the Commercial and Private Institutional markets except projects that require competitive sealed bids from several contractors on universal plans and specifications issued by specifying agencies such as architects or engineers.

Company dealers will have the first right to negotiate the sale of such projects but inability or failure to do so will give the Distributor and/or Company the right to quote prices and sell other contractors in addition to Dealer, with the understanding that the same price and terms will be quoted to all reliable bidders having an acceptable record of credit.

The Distributor and/or Company will use its good offices to recommend Dealer and promote the sale of such projects through Dealer whenever possible.

(c) Distributors and/or Company shall have the exclusive right to solicit and promote Weather-matic Turf Irrigation Systems and Company products in the Public Institutional market, except that Dealer shall have the right to negotiate the sale of such projects whenever possible.

Distributor and/or Company will favor and sell Company products to Dealer for Public Institutional projects whenever possible, but reserve the right to quote and sell other bidders as in (b) above. Distributor and/or Company also reserve the right to sell Company products direct to Public Institutions whenever bids are called for or sales may be negotiated on material only.

(d) Restrictions placed on Dealer in (b) and (c) above are due to the fact that specifying agencies such as architects, engineers or government bodies will not specify products that are not available to all prospective bidders. It is therefore in the best interest of the Company and its dealers to make Company's products available on equal terms to all bidders. Thus, Dealer is placed in the favored position of bidding on his own products.

(e) Public and Private Golf Courses shall be treated as an open market without any assignment of sales rights. Company products for such projects shall be made available to all bidders, including Dealer, but Company reserves the right to appoint and franchise Golf Course Dealers for specific regions with exclusive sales rights whenever it is in the best interest of the Company to do so.

(f) It is distinctly understood and agreed that Dealer will respect the rights of other authorized dealers and distributors and will not violate their rights or territories. In the event of a conflict between the parties, Company reserves the right to arbitrate the dispute and the decision of Company shall be binding upon the parties to such dispute.

15. *Bonafide Products:* To assure uniformity of the nature and quality of Weather-matic systems and to protect the trademark, image and goodwill of Company, Dealer, while utilizing the Weather-matic trademark, agrees to use only bonafide products made or supplied by Company and use other products only when approved by Company in the form of a written authorization, except that:

Dealer will be free to purchase competitive products for Commercial and Institutional projects on which there is general bidding on universal plans and specifications issued by a specifying agency such as an architect, engineer or government agency, but only after Dealer has made a bonafide effort to obtain approval of Company products under the usual "or equal" clause.

The employment or use by Dealer of any scheme or device designed to circumvent these provisions shall give Company the right to immediately terminate this agreement without advance notice.

16. *Cooperative Advertising Plan:* Company will share the cost with Dealer of certain literature, sales brochures, sales promotional material, building signs, bill boards and other forms of advertising as shown in exhibit (E). Company reserves the right to alter, modify, supplement or discontinue the Co-Op Plan at any time including share the cost ratios.

17. *Independent Contractor:* This agreement does not constitute Dealer an agent or legal representative of either the Company or Distributor for any purpose whatsoever, it being understood between the parties hereto that Dealer is to act as an independent contractor and is in no wise authorized to make any contract, agreement, warranty, or representation in behalf of Company or Distributor, or to assume or create any obligation or responsibility, express or implied, in behalf of, or in the name of, either the Company or Distributor.

18. *Insurance and Taxes:* Dealer will pay all of his own taxes when due at his own expense and will (a) keep all of its properties, which are of the character usually insured by companies similarly situated, including all inventories of materials furnished by Company and/or Distributor and as yet unpaid for, insured against loss or damage by fire, windstorm, explosion and other risks usually insured against by the owners of similar properties in amounts customarily maintained by such owners, but in no event less

than eighty percent (80%) of the insurable value of such properties, (b) maintain public liability insurance providing coverage against loss or damage for personal injury or death upon or in or about any premises occupied by his company, or occurring due to his, or his employees' maintenance or operation of any elevator, automobile, motor truck, or other vehicle, (c) maintain all workmen's compensation or similar insurance that may be required under the laws of any state or jurisdiction in which he may be engaged in business, or qualify as a self-insurer under such laws, and, (d) maintain such other insurance as may from time to time be customarily carried by companies engaged in the same or similar business. With each of the balance sheets and operating statements furnished the Company pursuant to paragraph 23 hereof, the Dealer will prepare and deliver a certificate describing the above described insurance then in force, the risks insured, the amount of coverage and names of the insurers.

19. *Headquarters:* Dealer will conduct its operation from an attractive, orderly, neat and well-maintained commercial establishment identified by an illuminated window or building sign furnished pursuant to the Co-Op Plan or approved by Company.

20. *Pricing Policies:* The Company is familiar with the costs of a dealer's operations and is familiar with the retail market of its products. Based upon such knowledge, the Company has ascertained that a dealer can most profitably operate by following certain pricing policies.

The Company urges Dealer to price Systems to its customers at not less than 50% and not more than 100% over its cost of labor and material excluding water meters, water service lines, fees, permits, electricians fees, etc. Company also urges Dealer to price these services at no more than cost plus 10%.

Company urges Dealer to price maintenance work on existing Systems at not less than 125% and not more than 250% over its cost of labor and at not less than 50% and at not more than 100% over its cost of material.

Whenever practical, Dealer will render service and maintenance on its existing Systems under the Annual Service Plan shown in Exhibit (F). On expiration of the new System warranty, said Plan will be offered to Dealer's customers on a year to year renewal basis at no more than 5% of the original sales price of the System. If said System has not been completely serviced for one or more years or has been allowed to deteriorate, thus requiring more than a normal amount of service work, Dealer may first recondition the System with the owner's consent on a cost plus basis as noted above before offering the Annual Service Plan.

21. *General Policies:* Dealer will at all times abide by and comply with the principles and policies contained in the Weather-matic Code of Ethics marked exhibit (G) and attached hereto.

Dealer will conservatively design and install all Systems in a competent and workmanlike manner to assure that all such Systems will adequately water all areas contracted for regardless of water pressure or climatic conditions.

Dealer will give his customers courteous and reasonably prompt service for maintaining Systems in efficient working order. Reasonably prompt service will be considered as having been handled within forty-eight (48) hours of notice during slack periods or within five (5) days notice during peak seasons of the Dealer's business.

Dealer will employ only sober persons of sound character with integrity and good morals. Any person in his employ found to be otherwise will be promptly terminated by Dealer.

Dealer will maintain adequate telephone and office facilities during normal business hours, answer all inquiries and make Systems available to all prospects, quote prices promptly, answer correspondence promptly, adjust customer grievances cheerfully, handle all customer contacts courteously, operate in a business-like way and generally do all necessary and within his power to create good will and maintain a good public image.

22. *Dealer's Warranty:* Dealer will sign and issue a guarantee to each of his customers stating that his Weather-matic System is guaranteed for a period of one (1) year from date of installation and acceptance by him; to be free of defect in workmanship or material; to adequately and completely cover all planted areas within the scope of its contract with customer regardless of water pressure or climatic conditions; and to cheerfully and expediently make any additions or alterations without additional charge if deemed necessary to fulfill this obligation.

23. *Accounting:* Dealer shall maintain a current record of all business transactions together with the necessary books of account within the scope of good bookkeeping practice and engage a reputable, accredited bookkeeping service on a monthly basis, said service to be acceptable to Company. Said bookkeeping service to furnish Dealer a balance sheet and operating statement monthly and to prepare all tax returns. Dealer shall furnish Company copies of his year to date balance sheet and operating statement every six months within sixty (60) days after closing books for each such period.

24. *Inspection:* Company shall have the right on reasonable notice and during normal business hours to inspect Dealer's premises, engineering, jobs, construction, and construction and service records to verify that all provisions hereof have been and are being complied with in respect to: (1) quality of engineering, (2) quality of installation, (3) neat and orderly premises, (4) caliber of personnel, (5) prompt service and repair work, and (6) good customer relations.

25. *Non-Delivery:* Company agrees that it will endeavor to fill the accepted orders as promptly as practicable subject to any causes of delay beyond Company's control. Dealer expressly releases Company from liability for any loss or damage arising from the failure of Company to fill any orders of Dealer.

26. *Hold Harmless:* Dealer shall hold harmless and indemnify Company from and against any and all losses, expenses, judgments, claims, costs, including reasonable attorney's fees, and damages arising out of or in connection with any lawsuit in which Company shall be named a defendant and which shall be based upon allegations of misconduct, incompetence or negligence by Dealer or any of his employees, agents or representatives.

Company shall hold harmless and indemnify Dealer against all claims for patent infringement arising out of Dealer's sale of Company products or systems and shall carry products liability insurance.

27. *Non-Waiver:* Failure of either party at any time to require performance by the other party of any provision hereof shall in no way affect the full right to require such performance at any time thereafter. Nor shall the waiver by either party of a breach of any provision hereof be taken or held to be a waiver of any succeeding breach of such provision or a waiver of this provision itself.

28. *Non-Transferable:* To maintain the high standards set forth by Company, this agreement is transferable or assignable only with written consent of Company.

29. *Termination by Company:*

(a) The failure of the Dealer to pay within thirty (30) days after the due date any sums due the Company or the Distributor under the terms of this agreement shall be an event of default under this agreement, and upon its happening, the Company may terminate this agreement by written notice of termination to the Dealer, to be effective fifteen (15) days after the mailing thereof.

(b) Upon the happening of any of the following events, Company may notify Dealer of such event; notify Dealer to rectify said event, itemizing the specific steps to be taken by Dealer. After such notice the events become events of default under this agreement and upon failure by Dealer to make the specified corrections within thirty (30) days after receipt of said notice, Company may terminate this agreement by written notice of termination, to be effective fifteen (15) days after the mailing thereof.

(1) Failure to purchase Company products in the amount or amounts stipulated in article 3.

(2) The use of un-bonafide, substitute or non-approved material as stipulated in article 15.

(3) Unauthorized use or violation of Company trademark as stipulated in article 8.

(4) Failure to issue and comply with warranties as stipulated in article 22.

(5) Failure to comply with policies stipulated in article 21.

(6) Failure to maintain current books of account and submit financial statements to Company as stipulated in article 23.

(7) The breach of any other covenant or agreement of Dealer herein contained.

(c) Upon the occurrence of any three (3) events of default under sections (a) and/or (b) of this article during any twelve (12) month period, Company may terminate this agreement by written notice of termination to the Dealer to be effective fifteen (15) days after the mailing thereof and Dealer forfeits any right to correct the last breach.

(d) This agreement will be automatically terminated without any right of notice upon the filing of a voluntary petition in bankruptcy by Dealer, or if Dealer shall be adjudicated bankrupt or insolvent or upon the execution by Dealer of an assignment for the benefit of creditors, or upon the appointment of a Receiver or Trustee for Dealer.

30. *Termination by Dealer:* Dealer has no right of termination during the first year of the term of this agreement. After the first year, Dealer may terminate this agreement by delivering to Company written notice of termination, to be effective on the ninetieth day after receipt thereof by Company.

31. *Non-Competing:* In the event the Company or Dealer terminates this agreement for any reason whatsoever, Dealer will not enter into the same or a similar business in competition with Company or any of Company's dealers or distributors, either directly or indirectly, in the state where Dealer's business is presently located, for a period of three (3) years following the date of termination of this agreement. The provisions of this article shall survive the termination of this agreement by either party and shall be of full force and effective and shall be enforceable by Company for three (3) years following the date of termination.

Dealer will obtain signed copies of non-competing agreements in the form shown in exhibit (I) from each employee occupying such key positions as manager, bookkeeper, sales engineer, salesman, engineer, draftsman, service manager and construction foreman. Dealer will mail one copy of each such agreement to Company.

32. *Procedures After Termination:* In the event of termination of this agreement, Company shall have the right to take over the territory assigned to Dealer and Dealer shall surrender all of its rights granted by this agreement, and shall thereafter refrain from using the Company's trademark Weather-matic in any way whatsoever, including use on signs of every kind or nature in or upon its place of business or business equipment and in advertising of any kind or nature, either directly or indirectly.

Dealer acknowledges that as a result of performance of this agreement by Company, Dealer will acquire knowledge of trade secrets of Company. Dealer agrees not to divulge any of these trade secrets either during the existence of this agreement or at any time thereafter. This provision shall survive termination of the agreement by either party and be binding and enforceable during the existence of the agreement and at all times after its termination.

Dealer shall surrender to Company all instructional or educational materials, operating procedural manuals, engineering manuals, management manuals, all printed forms, all literature, all sales promotional materials, sales kits and product samples furnished by Company. Dealer will ship all such materials to Company freight prepaid and on receipt of same Company will reimburse Dealer at his original cost or the then current price, whichever is lower, if in the opinion of Company said materials are useable.

Dealer will surrender and ship to Company freight prepaid all Company made products in Dealer's inventory at time of termination and Company will reimburse Dealer at his original cost or the then current price as published by Company, whichever is lower, less ten percent (10%) for rehandling and restocking, and less the actual cost of reconditioning if found necessary by Company. Company shall not be obligated to reimburse Dealer for obsolete or used parts so returned.

All capital equipment, tools and other inventory other than the above owned by Dealer shall be and remain the property of Dealer.

Nothing in this agreement including termination shall effect, modify or discharge any note, account receivable, conditional sales contract or chattel mortgage if there by any between the parties, contingent or otherwise.

33. *Authorizations:* In order to insure compliance with his obligations hereunder, Dealer has signed and delivered to Company certain letters as set forth in exhibit (J), and hereby authorizes Company, upon the termination of this agreement, however occurring, to fill in all blanks in said letters as Company may see fit and to mail said letters to the addresses so designated. Dealer shall be liable to Company for any attorneys' fees and other expenses which Company may incur in enforcing this agreement.

34. *Notices:* Any notice to be given by the parties under this agreement shall be in writing and shall conclusively be deemed to have been sufficiently given if deposited in a sealed postage prepaid and certified, return receipt requested, envelope in the United States mail addressed to the parties hereto at the following addresses:

Dealer: . . . .

                                 . . . .

                                 . . . .

Company:
                                 Weather-matic Sprinkler Division
                                 Telsco Industries
                                 P. O. Box 18205
                                 Dallas, Texas 75218

or such other address or addresses as the parties may hereafter from time to time specify in writing to the other party.

35. *Entire Agreement:* This agreement contains the entire understanding and agreement between the parties and shall not be modified or amended

in any manner whatsoever except by written agreement executed by the parties hereto.

In Witness Hereof, the parties hereto have executed this Agreement to be effective as of the day and year set out below.

Date ———————————, 19—

———————————————————
Dealer's Firm Name

Weather-matic Sprinkler Division
of Telsco Industries, a corporation

By ————————————————
   Authorized Signature

By ————————————

———————————————————
Witness

———————————————————
Witness

Attachments:

Exhibit

A   Potential Sales Formula
B   Initial Purchase Itemized
C   Current Price Lists
D   Current Conditions of Sale
E   Co-Op Plan
F   Annual Service Plan
G   Code of Ethics
H   (Deleted)
I   Non-Competing Agreement
J   Letters of Authorization

Additional Sources
for Franchise Information *

Are You Ready for Franchising? by A. L. Tunick. Published by the Small Business Administration. Available without charge from SBA field offices. Excellent guide to contract evaluation.

The Franchise Boom by Harry Kursh. New revised edition. Available in bookstores and libraries or for $9.95 from Prentice-Hall, Inc., Englewood Cliffs, New Jersey 07632.

The Franchise System of Distribution by Professors Robert S. Hancock and Edwin H. Lewis. Available for $2.50 from University of Minnesota, School of Business Administration, Research Division, Minneapolis, Minnesota 55455. A research study.

Franchising Today: 1967–1968. Report of the Third Annual Management Conference on Franchising, Boston College, 1967, sponsored by The Center for the Study of Franchise Distribution. Available for $15.00 from Farnsworth Publishing Co., 381 Sunrise Highway, Lynbrook, New York 11563.

How to Get Started in Your Own Franchised Business by David D. Seltz. Available for $10.00 from Farnsworth Publishing Co., 381 Sunrise Highway, Lynbrook, New York 11563. Directed to the person who is considering a franchise investment.

Partners for Profit: A Study of Franchising, published by the American Management Association. Available for $4.50 to AMA members, $6.75 to nonmembers, from American Management Association, Inc., 135 West 50th

* Compiled by *The Franchise Annual.*

Street, New York, New York 10020. This booklet is a research report on franchising by eight students of Harvard University's Graduate School of Business.

Continental Franchise Review. A bi-weekly. Available for $26.00 per year from Continental Reports, Inc., P. O. Box 6360, Denver, Colorado 80206. Features legal and financial aspects of franchising.

The Franchise Annual. Available annually for $2.75 from National Franchise Reports, 333 North Michigan Avenue, Chicago, Illinois 60601.

Franchise Journal. A bi-monthly magazine. Available for $3.00 per year ($4.50 foreign) from Franchise Journal Co., 892 West 16th Street, Newport Beach, California 92660.

Franchising Around the World. A monthly magazine. Available for $5.00 per year ($9.00 foreign) from Sutton Place Publications, Inc., 159-15 Northern Boulevard, Flushing, New York 11358.

Income Opportunities. A bi-monthly magazine. Available for $4.50 per year from Science & Mechanics Publishing Co., 229 Park Avenue South, New York, New York 10003. Regularly carries franchise articles.

Modern Franchising. A bi-monthly magazine. Available for $3.00 per year ($5.00 foreign) from Modern Franchising, 1033 First Avenue, Des Plaines, Illinois 60016. Features general-interest articles on the franchise field.

National Franchise Reports. A monthly magazine. Available for $13.00 per year from National Franchise Reports, 333 North Michigan Avenue, Chicago, Illinois 60601. Features current franchise opportunities.

Index